"I Am Cooking Something Else"

The Story of Oxford's legendary Magic Café

by Hafiz Ladell

"I Am Cooking Something Else"

The Story of
Oxford's legendary
Magic Café

by Hafiz Ladell

First published 2021

ISBN 9798492328382

Design and layout by Hafiz Ladell
for Magic Pocket Productions
www.magicpocket.org

Front cover photo by Hafiz Ladell
Back cover photo by Gerald Garcia

Contents

For Camilla,
my dear companion

Foreword

That apple you're about to crunch your teeth into: just pause a moment, if you will, and consider how it got to be there, sitting in the palm of your hand. There is surely a backstory, whether it has been picked fresh off your garden tree, or unwrapped from a supermarket baggie. It has travelled a distance, and in the process passed from one realm to another, fuelled by commerce or desire. And before that, it has been growing on a tree, fattening itself on sunlight, drawing subtle nutrition from the mysterious underground, up through the splayed and ravelling roots, the implausible tangle of couplings and collaboration. In this frozen moment, give thanks to all of that – then bite!

This thing they call the Magic Café, how did that come to be? I reached a point where I knew this was a story that needed to be told, and that it would be a tale only I could tell. And yet, next time I looked, I realised that, in order to tell this story properly, I would need to reach out – to enlist the cooperation and engagement of a wider world of association and friendship, without which this tale would lack all heart, all meaning.

And so it has come to pass. This account is, above all, framed in friendship. Through reaching out, my sense of self has both broadened, merging with a wider stream, and also found the means to trace its origin all the way back to the tinkling stream of fresh beginning. This story has become a powerful thing, an actor in a wider drama.

The spirit of friendship was first wakened in me by my childhood friend Crispin. Whatever happened to him, I mused, having unexpectedly come across his schoolboy picture on Facebook, a year and a half back. And whatever happened to the little boy sitting next to him? I hadn't seen either of them in a long while. So it was wonderful to meet up again, just a few months ago. Thanks, Cris, for being my pal, so full of encouragement, and thanks, too, to Gordon, for that serendipitous posting. That other little boy, I can now at last acknowledge, is my own childhood self.

My early years of adulthood were wreathed, Avalon-like, in legend-mist.

"I Am Cooking Something Else"

Thanks so much to Ian and Nigel Sjoholm for manifesting a photo of Loth-lorien, their hippy bus, forever anchored up on Rosudgeon Common. It was enough to tip my memories from fantasy into reality. And that curious character, the Archbishop of Rosudgeon: how utterly wonderful to have made contact with him once again. He's now known as Hari Das; after a lifetime of weirdness, he can still recall our little encounter.

People move around, and they may change their names, yet they persist, either embodied or in memory. My own name has shifted over the years, and I make some play with this theme. Is there any essential difference between Bhagwan Shree Rajneesh and Osho, or is this merely strategic rebranding? Since this unique individual plays a significant role in my tale, it might be a question worth pursuing, but I have tended to use the name appropriate to the period in question.

Places too may adopt a new identity. I will insist I was never in Mumbai, but I certainly passed through Bombay, on my way to Poona – or shall we say Pune? Some places keep the same name, and yet change fundamentally. I would say this is true of Berlin, which has become quite a different city since the removal of its dividing Wall. And I would suggest that it is also true of my own country, which has undergone much mutation during the half century in which my tale plays out.

Change and continuity, as ever, pursue their drunken dance.

My request for assistance with my project has garnered a rich response: so many lovely people have contributed to these pages, with their photos, stories, and reminiscences. I extend my thanks to all. Amongst these are some delightful pieces of well-honed craft: Premo's luscious evocation of the Medina kitchen; Jon's history of the Magic Arts; both Chris and Dominika's affectionate accounts of their Magic Café career; Cait's cheeky ribaldry. Let's sound a special fanfare to all from the Magic Café team who responded to my enquiries in one way or another: Andy, Bernadette, Bino, Cait, Chris, Colin, Cyd, Deja, Deki, Dominika, Dorota, Elaine, Jahan, Jamji, Jo, Justin, Kabita, Kathy, Lilia, Lucy, Maeve, Michelli, Renan, Rodrigo, Sharron, Sue Hughes, Supi, Tenzin, Tracey, Zoë. It has been a great pleasure for me to connect with so many old friends, and to realise that our shared experience has been so fondly remembered.

With each of my esteemed correspondents I have, by and large, held my pedant's instincts in check, withheld my red pen, recognizing that each grammatical quirk may encapsulate some essence of that original voice – with one exception: I have, I hope, succeeded in reinstating any missing acute accents in that all-important word, *Café*.

I am pleased to include many photos to illustrate this account. Some of these are my own snaps, but there was much that went unrecorded, in that busy busy time. Fortunately, some precious moments were caught by other curious lenses: thanks in particular to Paul Freestone, Gerald Garcia, and Kate Raworth for permission to use their images.

To illuminate my account of youthful questing I have drawn on various other sources: Martin Stott's fascinating archive provided precisely the image of Uhuru Café I wished for; Sarah Pethybridge (who, curiously, also features in Martin's photo) rooted out her old photos of Munchies and Slurpies and Greenham Common; thanks to Tenzin and Palden Tsering for their splendid memento of HH the Dalai Lama's visit to Oxford, and to Al Cane for sending the original file of his "Oxford – was it a dream?" photomontage; thanks to Sannyas Wiki and Osho News for various images relating to Bhagwan / Osho and the movement he inspired; thanks to Geetee at the Humaniversity for permission to use images of Veeresh; thanks to Ralph at the Natale Institute for images of Frank Natale. I am grateful to Creative Commons for a photo of the Dammtor Memorial, taken by Tim Tregenza. And the Oxford Mail was kind enough to allow me to use their wonderful photo of Don Smith.

Special thanks to my dear friend Kabira, whose correspondence over many years I have been able to mine for her unfailing insight, and who still maintains a warm-hearted concern for my activities.

My sister, Lindsay Mullaney, took up my proofreader's challenge: it turns out my text was not quite as error-free as I'd supposed. Thanks!

My dear wife Camilla: may blessings shower upon her!

Last, definitely not least, here's a heartfelt embrace for all of those who found their own special place at the Magic Café. I hope that this book may serve to entertain, broaden individual perspectives, and illuminate your own precious memories.

Oxford, October 2021

Photos by Paul Freestone

A Moment in Time

Saturday evening, December 20, 1997

Was I ever so excited? There is a tremendous vibrancy in the air. The room in filled with expectancy. This space is brand new, something borne out of imagination and suddenly manifest. The walls are glowing, freshly painted. Here is something to celebrate, a gift to the community. What could it be? What wonders might it bring forth?

By my side, my dear wife Camilla, ruby-robed and gorgeous, salutes the occasion, raises the glass: we are poised on a threshold. Sweeping off my paper cracker crown, I feel the power of this moment surging through me. There is only one thing I have to say:

"Ladies and gentlemen . . . I give you . . . The Magic Café!"

And the company assembled settle down to a sumptuous feast, with an abundance of good humour. The banter flows, and so does the wine. Palates are tickled, then sated, at least provisionally. There is a pause, while we gather our collective energy. Jon, as is his wont, has prepared a special ritual to engage the common will, to stoke the spirit of community. He calls it "Full Café!".

"Full Café!" is a cunning variant of Bingo. Each guest receives their own unique card, with numbers to cross off according to questions asked. Wizard-like, in festive fez and caftan, Jon delivers the carefully calibrated questions, and all engage, as if it were a competition. There is a sense that a winning call is imminent.

All at once a triumphant shout rings out, simultaneously, all across the room: *"FULL CAFÉ!"* It is a magical invocation.

Then there is pudding, and there is music. And there is a riotous eruption of fart-balloons: joyous, irreverent projectiles shooting across the room.

It is a celebration to savour, and bodes well for a successful venture.

Who was there, to witness and participate in this auspicious moment?

The room is by no means rammed. I'd taken the advice of the Fire Officer, concerned about any sudden rush towards the exit. The square footage seemed ample to me; nonetheless, caution suggested no more than half a hundred participants at one time. After allocating places to those who simply MUST be there, there were still some tickets available to purchase, for those tempted by the promised "auspicious sense of occasion". A small contribution to our coffers would be most welcome: the astonishing shape-shifting blitz of the last nine weeks had used up every spare penny – but surely all would not be in vain. This transformational process, all the comings and goings by which a shabby junkshop metamorphosed by daily increments into – well, into Something Else – had attracted much curious attention; and the air of expectation had already heated up into an encouraging head of steam. It seems fair to assume that everyone there was wholeheartedly present.

Who might we see, as we peer back in time to view that happy company?

Myself and Camilla, obviously. This was the fulfilment, in my case, of a long-held ambition, a vision that had been evolving and clarifying over many, many years, the product of a series of adventures on the wider cultural fringes. We'll be taking a closer look at these during the course of this book.

Also present: a close group of friends, which had coalesced around the turn of the decade, the time when I returned to Oxford clutching my vision close to my heart. Together, we had dreamed up the Barefoot Boogie – a dance event which offered an opportunity for shared celebration absent of sensory overload; there had been happenings and parties galore at the Garden Cottage in Elsfield, a delightful location which came complete with its own nature reserve, a full ten acres of wilderness; and, twice a week, tucked away in the Asian Cultural Centre on Manzil Way, the fledgling Magic Café had acted as a lunchtime focus – something like a clubhouse – for a developing community of artists, musicians, and creative people of all stripes – not the least of whom being that special class of heroes, mothers with young children.

Some had had occasion to make use of my catering services – Magic Feasts Vegetarian Celebration Catering, my means of subsistence over the past half dozen years. As this business had developed, so had my range of culinary skills, and my willingness to take on ever more demanding tasks.

Here were our good neighbours, Anthony and Ruth from the Inner Bookshop, for whom an adjacent café would make an ideal companion to their own niche business, a treasure house of esoteric literature. Several years previously they had moved away from the Cowley Road to this less obvious location – and their custom had followed. It was an encouraging precedent.

And, from just across the street, came our local Green Party powerhouses, Craig and Elise: invaluable help in surmounting the various bureaucratic obstacles in the way of business ingénus such as myself, as well as being amongst our most regular and enthusiastic customers. For many years, there had been nowhere nearby to find a cup of coffee: Elise had long been dreaming of just such a place.

Not least in celebrating this new arrival were the various members of my building crew, who had achieved so much in such a short time. My good friend Rob Valentine, Chief of Works, had proved the ideal factotum in elaborating my wishes and intentions into a practical schedule of actions. The last few days had witnessed a frenzy of coming-together. In truth, there were still a few loose ends to be tied up, final splashes of paint to be applied, but the relentlessly tight deadline had essentially been met. Now these guys were ready to party.

It was quite a moment – and a reminder that not all moments are equal. This, for example, is the moment when my discourse appears to swing wildly, from describing a very special time in my life to invoking some fundamental principles of physics. I am using the word 'moment' as a lever, to switch the thrust of my argument, having been reminded of my schoolboy science lessons, in which many of the essential underpinnings of scientific method were committed to memory by rote repetition, on pain of public shaming, or worse.

Thus, I recall that the operating principle of the lever was elucidated by Archimedes, back in the third century BC. Archimedes is a true star: a scientist and inventor of such lucidity and practicality that his eponymous ingenious device, the Archimedes Screw, is still irrigating fields the world over. As for his principle of moments, who could forget:

"The moment of a force about a point is equal to the force times the distance from the force to the pivot"? Or something like that.

It is to be my contention that the establishment of the Magic Café, on Magdalen Road in the heart of East Oxford, was, in its own particular, special way, a world-changing, epic event – for all of those who partici-pated in it, either as staff or as customers. Something worth writing a book about, at the very least.

Hooke and Boyle: we'll be joining these two clever Fellows for a coffee or two later on . . .

While those long gone physics classes are still on my mind, I'd like to invoke yet another of those principles of mechanics that remain ingrained in my memory. It's a local discovery, honoured by a memorial on Oxford High Street, on the wall adjacent University College, which commemorates the achievements of the "the two Bobs", Hooke and Boyle, both titans of experimen-tal science. Doubtless fired up by the potent brew available in the Queens Lane Coffee House just over the road – it's amazing how stimulating a good café can be – these two each succeeded in laying down their own laws. Hooke was given to pondering the characteristics of springs. You can imagine him sitting across the table from his friend, pulling a coil

4

this way and that, testing it to breaking point. His conclusion:

   "Hooke's Law states that the extension is proportionate to the load, provided that the elastic limit is not exceeded."

Notice how I leap with abandon from swings to springs!

I love metaphors. I love how they permit a mental gear switch, a sudden shift from rational analysis to airy fancy, or even high-falutin' nonsense. This is a source of much delight to me, and it is also fundamental in considering that all-important word, Magic.

By Magic I do not mean the art of prestidigitation, in which the observing eye is fooled into perceiving something that manifestly cannot be true – trust me, the lovely lady always escapes unscathed; nor do I refer to the so-called Dark Arts, as practised by thelemites, the assertion of the individual Will via occult practice. For me, Magic is something best understood by children, in their limitless capacity for creative play: *"You be Batman, I'm Robin . . ."* Something becomes true, because we say it is so. Maybe even "War is Over (if you want it)".

It was a guiding principle for me, in configuring my Magic Café, that it should be a place where children might feel at ease, welcomed as an essential part of a shared community space, with all the concomitant benefits this might bring to over-pressured parents. Seeding the eager, irresistible request – *"Mum, can we go to the Magic?"* – always seemed like the best possible business strategy.

See, I'm staking out my patch here, giving some sense of who I might be.

I can be mercurial, my mind careening off at wild tangents; some might call this my Gemini nature. Astrology? Well, I'd like to say it's really not my thing. I'm no stranger to the methods of rational enquiry, and it's no accident I've gravitated towards this famous seat of learning. I've never developed any ability to unravel the arcana of the horoscope, the geometry of cosmic forces. Nonetheless, I have derived considerable benefit over the years from the observation made by my dear friend Kabira (who is an astrological adept) that I have "Mars in Fish".

It's a metaphor, of course. Mars, the vigorous, creative force, is envisaged as a powerful fish, a pike perhaps, lurking in the shadowy depths of the river, hidden away among the reedbeds. Suddenly, there is a commotion on the

surface of the water, a great splash, a glinting of sunlight upon scales, ripples spreading outwards . . . and then, he is lost from view once again. It makes sense to me: helps me to understand that I shouldn't feel worried if my creativity is not always apparent, that there is likely to be much going on beneath the surface, invisible. Mr Pike has his own agenda, which ought to be respected. Should he be required to show up for duty day after day, at the appointed hour, that might become a problem.

Clock-time, apparently so integral to our social and business life, is an imaginary conceit: a pit-prop of the industrial age, or a pill you are obliged to swallow in order to participate in the arena of commerce.

An astrological mindset would view things differently: that the psyche is being pulled this way and that by various specific, albeit imprecisely definable, cosmic forces, each with its own imperative and periodicity. From a rationalist point of view, this might well seem unfathomable nonsense.

And so it is with some trepidation that I must admit that, in the weird and wonderful life which informs this current inquiry, the crucial decisions, the pivotal moments, have been determined not by careful deliberation, a rational consideration of possible consequences, balanced measurement of costs against possible benefit, but by methods which laugh in the face of reason: a deeply pondered selection of tarot cards, an I-Ching reading generated by the tossing of coins, a spinning pendulum, or simply by "following my feelings".

History has always been my special subject of study. Here is an inexhaustible well of mystery: the attempt to plot a narrative from what once was, to a more recent state of affairs in which "normality" has become something quite different. What we consider as normal, as we enact the customs of our everyday lives, is a deeply conditioned construct, which may from time to time undergo seismic upheaval: sudden, unforeseen change, followed by a frantic rush to reconstruct a fabric of consensual understanding, the safety net of common-sense.

As taught in schools, history can be a dry affair: schematic categorisations, tracking the elaboration of, say, property rights against state intervention; or else it is called up as a useful tool for national myth-making, explaining the glorious imposition of imperial dominion over imagined lesser races. Rarely does it succeed in tracing the deeper motivators of change: the irruptions of the spirit, and of the heart. Thus, the splendid but brief cultural efflorescence of Medici Florence is swiftly overturned by the Bonfire of the Vanities – Savonarola's purgative iconoclasm; the stable civilisation of late antiquity is suddenly swept away by the rampaging zealotry of Islam; and the supposed "Evil Empire" of communism, which formed the bedrock of geopolitical understanding throughout half my lifetime, quite unexpectedly dissipates and vanishes, like morning mist under the rays of the sun.

We can but marvel at how the human spirit, as it responds to the exigencies of the age, evades the strait-jacket of the tick-box culture: the insistence that if a thing be not this, then it must be that. Me, I'm always looking for the box marked "Something Else".

Hence my insistence, as I attempt to formulate my account of the dear old Magic Café, tracing the genesis of a vision and its historical trajectory, that there is so much more to be said, beyond that dry, dismissive categorisation: Vegetarian Hippy Business.

Bear with me; it's a good story. There's an odd fish of a hero, a jolly band of companions, and there is some sort of quest, or voyage of discovery . . .

And so, like Columbus with his three little ships, I set my course upon the open Ocean, trimming my sail to the prevailing winds, heading ever westward, boldly going . . . confident in the approbation of my monarch, and with the chancer's faith that all might somehow be well.

Would stores suffice? Would my carefully considered gift to the Emperor of Japan be well received?

What new lands and strange peoples might I discover? Or would I, as some supposed, merely tip over the edge of the world, never to be seen again?

Now perhaps you're growing anxious, wondering: how far can we stretch this metaphor before it too breaks asunder, with loss of all aboard?

Be not a-feared . . .

"Anything You Want"

The world of my childhood was shaped very largely by my older siblings, from whom I inherited, in due course: comfort blanket, dinky toys, board games, books, and a disparate collection of pop records – all of which provided ample amusement for a curious but introspective boy, roaming far in his imagination, safe within the bounding walls of the family Playroom. Also within reach: a large wooden trunk, filled with mysterious evidence of a world long gone, an ancestral hoard featuring relics of Empire, musty union jacks, crusted opium pipes, old-time curios divorced from context, and sundry inexplicable knick-knacks.

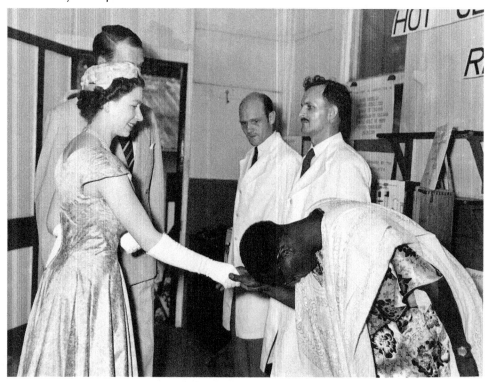

A photo, proudly displayed, commemorates the moment when the youth-ful Queen Elizabeth proffers her immaculately gloved hand to accept the graceful obeisance of an exquisitely robed black man. Two white men in well-ironed lab coats stand alongside. One holds himself ramrod straight, eyes forward, scarcely daring to breathe. The other is my Uncle Bill, whose gaze is transfixed by the conjunction of black hand and brow with monarchical glove. What is it that he sees? The occasion is something to do with a hospital in Nigeria, for which Uncle Bill is receiving royal approval. But the days of Empire are numbered.

An age was passing; Churchill dies, and the teeming cranes of London dockland bow their heads in gratitude to the saviour of the nation. A legend has gone before us; change is in the air.

Mop-topped Beatles engage the affections of my excited sisters: *"they're singing in French!"* But it is the insistent, raucous voice of a young American singer that catches my attention: again and again I play this record, each skipping reel of rhyme imprinting itself on my fledgling awareness. Something important is happening – The Times They Are a-Changing. There are so many great songs on this elpee, all delivered with passionate engagement, each of them opening up a moral drama: asking questions, posing riddles, offering no easy answers. Here is a seedbed of powerful ideas: righteous struggle, racial victimisation, desolate dustbowl tragedy, the faceless tyranny of capitalism, the fickleness of romantic yearning, the capriciousness of fate, the dubious nature of national mythmaking. These are subtly crafted songs to last a lifetime, supporting endless reflection and meditation, ever fresh with insight.

My brother, who had contributed this record to our playroom, went on to train as a lawyer, in order to pursue the struggle for Civil Rights in America, eventually pleading his cause in the U.S. Supreme Court. Me, I caught the history bug. I needed to understand what, or who was driving the process of change. Who, after all, was in the driver's seat?

Not that the process of change was much in evidence in the provincial town in which I spent my childhood and youth. Preston was proud of its rootedness in tradition, measuring out the passage of time in discrete 20 year intervals, each Preston Guild an occasion to stage the time-honoured ritual of civic procession, from then until now.

The shifting tides of fashion were held at bay in the school playground: black-clad, cane-wielding schoolmasters kept a strict eye on hair length, as it impinged ever closer on the shirt collar. Suddenly there was something irresistibly attractive about long hair.

In the summer of 1970 I had occasion to be on the ferry across to the Isle of Wight: it was a family visit to see Uncle Bill, newly in retirement. Travelling with us were a host of colourful young people, many of them barefoot, carrying guitars and rucksacks, all headed for the Festival to witness Jimi Hendrix, the Doors, The Who – so many luminaries of the current Pop scene – and – perhaps even more important – to all be together in one place, a hippy ritual of community. Woodstock had occurred just the year before, and with it a new paradigm had spread like wildfire among the youth of the Western world. In this emergent culture, long, unruly hair was the essential token of membership. I was fascinated.

But our few days on the island were spent with aunt and uncle in their sedate retirement cottage. Over breakfast the Daily Telegraph was, as ever, carefully perused: there were outraged letters suggesting that this gathering of rebellious youth all in one place would be a good opportunity for some sort of drastic, surgical action. There was no discussion of what might have provoked such a shocking spectacle. It was only many years later that I understood how this manifestation may have been set in motion.

In our family there was always something hush-hush about Uncle Bill's career trajectory, following his return from Empire. When we visited his home on Salisbury Plain my brother and I were treated to privileged access to an immense area of wilderness (which haunted my imagination long after), following which we were offered the unaccustomed luxury of real Coca-Cola at some sort of clubhouse. This was indeed Porton Down, where Uncle Bill was employed in a senior position, conducting scientific experiments into dangerous toxins. In these latter days, less obedient to the strictures of national security, it has, appropriately, acquired considerable notoriety. Disturbing stories have been emerging about what was really going on there.

One of these experiments was code-named Operation Moneybags, a punning reference to the object of study. In that pre-decimalisation age, the British currency, Sterling, might still be referred to as LSD – pounds, shillings and pence. Of course, these initials had now assumed a quite different significance. Uncle Bill's job remit was not merely to serve the defensive interests of the realm, but also to explore the possible weaponization of such new chemical agents as were being uncovered by science. Apparently, he had a track record of self-experimentation. And he was bold enough to wonder: what might happen if an elite group of commandos were dosed, under "controlled conditions", with that curious compound, lysergic acid diethylamide?

The results were duly documented in a fifteen minute Ministry of Defence film report, never publicly broadcast, but now widely distributed in various formats on the internet. First we see the squad performing a well-co-ordinated operation across the open country of Salisbury Plain, against some putative "terrorist gang". Next day they repeat the exercise, having first imbibed a cup of Something. That day's filming reveals very different results: for anyone who has themselves experienced the effect of that remarkable substance, these are highly amusing. Most of the squaddies are convulsed in hysterical delirium, paying no attention as a supposed terrorist wanders through this dissolute rabble. We see an officer reporting back to base, quite accurately: *"I am wiped out as an attacking force."*

What interests me most, though, is the footage of the subsequent debriefing, as the participants discuss their peculiar experiences. They are excited, elated even; they will never have experienced anything like this in their lives. Next day they will repeat the exercise again, but without their special refreshment. Life goes on – but can it ever really feel normal again? This took place in 1964. Subsequently, more interesting uses would be found for LSD: the genie was out of the bottle.

I felt certain, as I read through the paperbacks on my brother's bookshelf – Hermann Hesse's Steppenwolf, Carlos Castaneda's studies of Mexican shamanism, Aldous Huxley's Doors of Perception – that I would make my own appointment with that genie at some point; but perhaps not in obstinately monochrome Preston. Meanwhile, I doodled ever more hirsute faces in the margins of my schoolbooks, and started to accumulate my own gathering of cultural goods.

It must have been the New Musical Express that tipped me off about Arlo Guthrie's Alice's Restaurant. On one side was a more-or-less undistinguished set of folky tunes, but what made this record unforgettable was a tune that ran over the whole of one side, a catchy finger-picked rag that accompanied a hilarious monologue that seemed to encapsulate the embattled sixties youth subculture, caught between the incomprehension of straight society and the very real threat of military service in the Vietnam debacle. There could be very real consequences for letting your hair grow out.

Ever and anon the chorus would come around on the guitar, and then somehow it would be a song about a hippy community restaurant, a place where "you can get anything you want".

I was intrigued by the idea of a restaurant that might supply "anything you want". What, come to think of it, did I want? It had become clear to me that the standard offer, so dismissively summed up as "straight society", held no attraction for me. There was, so I had come to understand, "something else" – if only I knew where to look.

The closest thing to a hippy hangout that Preston could offer was the absurdly-named "Palace Hotel": essentially a dingy second-hand record store with a café upstairs, where a mug of tea and a baked potato would have to stand in for "anything you want". There was a certain frisson to be enjoyed, going in there with my schoolmates, hoping that my coloured shirt might serve as sufficient evidence of counter-cultural commitment. But I knew I was fooling myself: this was certainly no portal into another dimension of being.

Just beyond the railway station I came upon a small shop that stocked, alongside a small range of hippy signifiers such as brown rice and patchouli oil, a selection of publications still waving high the freak flag of Alternative Culture, notably International Times and Peace News. Top story on the inky cover of IT was a feature about a long-haired commune in Germany where everybody got naked and engaged in some sort of collective therapy: full-force screaming, with everything shamelessly hanging out. Now, this sounded much more enticing – if only I might somehow cast myself free from the dead weight of parental expectation and cultural conditioning.

As it was, I was all set to go "up" to Oxford University. My mother had bought me a life membership of the prestigious Oxford Union. It wouldn't be long before my train was heading out of the station, rolling down the track . . . would I ever dare to pull the emergency chain?

12

Splat!

On the seventh day, so we were taught, God took a rest, but everyone else had to go to church. Ours was a Catholic family, so we would all bundle into the family microbus and go to Mass. Our church was called the "Blessed Sack": a recent construction in austere Byzantine style, built to serve the local working-class community. Both my parents had moved to the area shortly after the war, so we were considered to be posh middle-class interlopers.

And yet, here we all were, brought together under one roof, to celebrate the ritual of communion. Essentially, it's a shared meal: breaking and sharing bread among companions – although, oddly, it's only the priest who gets to drink the wine.

It's a celebration rooted in the depths of time; participants in the ceremony are joined in spirit to all those so gathered throughout the ages. Except – in an effort to meet the challenges of modernity, the Roman Catholic Church had recently undergone a massive upheaval both in doctrine and practice. The new liturgy introduced by Vatican Two had dispensed with the magical mumbo-jumbo of the Latin rite. Proceedings were now conducted almost entirely in the vernacular language, by a priest no longer turned towards the sacred shrine at the head of the nave, but facing back towards the congregation. No longer was he (always he, of course) addressing the deity on high, interceding on our behalf; now it was to be far more of a collective effort, with the priest as conductor, engaging our attention and directing our prayers. The ritual had been turned back to front; some might even say upside down. It was all: *"Eyes down for a Full House"*.

There was something fishy about this religious malarkey, no matter how much it might be esteemed (in curiously different ways) by my mum and dad. Nonetheless, I wasn't ready to ditch, as so much stuff and nonsense, the whole arena of spirituality. In the books I read there was much to ponder, and when I first learned about zen it was a kind of satori moment: *"ah, this!"* Here was an approach to the divine that cut a swathe through all the flummery and nonsense of religious practise. Shortly afterwards, dutifully cycling to Sunday evening mass, I stopped off by the bridge over a quiet stream and realised that this was where I wanted to be, right here, right now. I was through with church.

Oxford proved a revelation, but unfortunately not the one I hoped for. Even a non-traditional college such as St Catherine's, where I had gained a place to study History, was dominated by oafish individuals with an over-privileged sense of entitlement. I'm sure you know the type. I found it hard to feel at ease with myself in such an environment, for all that the fabulous buildings and institutions I was surrounded by seemed to promise that this was indeed a pinnacle of attainment. To fortify myself against this overload of expectation, I worked at constructing a new persona, who was called Franc – an article of common currency. Franc did his best to shun orthodoxy, declared himself a vegetarian, spurned the bar crowd, wore shabby sneakers in winter and went barefoot to tutorials in the summer. Fortunately, there were others of a similar disposition, easy to spot by their hair length. Our favourite bonding exercise – surprise! – involved passing the spliff. Very often the chosen rolling board – an elpee cover providing the ideal base for joint construction – would be Arlo Guthrie's Alice's Restaurant, and we would smoke ourselves silly, joining in with the chorus when it came around on the guitar, and familiarizing ourselves with the endless progression of artfully delivered catchphrases.

For a brief, shining moment I enjoyed local notoriety as lead singer in a punk band, Marius and the Firebombers. I took my name from the fellow who (allegedly) burnt down the Reichstag; I really couldn't explain why. After two thrilling episodes of on-stage crowd-baiting and mayhem, our budding career was cut tragically short by the sudden death of our bass player Ray in a punting accident. That was a big shock.

Meanwhile, my studies, my intellectual training, had assumed the character of an irksome day job. My fellow would-be historians were evidently either irredeemably straight or insufferably snooty. Some were even girls!

No wonder I was a lonely boy. I took refuge in the foggy ceremony of passing the spliff, but I really wasn't having much fun.

One evening, my bandmate Nigel, an ardent acid head, offered to split a little pink pill with me: half should be enough, he reckoned, for a neophyte like me. Some time later, some intestinal awkwardness persuaded me to venture to the staircase loo. Embodiment posed such peculiar challenges! Some further time later, one of my fellow psychonauts, presumably having registered my absence, discovered me curled up in a corner of the wash-room, amidst a pulsating geometry of tiles, burbling in wonderment: *"This is real . . . This Is Real . . ."*

The doors of perception had swung open. The parameters of being had shifted.

A small group of my friends coalesced around the shared activity of cooking for one another – one way of avoiding the daily parade down the foodline in the college canteen, "Esso Hall". We had each declared our-selves vegetarian, which in those days bore the satisfying implication of weirdness, a refusal to subscribe to behavioural norms. Together, we explored the possibilities of the "brown rice revolution", cooking up our own connec-tion to the countercultural reformulations of the 1960s, our touchstone of authenticity. A favourite source of inspiration was The Vegetarian Epicure by Anna Thomas, an adventurous journey into this new cuisine.

Published in 1972, a time when vegetarianism was just emerging from a faddist ghetto, an austere and dingy realm inhabited by Difficult People, Anna Thomas stakes a bold claim for its recognition as a potential garden of delight, drawing on all the many flavours of California.

Her book is beautifully presented, illustrated with engaging cartoons, and her text flows effortlessly from poetic evocation to clear and responsible description. She presents a wide variety of recipes, with a notable emphasis on dairy-based dishes. Aesthetics are paramount: *"a well-designed meal is suited to the season, to the location, and to the tastes of the diners . . . the parts should contrast and complement one another in a lively way, but the result should be a harmonious whole"*. She also makes it clear that she is a bit of a pot-head: *"If you have passed a joint around before dinner to sharpen gustatory perceptions, you most likely will pass another one after dinner, and everyone will know what that will do – the blind munchies can strike at any time"*.

I gained a lot working from these recipes, not least a willingness to learn from experience, and the sense to allow enough time for preparation, particularly when attempting an unfamiliar dish. I came to realise that not every one of my pals had the same degree of patience and commitment.

By the time my final exams rolled around it was dawning on me that the most important part of my college experience had in fact been the time spent hanging out with my mates, cooking together, getting high. I made no attempt to plan for the next stage of life, pointedly avoiding the careers fair meat market. My ambition had instead crystallised around a self-chosen project: blowing my brains. This was to involve much more than simple inertia: it was a dedicated, deliberate casting away of the anchor of rationality. No doubt I was inspired by the inscription on Steppenwolf's ticket for the Magic Theatre: *"For Madmen Only – Price of Admission Your Mind – Not for Everybody"*.

That year, midsummer fell just a few days after finals, offering a choice of break-out destination: festivals at both Stonehenge and Glastonbury. The first vehicle to stop for my outstretched thumb was heading Stonehenge way, so that's where I duly pitched up.

I had attended a couple of the commercial festivals at Reading as a teenager, but had no real conception of what a free festival might portend, beyond Nigel's excited and unreliable recollections. Stonehenge Free Festival really was an eye-opener; my mind was well and truly blown. I can offer no dispassionate, objective assessment. Shortly after establishing my campsite, and wasting no time in availing myself to a quarter of hash openly on offer, I set myself down in front of the pyramid stage and tuned in on the festive hubbub. An announcement came over on the main PA: *"Guy down here has five red stars to swap for a quarter of hash; first up gets them"*. My recent purchase proved just the ticket: I stepped up smartly, scored my prize. I handed over one of my tabs as consolation to the next in line; it seemed only fair. I was sorted!

Here was an impromptu settlement of several thousand people, in the midst of the high, wide plateau, open to the elements, with the ancient, enigmatic monument just across the way bearing mute witness to the passage of time. Nothing silent about this gathering: wandering through the assorted tents, tipis, improvised stalls, bizarrely painted vehicles, campfire circles, a constantly shifting soundscape played tribute to the spirit of Jimi Hendrix, blowing wild and free. On the main stage, a progression of absurdly named bands shaped their entertainment around the certain knowledge that their audience would all be tripping, responsive to their throbbing, loping rhythm. As darkness fell, the banks of coloured lights around the stage took up with the beat, pulsing blobby cartoon lettering, spelling out: *LOVE . . . SEX . . . LOVE . . . SEX . . .*

Solstice dawn was particularly splendid that year, so I'm told. I'm sure I was there, in the inner circle of stones to receive the solar blessing, but by that stage, overwhelmed by an excess of stimulation, my memory circuits had more or less ceased to engage.

What strange, wonderful place had I woken up to? From out of an adjacent tipi emerged a Celtic prince, wrapped in flowing cloak with hair to match, followed by his Guinevere, and by his faithful hound. No doubt they were on a quest for breakfast. Others too were stumbling around with the same idea, not all of them in a conventional state of consciousness. Hearty food was available from a variety of outfits, from more or less well-organised catering caravans to a more basic offer at the free food campfires, which specialised in hand-pressed chapatis baked over hot stones. Hygiene was evidently not a major concern; but there was, overall, a sense of welcoming and generosity. Prominent on many of the menus displayed was a selection of hallucinogens. Were these starters or finishers?

Who were all these odd characters, so open in their eccentricity? How long might it take to evolve into such a being? It was evidently infectious: I made friends with a group of lads fresh from school, who had pitched their tent next to mine. Rapidly concluding that they needed to readjust to circumstances, they had nipped back to Amesbury to take advantage of an opportune jumble sale. On their return, their identities had already start to mutate. As for me, for some reason I had come to this festival all dressed in drab. The boys called me "Black Frank". True to form, I was already busy trying to squeeze all I had experienced into a frame of reference I could comprehend. How to account for this untrammelled state of independence, untroubled by the uniformed police, who by some tacit agreement ventured no further than the car park by the site entrance? How could such rampant derangement of convention persist alongside a culture of normality that had only just elected Margaret Thatcher as prime minister, pledged to uphold law and order and restore accepted standards of common sense?

Was I simply thinking too much? *"I just don't know what to do with my brain"*, I sang to myself back in Oxford, borrowing from Burt Bacharach; *"it's the one thing that's driving me insane . . ."* I needed to put some work into this; fortunately, I had some friends with apparently similar intentions. *"All Hail Discordia"*, proclaimed the message scribbled on the walls of our squat – one of a series that provided a squalid home base to our collective endeavour.

This is not an easy period in my life to write about. There is a temptation to present it as some sort of jolly, out-of-it romp. No doubt fun was had; drugs were certainly consumed, in quantity, and poor judgements made in terms of company kept and activities undertaken. Over the course of a year and a half, I think it's fair to say that it wasn't so much my brains that were being pummelled, it was my spirit that was suffering. Had it not been for the support of some trusted, caring friends, I might not have made it through, or been sucked under. Now, I recognise the need to acknowledge the kindness that was shown me in that difficult time.

Throughout it all I kept up with my cooking, although any attempt at fine cuisine had more or less collapsed. The prevailing dish du jour was called Splat – after the sound made as it dropped onto the plate. Splat requires very little finesse to prepare. The essential ingredient is lentils, plus whatever else happens to be available. It kept us going, and no doubt was gratefully received. After all, the most important thing about cooking is that it's something you do for other people – it's testimony that you care for them, and they will for sure reflect that on back onto you.

An Initiation of Sorts

Hey Hey I'm Stuck in a Box

Listen to me, somebody please
Gimme some affection, some attention, some time
I know I don't invite it, always hiding
And you got enough problems to care about mine

Hey Hey I'm stuck in a box
Busting my head on a paradox
You wonder why I wear odd socks
But I can't recall what I never forgot

Who am I? Well I know my name
That's as far as I'll go for definition
It's a hustling world, nobody's to blame
Everybody got their own superstition

Hey hey I'm stuck in a box
Busting my head on a paradox
You wonder why I wear odd socks
But I can't recall what I never forgot

Memory is such a strange thing. I notice that I don't have any written record of this song, but it pours straight out onto the page, and I am instantly carried back to a very specific time and place, where I played it for myself, over and over, in my hermit's caravan, my immobile home, on Rosudgeon Common down near the very toe's end of Cornwall.

If this was a box, then it was at least a quite delightful one, for a young man desperate to reconfigure his battered spirit, away from the clutter and nonsense of a sleazy city lifestyle. Here was as much clear space as one could wish for, accentuated by the absence of any furniture, apart from a couple of sofa cushions and a low Japanese-style table. Hessian sacking covered the walls, some unpretentious carpeting the floor. An enormous window, the whole of one side of the structure, looked out onto a wilderness of gold-flecked gorse bushes. Amidships was a wood-burning stove, capable of brewing up a kettle or a simple pot of splat. There was also some basic kitchen provision, although without any connection to water, gas or electricity. A large, comfy bed nestled behind a partition wall. Open the door, and an immense view beckons, the gaze leaping down to the glistening Atlantic just a mile or two distant, beyond the headland overlooking Prussia Cove; and from thence to the wide horizon reaching to the very edge of the sky.

It was possible to spend a whole week here without seeing anybody, apart from a poacher emerging from the bushes, gun in hand, on the lookout for an incautious rabbit. But if I was looking for company, I could invite myself

round to the hippy bus parked up on the other side of the gorse thicket, which acted as a sort of clubhouse for the small community resident on this patch of common land. Wonderfully, this was named Lothlorien, after the enchanted elven forest in Lord of the Rings. According to legend, it had even carried Ian and Clare, whose home it was, all the way to India and back; but it seemed unlikely now to escape a slow decline into the rutted trackways of Rosudgeon Common. If ever a metaphor for the sixties dream were called for, surely one need look no further.

Nonetheless, the wisdom of the East was yet in evidence. Not content with pass-the-spliff, those assembled in the compact kitchen area at the back of the bus might indulge in a poky chillum, a sort of inverted volcano filled with a mixture of tobacco and hashish. There was a special ritual to go with this. Wrapping the saffy, a disreputable neckerchief, around the end of the pipe, it would be raised to the brow, the third eye, with the sacred invocation: *"BOM SHIVA!"* – All hail the Cosmic Destroyer!

Sucking the fierce smoke into my lungs, my bodily co-ordination abruptly shut down, and I keeled over onto the floor, motionless. In my mind, I wanted to say *"nothing to worry about, I'm still here"*, but the words just wouldn't come.

Mostly I was content with my own company, roaming the tracks and byways that led me down to the rocky shoreline at Prussia Cove, or striking out across the farmland, heading towards the picture postcard fishing village of Porthleven. My spirit opened up to the wonder of the natural world; I discovered a special source of delight, watching the pellucid  play of blues and greens, ever-shifting, in the breakwaters and rockpools at the edge of the ocean; and on my way back home I gathered up an armful of dry branches to fuel my stove.

Strumming my guitar, I sang out my song to these four walls, the ceiling and floor: my lovely box. How come I felt so stuck? What was the paradox? No matter how I tried to restructure the final line of my chorus, it obstinately refused to budge: *"Can't recall what I never forgot"*.

I was expanding the parameters of my quest for meaning. Apart from the I-Ching, referenced in my song lyric, most days I would devote much time to exploring my pack of Tarot cards, the dynamic Book of Thoth painted by Lady Frieda Harris under the tutelage of Aleister Crowley. I laid out elaborate spreads, wondering how the interaction of cosmic forces on display might correspond to my current psychic situation, paying little regard to the actual sameness of my day-to-day routine.

Time there also was for the mysterious practice of meditation. Sit down, close the eyes. What was supposed to happen? Was I there yet?

I had occasion to hitch back to Oxford for a couple of days, and on my return, early in the morning after a chilly night spent huddled in a cowshed just outside Plymouth, I discovered that a large box van, gaily painted Indian-style, was now parked up in front of my caravan, blocking the view down to the sea. I had new neighbours: a handful of Premmies, devotees of the Indian "boy-god" Maharaji, together with their joyous three-legged dog. And this wasn't all: a short distance along the track from Lothlorien, a faded green tent had appeared, with an awning stretched out in front, and a neat sign stuck into the turf announcing "Sunshine Healing Ashram". What might this be?

I had by this stage managed to procure a gas cylinder to power the small oven included in my kitchen. It occurred to me to bake a tray of flapjacks, from the gleanings of my wholefood larder; these I bore through the gorse to greet the newcomers. I was met by a stocky middle-aged man with diminished hairline, dressed in a denim jacket on the back of which was displayed the sequinned outline of a butterfly – evidently the work of his young acolyte and lover, Sue. Both graciously accepted my offering.

This was "Baba Jock", also known as the Archbishop of Rosudgeon: the first man I had met who provided clear evidence that there was indeed a whole universe to explore, a path to strike out on, way beyond the frontiers of reason. He bade me welcome, and supplied me with some fresh ideas, plus some interesting material to peruse. I was given to understand that his was essentially a healing mission, albeit one conducted on a scarcely conceivable esoteric plane. Some might describe him as a prankster, a shape-shifting agent of change. He had a power in him, a force.

What was he doing here on Rosudgeon Common? Had I summoned him up, together with the busload of premmies, by the magnetism of my spiritual yearning? He was in fact well known to my neighbours, so much so that he had adopted the Common as his own diocese. With child-like glee, he described how a small payment to the Universal Life Church (Modesto, California) had secured him his archiepiscopal title, while a simple quiz (What was the name of Adam's wife? . . .) had earned a diploma as Doctor of Divinity. He was hereby authorized to ordain as minister of religion anyone who might so wish. I duly received my small piece of card, entitling me to perform offices of baptism, marriage, and funerals, as did most of my fellow residents. It was probably the most religious community this side of Truro Cathedral.

Jock was keen to broaden our horizons: this little community had gotten a little too sleepy. Driving the Ji-mobile through the little sunken lanes of rural Cornwall, with the mesmeric devotional Ji-music playing through the speakers, we made our way to a village fete. Pausing only for Jock to clip a white clerical collar over his purple shirt, we piled out onto the green, an exotic crew chanting the Hare Krishna mantra.

Not long afterwards, Jock busied himself under the hood of Lothlorien, checking through her secret parts, all those tappets and gaskets. In due course, a steady throbbing rumble announced that there was life in the old girl yet. A general invitation was extended through the Common: who fancied a trip to the Elephant Fayre? There was to be a festival on the ancestral estate of Lord Eliot, whose family coat of arms was topped by an elephant's head. This was at St Germans, at the other end of Cornwall, perhaps an hour and a half distant. And so we all piled onto the bus, Jock at the wheel, holding this powerful beast steady. As we pulled onto the main highway, he sucked deeply on a mighty chillum, blowing out a dense cloud of smoke.
"Bombalay!"

The Elephant Fayre was certainly a delightful event, well-managed and spread comfortably across the landscaped grounds. His Lordship dropped by to say hello, the hare krishnas were offering their delicious dinners, and I had my first sighting of a new sect of red-robed hairies, each wearing a set of beads emblazoned with yet another guru. Jock wasn't too flattering about this lot, but I wasn't properly paying attention – there was so much else going on. To help things along, I shared a bag of Mexican mushrooms, then rather regretted choosing to watch the simulated Viking attack on a Saxon village – real blood was shed! Never mind, there was some great music to enjoy in the estate quarry. All in all, it was a wonderful couple of days.

Still pondering my lyric, the song playing constantly in the background of this chapter, I tune in on this young fellow, so wary of having an identity imposed upon him, of surrendering his fate to the force of the river's raging current. So easy to be sucked in, to be swallowed up in the hustle and bustle, the hassle and baffle. And now the stream has sought him out, invited him to taste the waters; Rosudgeon was not such a backwater after all . . .

"Tell Me Who You Are"

I returned to Oxford at the end of summer and wasted no time in registering at the Job Centre as a Minister of Religion desirous of employment. If, as anticipated, they had nothing to offer, so much the better. There were surely many other things I could be getting busy with. First, though, I needed a home base. It wasn't long before the ideal opportunity presented itself.

The Charles Street Collective had originally comprised three adjacent terraced properties operating as a single shared household, in accordance with the radical communitarian vision of that era. A total of twelve members, each with their own room, would share cooking and domestic duties, and cultivate (or otherwise) the garden space as a single unit. Recently, one house had declared autonomy as a separate feminist republic, but continued to accept calls on the shared payphone in the main living room. The three houses shared a common landlord, who was, in theory, amenable to this arrangement, as long as the rent was paid on time. In practice, his attitude was hands-off to the point of negligence. The properties were in a poor state of repair and a tense stand-off with "Mr K" prevailed: rent was being withheld. Still, the household enjoyed a reputation as a groovy place to live; I was anxious to make a good impression.

The crucial interview took place in the shared living room, a distinctly shabby venue with no furniture besides a table, and no means of heating apart from the chimney fireplace. The chairs, apparently, had all been chopped up during the previous tough winter and fed into the fire; the landlord was still very cross. Social life was perforce conducted close to the floor, slumped on grubby sofa cushions and beanbags. Two or three cats sought out the most comfortable locations and welcoming laps. Across one wall, a large pseudo-cabbalistic pentagram loomed disconcertingly.

My would-be housemates were of a similar age to myself, but otherwise fairly disparate; some even had proper jobs. Each held the power of veto. As my interview progressed, I became uncomfortably aware of the unstable power dynamic in the room. Fortunately, I had the sense to play my strongest card: I loved to cook. This was a winning gambit: cooking was, after all, the bond that held this house together, even while plaster peeled from the walls and rain seeped through the damaged rooftiles.

In my first few weeks as resident I barely moved from the living room – apart from painting an evocation of Prussia Cove in my little bedroom, a wall of splashing blues and greens. I took possession of the shared record collection, selecting the ongoing entertainment while a steady progression of eccentric characters knocked for admission. In the evening came the high point of the day, the shared meal. This was, of course, vegetarian, with a strong reliance on Splat. Nonetheless, every day might offer some fresh revelation, as each resident, engaging their individual predilections and tastes, endeavoured to provide an attractive and satisfying plateful, nourishment for both body and soul. Supper was what brought us together, framed our collective identity.

Our kitchen was rudimentary, but it did boast a pressure cooker, so we were by no means restricted to the humble lentil. Arrayed across the pantry shelves was a wide variety of pulses in all their distinct colours and shapes, plus a host of little jars containing all the herbs and spices that the wholefood shop could supply. For me, it was as good as a playground for my budding culinary imagination.

Wholegrains, cereal flakes, legumes; more exotic items such as miso and tahini . . . most of these ingredients are now readily available in a larger supermarket, but in this well-thumbed booklet they are treated with a self-conscious awe. Using these products – such is the implication – will be a badge of your own weirdness and a gateway to an exciting new lifestyle.

It's a helpful beginner's guide, not least in the *"crazy diagram"* on the last page, intended as license to experiment. All recipes are mutable: what might happen if you add an extra egg, a bit less flour, oil rather than butter, milk instead of water? Look closely enough, and you will find this empowering message: *"anything is possible"*.

Most likely, all of these kitchen goodies came from the same source,

Uhuru Wholefoods on the Cowley Road. Together with its affiliated café on the opposite side of the road, Uhuru's was the epicentre of the East Oxford "alternative scene". From its foundation in the mid-70s, it had been pioneering a new business model, based around the principle of cooperation as an alternative to capitalist rapacity. This reached all the way from its non-hierarchical collective governance to the preferred "third world" suppliers of such goods as coffee and olive oil. Shopping for essential wholefood ingredients might thus become participation in a worldwide revolution, encouraged by the consciousness-raising messages on the store-filled packages. Extra cred-points accrued from volunteering for packaging duties, or by diving shoulder-deep into the bran-tub to mix the signature product, Uhuru's Muesli Deluxe. Both of these activities were fun, but what I really aspired to was to be trusted with cooking duties in the café. In my earlier, more dissolute days I had been too timid, or disorganised, to step up; now I considered myself up for the challenge.

The remodelled Uhuru's Café in 1982, at the time of the Falklands War.
Photo courtesy Martin Stott

While I had been away, the café had been substantially remodelled, to bring it more into line with accepted standards of health and safety. It had always had a reputation for being a bit rough and ready: the only way to close the oven, for example, had been to wedge the fire extinguisher against the door. Those days were gone: a newly spacious kitchen area now hosted a proper kitchen range, and toilet facilities had been doubled to enable gender differentiation. Also, in the interim, the Uhuru collective management had undergone a fundamental shift, in line with radical culture in general. Easy-going, lackadaisical "alternative" lifestyles were no longer cool; now was a time for rigorous organisation, to take a principled stand against the root of all evil, whose name was Patriarchy. The hour of the Radical Feminist had struck, and, in Uhuru's at least, she ruled the roost.

Okay, cool, I reckoned: right on, Sister. I duly showed up for duty, given free rein to design, prepare and cook a full lunch menu. How much fun this was, to bury my hands in a mixing bowl, to stir a giant pot of bean stew, to chop the salad vegetables, to guess the quantities for a cake recipe. It felt like coming home. **This** was what I wanted.

From my activist housemates, I became aware of a wider world of struggle, in which my enthusiasms might play a role. Radical Feminism had recently turbo-charged the anti-nuclear movement, in its campaign against the cruise missiles being introduced by the Thatcher government. Peace Camps, standing sentinel outside the gates of many of the key "defence" establishments, provided a focal point for protest actions. Greenham Common emerged as the model for women's self-organisation, and a new system of rapid response, the phone-tree, was developed which could mobilise activists to counter any fresh outrage. The coin-operated phone-box in our living room served as one such link in the chain of communication.

It was time to challenge long-standing traditions of gender roles. I was happy to offer my support by keeping the pot well stirred, while the sisters did the "heavy lifting" – putting themselves on the front-line of confrontation, no doubt looking forward to a heart-warming bowlful of bean stew, fuel for their indomitable spirit.

The bigger the pot, the more fun it was, so it seemed to me. But there was a correct order to be observed, or to be learned. In preparing the breakfast porridge, for example, it was vital not to add the oats before the water was boiling: burnt porridge would be no one's idea of a restorative feast.

Bravehearts keeping vigil on the airbase perimeter, doing their best to stay warm.

Such mistakes, I came to recognise, were the product of overweening confidence, or rampaging ego. Here was no place for preening kitchen tyrants; our mission was to support the chilled and hungry brave-hearts as best we could.

I was beginning to comprehend the importance of being organised. Somebody needed to think it all through in advance, so that sufficient store of oats might be loaded onto the bus, or that the same sack of onions wasn't expected, by some impossible magic, to be used twice over. There was certainly a place for improvisation, but only if supplies permitted. A sudden demand for cheese rolls could only be met if a speculative order had been placed with the baker a couple of days before departure, and the bread duly picked up and stored appropriately. A clear head was required to anticipate all that might be required on an expedition headed far away from any source of supply.

One thing that was sure to be appreciated, as the necessary complement to a hot mug of tea, was a chunky piece of flapjack. These needed to be baked in advance, sliced into more or less uniform portions, and boxed up in large plastic tubs. Bean stew, mugs of tea, and flapjacks: such was the standard offer from the Munchies and Slurpies Action Support, roving caterers to anti-nuclear protests across the region, championing the cause of alternative energy at all manner of gatherings, and source of an immense amount of satisfaction to all those who took part in its operations.

Munchies and Slurpies was the brainchild of Steve Wade, a former Charles Street resident and passionate advocate of ecological energy systems. His company, Wind and Sun, has over the years become one of the country's leading providers in this sector. In the beginning, he recognised the need to spread his vision. A powerful minivan was procured, together with a catering caravan which could be towed wherever it might be required. On board would be not only a willing crew, with sufficient supplies for the envisaged catering operation, but display boards, posters and flyers providing information about the latest necessary steps towards meeting the challenge of changing times.

As is generally the case with collective endeavours, duties and responsibilities were by no means equally distributed. How many people might be willing to drive such a cumbersome load – or were properly qualified to do so? I considered my skill set to be relatively modest – why had my practical education been so limited? – but I could offer a willing pair of hands with the vegetable chopping, and was ready enough to help out with the various tasks. There was such a romance to setting up in the middle of a field, building a fire in our half-sliced oil drum, gathering the wood supply, getting out the chopping boards; in organising the serving counter at the back of the caravan, arranging the circus-style signboards over the top of the hatch,

meeting the requests of the first eager customers – *"mug of tea and a flapjack, please"*; and in being an active participant in whatever celebration of community conscience happened to be in play.

Events attended were various, ranging from crunchy demos to genial gatherings: Greenham Common, Upper Heyford, Molesworth all hosted Peace Camps in need of succour; Glastonbury, Cropredy, Rougham Tree Fair, Otmoor were each unique iterations of the festival model, occasions to spread the message, boost the funds, and have a real fun time. Somewhere in the middle was a remarkable happening known as the Cosmic Counter Cruise Carnival, which was the product of an uneasy coalition/collision between the Greenham Peace Camp and the Free Festival movement. That year, as Stonehenge festival drew to a close, a decision was taken to decamp immediately to Greenham Common. Thus was spawned the Peace Convoy, soon to haunt the imaginations of Conservative voters throughout the country, the very image of rampant anarchy.

29

So there we were, part of an instant village complete with its own post office and street names, serving up bean stews, mugs of tea, flapjacks, just a few yards from the chain-link fence. We had some competition: *"Get your chemical breakfast here!"* was one early morning barker's cry. It was all rather chaotic, sitting very uneasily with the self-denying austerity of the Women's Peace Camp. One morning, after a night of relentless psychedelic jamming, part of the fence was vigorously assaulted with sledgehammers, bringing a substantial section of it tumbling down. Shortly afterwards, hundreds of police invaded the site, corralling us all by the stage. **"Sit down"**, ordered the women, keen to avoid an unruly brawl; all obeyed, allowing the police to wade into the crowd and haul away seven hairy hippies – the Greenham Seven.

More troubling for my own conscience, over the long term, has been my careless attitude to hygiene at this event. Sanitation at festivals has always proved problematic; this was worse than most. Soon, I was making repeated trips into the woods, feeling distinctly unwell. I realised I really ought to go home. This sensible policy then got mixed up with the perceived need to replenish the flapjack supply. Back home, I endured repeated bouts of bowel-wringing; then I forced myself into baking duties and returned to the carnival carrying these dubious goods. This was undoubtedly the most shameful moment of my catering career.

Now would be a good point to examine the relationship between conscience and consciousness. The two words have the same etymological root, of course. Both relate to knowledge. There's a story in the bible, concerning a certain tree, which has had great resonance. Knowledge is power, according to Mr Bacon. But it comes hand in hand with responsibility. Innocence is lovely, but it has no creative potential. *"It's never too late to have a happy childhood"* proclaimed the banner customarily unrolled at Peace Convoy gatherings. The resolute women encamped at Greenham had rooted themselves into the unquiet knowledge that, just a few yards away, beyond the perimeter fence, was siloed the potential for global destruction.

The premmies I'd met at Rosudgeon had taken refuge in the Knowledge imparted by their guru, Maraji: All is Love. I was suspicious of gurus, wary of faith in general. But I was eager for knowledge, tracking it down in the secret corners of the library, attempting to draw some coherence from out of the murmurings of the mystics. I was looking in the wrong place, as I was about to discover. Knowledge comes from experience.

A cosmically-inclined friend from college had recently returned from India, where, according to the stories he related, he had undergone a mar-vellous, transformative experience at a certain ashram. Now he had attached himself to a community of like-minded souls who were creating a hub for meditative energy in the North Wales countryside. I was curious, so I accepted his invitation to come visit, booking a ticket with National Bus. In due course I found myself in a very pleasant location, not far from the coast, where an old hunting lodge had been repurposed as a commune for disciples of Bhagwan Shree Rajneesh, the controversial Indian guru. All were robed in red, wore a set of beads around their neck, and were generally quite hairy. I had, you may recall, noticed some of these at the Elephant Fayre.

It was a most pleasant weekend: I shared the hash I'd brought with me (not realising this was officially discouraged), took part in a massage workshop (touching other people!), and offered to prepare a meal for the community – if memory serves me right, this was an unlikely pastry pie, filled with black-eyed beans in a bechamel sauce. My cooking may have been experimental, but it was well received, and as I headed back to Oxford I could enjoy the sense that my horizon of possibility had opened out, become more enticing.

Next day, I went shopping for a new T-shirt, perhaps to celebrate my altered sense of self. Shopping in those days was conducted at Stuff Central, otherwise known as Woolworths. There was a technique which I had learned from a friend: how to wrap a sense of ownership around any object before removing it from the shop without the inconvenience of having to pay. This is, of course, also known as shoplifting, as was shortly to be made clear. Perhaps I hadn't exercised sufficient focus in my play of mind over matter; on my way out into the street I was accosted by the store detective and obliged to return to his little office. I had taken the precaution of removing any means of identity (my library card) before I entered, so that, on being asked my name, I replied: *"Robert Davis"*. The police were called, and in due course I found myself remanded in the police lockup.

In the middle of the night I was hauled out and the interrogation was repeated. This time I gave the answer *"David Roberts"*, so that it was as David Roberts that I was conducted, in the back of a Black Maria, to Oxford Prison. These days this historic building has been transformed into a posh hotel, but it was soon apparent what an involuntary guest of Her Majesty might expect. Most fundamentally, there was an absence of doorknob on the door. My two fellow cell-mates and I had blundered our way, by ill-luck or folly, into a dark and dismal place that stank of staleness and thwarted opportunity. Time hung heavy. I did my best to meditate, cross-legged on my mattress, and rehearsed my false identity again and again until it appeared no more than a confection of holes. By next morning I had had enough. Ordered to appear before the Governor, this time round I was Francis Stainthorp; it was Francis Stainthorp who appeared, in mercifully short order, in front of the county court magistrate. Francis Stainthorp, so my duty lawyer pleaded, was *"a private student of religion"* who had somehow stumbled off the strait and narrow path; compassion was requested – and duly awarded. I was sternly admonished to stay out of trouble, a token penalty was imposed . . . and then I was released into the brightness of the day, a free man once more.

Back at Charles Street, I had of course been missed; and then the police had come calling, asking for David Roberts, or maybe Francis Stainthorp. I had sown sufficient confusion for them to return to base little the wiser. There was opportunity for my housemates to remove anything which might have drawn unwanted attention, thus sparing me the shame of drawing my friends into a legal morass.

The next day, scrubbed well clean of prison-aroma, I was back on the street, glad to be able to fulfil a prior commitment to stand up against Corporate Capitalism. I was carrying a cleverly sloganned cardboard sign ("NUKE FUEL SLAVE LABOUR") under my arm, on my way to picket Rio Tinto Zinc, whose representatives were in town to recruit the nation's best and brightest to organise their strip-mining operations. There was an un-expected voice at my shoulder: *"Francis Stainthorp? – I've been told to keep an eye out for you; you don't want to get in any trouble, do you?"* It was a police officer; evidently, I was a marked man.

I had fallen in with the protest crew. Who could deny that voices needed to be raised? Next stop offered the possibility of a genuine confrontation. All through the summer Britain had been at war with Argentina: the entirety of the Royal Navy had been despatched to the South Atlantic to reclaim a couple of scrubby islands which had been seized by the dastardly foreigner. It had been a shockingly desperate affair, its viciousness masked by official censorship. But now we had emerged victorious, and Resurgent Britannia was set to parade through the City of London. There was a plan, I learned, to disrupt such proceedings.

We convened somewhere in the East End; apart from one or two of my Oxford friends, here were people I had never met before, so we spent the evening performing bonding exercises and attempting a trial run in a local cul-de-sac. Those truly brave, willing to risk serious bother, arrest and imprisonment, committed themselves to a collective dash into the path of the procession, intent on fastening themselves into a padlocked chain which might force the oncoming army to an abrupt halt. I, more cautious, elected myself to an observer's role; I had had enough of prison cells.

Next morning, we walked out separately, headed towards our agreed rendezvous. In the street was an air of excited expectancy, and a strong police presence. As I walked past one officer, I caught a snatch of their walkie-talkie messaging: *"he's just progressing up the road . . ."* Shortly afterwards, a burly officer called me to a halt, ordering me to turn out my pockets and explain my shifty presence on such a patriotic occasion. My empty pockets, and my noncommittal attitude, provided no cause for detention, but it was apparent, as I mingled with the flag-bearing crowds gathering at the barricades, that our plot had been well and truly rumbled. It was, in fact, an extremely effective exercise in proactive suppression of public unrest. All would-be perpetrators had been detained prior to their intended protest, so that no rumour of dissent ever entered into the newspaper coverage. The victory parade could be presented as a scene of unalloyed joy. Surrounded by the cheering throng, I sought to make myself inconspicuous: as an emblem of my shame, I purchased a union flag and waved it disconsolately.

It is tempting to draw a connection between the prevailing wartime unease of those times and the increasingly incendiary graffiti appearing on the Cowley Road: *"Burn Men"*, for example. As local standard bearers for the Radical Feminist cause, the mood of the Uhuru Women's Collective had shifted away from grudging tolerance towards open disrespect. One morning, as I arrived for my shift in the café, I was astonished to read the sign on the men's toilet, which now stated *"Men & Other Worldwide Diseases"*. I declared straight away that I intended to remove it, and, not being met with an outright rebuttal (suggestive of a certain ambivalence amongst the collective about this new turn), I duly turned up next day equipped with paint and brush. Out went the offending sign. I had crossed a Rubicon.

The response was rapid, immense. I was ordered off the premises, banned forever. The very personification of Patriarchy . . . was my own self!

Fired up with so much donated energy, I went to see my sannyasin friends who lived in the semi-derelict house next door. I was possessed by a marvellous clarity: confronted by such rampant absurdity, there was evidently no need to hang on to the vestiges of normality, of rationality. The world had an immense tolerance for craziness. That thing which had been tempting me for the past several weeks was suddenly mine for the taking. I was going to offer my submission to the Master, to become a sannyasin of Bhagwan Shree Rajneesh.

Through such peculiar twists and turns, like the convoluted coils and spirals of a river whirlpool, a life's course may flip direction and the world is transformed. No wonder history lessons had never quite made sense.

For narrative purposes, I am now fast forwarding my account by a full year and more, to an exercise in which my identity is once again to be quizzed, with increasing intensity, over a ten-day period. This will take place at Medina, the headquarters of the Rajneesh movement in England, and will be called the Satori Event.

There is a very simple structure, which is repeated again and again throughout the day, pausing only for frugal meals and physical exercise. Participants are grouped in pairs for a forty-minute session, swapping roles every ten minutes. Sitting on cushions facing one other, close up, one poses the question: *"Tell me who you are"*. He or she then remains silent, impassive while the partner attempts to provide a convincing answer. Then the roles are reversed, again and again, partners changing for each new session.

There is so much to say – and still there is no answer! Personal history, family details, are recounted, but the mystery remains. The realms of metaphor are opened up and explored – all those hills and valleys, rivers and oceans, fortresses and palaces – but who was it lived there, who inhabited those realms? Metaphysical constructs are invoked – the soul, the spirit, the heart, the physical self – but none seem to speak with a true voice.

This is trickier than you might think!

So much is said, and heard, and yet all remains unresolved – unless the moderator, sensing that a participant might be poised on the edge of transcendent resolution, throws another corker into the play: *"What is Love?"*, for example.

It's a revelatory technique, not least in pointing up the impossibility of self-definition. There is always more to be said.

So, why fixate on being consistent? It's a point well-captured by Walt Whitman, the hippies' favourite transcendentalist poet:

> *Do I contradict myself? Very well, then, I contradict myself;*
>
> *(I am large. I contain multitudes).*

Hejira

What was it that first attracted me to this notorious Sex Cult?

Well, I was still a terribly lonely boy, weary of carrying my burdensome, metaphorical sign – the one that read "Hands Off" – through all those wasted years, even bringing it with me into the famously sociable Charles Street. Was there even a point in pursuing spiritual enquiry without first engaging with this?

Rajneesh – Bhagwan as I learned to call him – had a very attractive, insightful line on this. There was, he boldly asserted, no inherent contradiction between sex and spirituality; they were in fact entirely complementary. Moreover, he developed and encouraged a wide range of strategies to enable the truth of this to be appreciated. Here was a faith that could celebrate the full potential of being human. And there was a large community living out this vision, evidently having a wonderful time. I could do with some of that!

The Price of Admission? Sannyasins committed to four undertakings: to wear only "sunrise colours" – red, maroon, orange, cerise; to don a set of beads carrying the master's portrait – the mala; to meditate for one hour a day; and to adopt a new name chosen by the master. All in all, it offered the chance of a fundamental reset, a fresh beginning. Yes, I was ready for that, too.

Sannyas Central in England was called Medina Rajneesh, a large property deep in the Sussex countryside, built around the turn of the twentieth century in the Tudorbethan style. Its original purpose as a preparatory school for boys remained much in evidence, though now overlaid with a playful new age wackiness, which in the couple of years of the commune's existence had done much to instil a special charm. Had the term yet been coined, it could well be described as Hogwartian; it was a very British fantasy of communal living.

My first visit came just a few weeks after I had started to attend gatherings in Oxford, still getting to know the ten or a dozen local sannyasins. Molly, who hosted our weekly meetings, was to be initiated with her new name, Sohani, so we piled into a small van and headed across country. On arrival, I had my first taste of the visceral power of a whole community dressed in red, like plunging into a collective energy field. All was soft, warm, loving – if only I could allow it in. The evening sannyas-giving ceremony culminated in a marvellous, ego-stopping dance, for which the excellent resident band played a succession of simple devotional songs that tuned us all onto the same delicious wavelength – the way of the heart. When the music stopped, all merged into a lovely pile of bodies, hugging and being embraced. I was utterly bowled over. *"This is where I want to live"*, I told myself, *"this is how I want to be"*.

Just a few weeks later, it was my turn. *"How did you get your name?"*, I've often been asked, as the apparent mismatch between my name and national identity demands some explanation. This allows me the cheeky reply: *"It came in the post"*. I'd received a large envelope from Oregon, USA, addressed to Swami Antar Hafiz. This was to be my new name, printed at the bottom of an embossed certificate, together with a helpful guide as to its meaning: all male sannyasins were Swami (women were Ma), which implies being master; Antar means "Inner"; Hafiz is a sufi word for God, in his aspect as preserver. This was a lot to swallow!

Many sannyasins can relate how they were personally initiated by the master's mystic thumb, pressing into the third eye point on their brow, triggering a precious glimpse into transcendence. I would have to make do with a deputy digit, courtesy of one of the big-haired mommas at Medina. But I had made my jump: I had elected to submit to the will of a purported enlightened being, and to the community dedicated to his vision, as directed by his earthly representatives.

Bhagwan, it's worth noting at this point, had responded to the feminist moment by appointing a team of women as principal directors of his organisation. Chief amongst these, Big Momma herself, was Ma Anand Sheela, officially Bhagwan's secretary. Medina was headed up by Ma Poonam, a benign dictator. This was in fact Matriarchy in action.

The day after my sannyas ceremony, I joined the entire community on a coach trip to London. Much to my embarrassment, I was called out by Poonam for wearing a black donkey jacket: my transition to red-ness was not yet complete. We were set to process through central London, to announce the launch of Britain's newest newspaper, the Rajneesh Times, and to present a gift of flowers to the visiting vice president George Bush. This was a very different demonstration to any I had previously taken part in! Despite my lack of red coat, I joined in with the collective convulsion of happiness, as we paraded our message of "Love, Life, Laughter" through the streets.

I returned to Oxford with my beads, sifting out any noncompliant clothing from my meagre wardrobe, and devoted myself to cultivating my new identity. I was grateful to have the support and encouragement of the local sannyasin community: small though this was, it fostered a sense of group belonging through a regular programme of gatherings and meditations. Bhagwan had developed a wide range of meditation techniques which differed markedly from the traditional method of silent sitting, vipassana, to cultivate a state of detached watchfulness. The chaotic lifestyles of modernity required a new approach; there was simply too much going on in everyday life to expect the psyche to arrive readily at stillness. Instead, a vigorous, rhythmic soundtrack encouraged the fullest expression of thoughts and emotions, via a succession of physical exercises, before subsiding to a more quiescent state. In short, they tended to involve noisy cathartic expression, definitely not the sort of thing your neighbours might willingly tolerate.

Sohani enjoying the freedom of Port Meadow

There were techniques more suited to domestic practice, but for these hardcore methods, notably Kundalini and Dynamic, we needed to hire a local community centre. Afterwards, lying down in a sort of afterglow, we would listen to a recording of Bhagwan speaking, allowing his voice to resonate in our clarified consciousness. Then we would pack up the hall and head for supper. Meanwhile, Sohani had been busy at home preparing a wonderful feast for us all.

For me, it amounted to a marvellous package, in which the shared meal, the ritual feast, was by no means the least important. After the mental and emotional clutter had been acknowledged and allowed full expression, what remained was a receptivity, an open-ness, and a sense of gratitude. These were all gifts which might best be shared over a meal prepared with love. It was a proper communion.

Sohani drew much of her culinary inspiration – notably her cheecake recipes – from the Moosewood Cookbook (1977) by Mollie Katzen. Despite the authorship, this is very much the product of collective endeavour, the pooling of traditions and cultural backgrounds at the eponymous restaurant in upstate New York. As such, it epitomises the wholefood approach to cooking – I could imagine this food being on the menu at Alice's Restaurant.

The unifying element is supplied by the presentation: each page is lovingly hand-written in a cheeky, friendly style, embellished by quirky cartoons and illustrations, a pleasure to linger over. As a whole, the book opens up a wide range of possibilities, with signposts leading off in many directions.

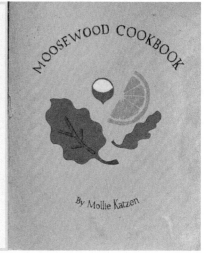

For an extra blast of transformative Bhagwan energy, a weekend workshop at Medina was recommended. This was a big source of income for the Commune: a wide range of seminars and trainings was offered, led by a team of skilled therapists and facilitators. For someone like myself, habitually unemployed, this posed a financial challenge. Making this explicit, I was instructed by Poonam to get myself a job.

There is a big difference between getting a job and committing to a career. For some reason this escaped me entirely. In the course of a hitch to Reading one day, a driver helpfully suggested that I should become a nurse. This was not something I had hitherto shown any interest in; nonetheless, I accepted this as Cosmic Advice, and duly applied for a three-year nursing training at the John Radcliffe hospital. Rather surprisingly, I was accepted. When, shortly afterwards, I was informed that second thoughts had been had, I made a determined effort to reinstate myself on the course. What was I thinking?

It was soon apparent that nursing, estimable profession though it be, really wasn't what I wanted. Put most simply, I couldn't be a servant of two masters. There was something I was most keen to do at Medina, and my demanding work schedule just wouldn't allow the necessary time off. That was the Satori Event. *"Tell me who you are?"* Well, I definitely wasn't going to be a Nurse.

The dynamism of emergent spiritual and religious movements is generally expressed through a narrative of expanding frontiers, be these internal or external. Sannyas, it soon became apparent, was not in the business of remaining in the same place. It was already two years since its centre of operations had uprooted from the legendary ashram in Poona, India, to enter a radically new phase of activity. The emphasis was now on building a new society from scratch, a model community in the middle of the Oregon bad-lands. An extensive property had been purchased – the Ranch, also known as Rajneeshpuram – space enough to manifest the boldest of dreams. To meet these new circumstances, hair was to be trimmed back, flowing loose robes were exchanged for thick puffa jackets (red, of course) more suited for the fierce Oregon winters, and practical skills such as construction and road-building were enthusiastically embraced by quondam pioneers of spiritual exploration. True to feminist form, women were allotted privileged status in controlling the heavy diggers and earthmoving equipment. Happy smiles remained in place; team spirit was overflowing in the thrilling videos we watched, relaxing after Sohani's delicious dinners. See the hillside explode, to make way for the new runway for Rajneesh Air!

Bhagwan himself had gone into silence. His presence on the Ranch was restricted, apparently, to a daily drive-by in one of his growing collection of immaculate Rolls Royces, an opportunity to greet his slow but steady

progress with outbreaks of frenzied joy. It was very much Sheela's show: she called the shots, quite literally. Having provoked some confrontation with the local residents, selected commune members had been equipped and trained in firearms use, a red-clad police department to be known as the Peace Force.

Furthermore, the easy-going exploration and expression of sexuality which had been fundamental to the sannyas lifestyle had been substantially reined back, as a clear-sighted response to the AIDS pandemic. Sheela had showed up in London to share her unwelcome message: obligatory condoms and rubber gloves for all sexual contact.

Ma Anand Sheela

Our little centre in Oxford was under some pressure from Poonam, for not being dynamic enough. Perhaps Oxford was simply too much of a "head-town". I took up an invitation to visit our Bristol equivalent, Udgatri, which had recently acquired a substantial property on the side of Brandon Hill, to see what might be possible. This was a decommissioned police station, with plenty of space for group meditations and gatherings, as well as still boasting a couple of lock-up cells. About a dozen commune members travelled in daily from their shared house, pooling their energy and skills to create a welcoming space for the flourishing local sannyasin community.

Most exciting for me was the delightful little café, with access to an outside patio area, which was evidently just waiting for the right person to take it in hand. While I was there, I took the opportunity to bake a cake, which went down well.

But perhaps there was another café opportunity in Oxford. As I'd anticipated, the intimidating regime imposed by the Uhuru Women's Collective had driven away all but a hardcore of committed supporters and guilty men. The café had been obliged to close for want of custom, opening only for special women-only events. It seemed a terrible shame, given the amount of voluntary effort that had gone into refitting the premises. From a friend – okay, a girlfriend (!) – I learnt that a new collective had formed, men and women both, proposing to rent the premises under the name Wholemeal Café. Allowing my misgivings to be overridden by womanly wiles, I agreed to help out with cooking duties.

The Uhuru Women, learning of this outrage, stamped their Doc Martens down hard, demanding that I be purged from their property. Wholemeal responded with admirable principle, declaring that it was their right as renters to conduct their business without interference. The upshot was, the fledgling café closed down, and the premises once again reverted to sorry desuetude.

I had managed to close down the local community café. Here, surely, was a karmic debt waiting to be redeemed.

It felt like time for me to move on. Funds I'd saved from my brief nursing career had been spent on a ticket to the Summer Celebration on the Ranch, a more-or-less obligatory token of my commitment to the faith. It was understood that I would move to Bristol, to Udgatri, on my return.

The Celebration, held under the wide, suddenly very hot skies of the Oregon semi-desert, certainly provided an expanded horizon for me. Thousands of red-clad devotees, all in one place, and I was a part of this awesome undertaking! Bhagwan appeared each day, to sit in silence with us, and we celebrated our good fortune at being in his presence. I explored the rapidly expanding township, took part in the daily meditation program, enjoyed the generous meals served up by the extremely efficient commune kitchen, and helped out with the washing-up operation afterwards.

Meanwhile, Sheela was engaging with representatives of the worldwide movement, laying down the template for the next stage of its evolution. When I arrived back in Bristol, to take up my place as a proper commune member, it was to the news that time had been called on this little centre. In just a couple of weeks all who wished to would be moving to Medina. Centralisation was the new policy.

I had barely time to get used to the strangeness of not having my own room to take refuge in, barely time to accustom myself to the responsibilities of café management. Still, this was very much a culture of "one day at a time". I would get used to that. Two weeks later, I was on the bus headed for Medina, alongside my colleague, Jivan: "two thin cooks".

Herringswell Manor, aka Medina Rajneesh

I was very much a new boy, and was allowed the privilege of a guided tour of the estate. Apart from the main building, which housed the kitchen and eating areas, plus two storeys of dormitories, various other structures were clustered around the entrance driveway: a smaller building dedicated to the 20 or so children, for their sleeping and teaching needs, a laundry, a small shop selling knick-knacks and sweeties, a communal clothes store, and an extensive garage caring for the disparate fleet of motor vehicles pooled by residents. Slightly removed was a complex of newer structures reserved for therapy group activities.

There was, I was informed, one person I really must meet – the resident witch, Jaya. Jaya was currently Tools Mama, supervising the communal store of useful implements around the back of the garage, making sure that each item returned to base after being used. It would have been easy to mislay things in such a large household! But she was also available for on-demand psychic readings. We introduced ourselves, and a tarot pack was produced.

The first card I pulled out was the Queen of Swords – swords, the suit for mentality, the intellect. *"Ah, the Old Nag"*, she observed, with a gentle Irish lilt.

Second card: The Fool – Zero the Hero. *"And that's you"*, she said.

"No more cards. Two's quite enough". She was, of course, absolutely right. This particular conjunction has kept me busy throughout my entire life.

I was happy to be set to work on kitchen duties. Down in the basement, to sort out a fresh delivery of provisions, I met an ebullient young Italian woman named Premo. She struck me as being very much at home. As I recklessly wrapped sticky tape round and around an unruly box, she called me to order: *"you think the commune's made of money?"*

I'm glad to say that I have remained in touch with Premo, on and off, down the years. Asked to contribute to this current book, she was kind enough to provide the following impressions of her own time at Medina. She had evidently been living there for some time before I showed up, after having settled in London following taking sannyas in Poona.

Medina was a true dreamland for me (and surely for many of us) – in spite of anything that could be said about Poonam and some of her ways. I worked in the kitchen from the very beginning and for quite a long time; when I asked to join the Commune I was first told that I could do so only if I got an outside job, and for a while I worked with a catering company that had an ongoing gig making meals for construction workers at building sites. Every day I would leave at 6am in the misty, chill Suffolk morning and spend 7 hours frying eggs and bacon and heating up baked beans from gigantic cans, making toasts, then washing dishes and starting the midday meal preparation (more gross stuff like macaroni cheese, deep-fried things, and such). During the weekend I would help in the Medina kitchen. After a couple of weeks, Vira – the tiny, sprightly German powerhouse who ran the kitchen at the time – told Poonam, "you know, I really need Preemo in the kitchen" and Poonam replied, "Okay. Tell her to quit her job". I had tears in my eyes that afternoon when I received the news, it was one of the greatest days in my life.

Ma Premo

Medina kitchen was impeccably organized but I added my own contribution when I colour-coded all the cleaning supplies and sponges and cloths – in order to ensure top hygiene standards – and even made a laminated board illustrated with drawings that showed all the purposes of each colour sponge or cloth. Some people were very resistant to the colour-coding, though.

On warm days we would take our cutting boards, knives, aprons, and bins full of produce, and we would go sit outside in a vivacious and giggly circle, prepping the veggies and yakking and laughing and gossiping away (not the "mean" kind of gossip, but more of a quite loving and light-hearted storytelling).

I remember one funny episode related to the cooking of spaghetti: I was horrified when I saw that the spaghetti bundles were cut in two "because they were too long to fit" and because "they would cook faster". I took a bundle, climbed on top of the cooks' stool (our stoves were high, and some of us cooks were tiny) and demonstrated how it's done by circling the bundle halfway down its length with both hands, giving it a little twist in opposite directions while holding it right in the middle of the boiling pot, and then releasing it so that it would fan evenly, gently sinking into the water as it softened. Premananda looked quite impressed and said, "wow! She's done that before!"

Veggie shopping was my favourite: We would take a flatbed truck to the wholesalers' farmers' market and load gigantic amounts of fruit and veggies and fresh dairy and all sorts of things. We had the most *amazing cellar below the kitchen, a real labyrinth of cool and well-aired stockrooms.*

Also it was amazing that we dined in these spectacular rooms, hand-decorated with vintage stencils of birds and vines and foliage, with giant bay-windows . . . I loved them!

The menus were always incredibly varied and featuring dishes from so many different traditions – from Yorkshire pudding (vegetarian version of course) to lasagna to Indian curries and Japanese delicacies . . . And the bread! Oh my god, the bread!!! We had amazing bakers. On visitors' Open Days we had Cream Teas with the most incredible spread of delicious cakes, scones, homemade jams, pies and rolls . . . we as residents were not allowed to partake, as visitors of course had priority . . . but it was sooo good to look at it all!

It's a delightful evocation, in which Premo's understanding of the central role of the kitchen in commune life shines through clearly. Mealtimes are an opportunity for coming together, to be enjoyed in a civilised and relaxing atmosphere.

It's also evident that not everyone really knew what they were doing, that a constant process of improvisation and adaptation was in play. At the time I really didn't appreciate this: I was simply overawed by the complexity of the operation, and lacked the self-confidence to assert my own experience.

But perhaps the strongest flavour here is one of nostalgia, for a lost paradise. Already, by the time I arrived, this was visibly slipping away. Medina, suddenly obliged to find room for commune members from all the smaller centres, now closed, was bursting at the seams. The cosy community that had grown together, the close-knit bonds of friendship built through shared endeavour, was confronted by drastic upheaval. Poonam herself had been deposed, ordered to taxi-driving duties on the Ranch – doubtless in the interest of her spiritual growth. A colleague of Sheela's was now in charge: she seemed genial enough, but this was an uncertain new world. I'm sure I wasn't the only one to feel challenged by the unfamiliar situation I now found myself in. Nonetheless, the governing ethos was to Celebrate Everything – so that's what we did. We understood that sannyas wasn't supposed to be an easy ride. This was a daredevil adventure into the unknown, trusting in the wisdom of the Master.

It soon became apparent that there was a master plan to co-ordinate all the communes around the world in a single, tremendous transformational effort. Apart from the Ranch, there would be just one multi-campus European commune, together with similar centralised communities in Australia and Japan. The specific plan for Medina was to convert it back into a school, where all the children from the European communes could receive their education, freeing their parents to concentrate on their spiritual engagement. There was no time to lose!

The beautiful stencilled paintings, so beloved of Premo, were amongst the first things to go, covered over in a uniform wash of brilliant white. The grand piano in the parlour was manhandled up the stairs, and the immaculately polished parquet floor was hidden away under linoleum sheeting, hammered into position by barbarous nails.

It was all change in the kitchen, too. In place of the lovingly constructed menus, respective of local foibles and sensibilities, there was to be strict co-ordination with the rest of Europe, using a three-week (later expanded to four) rota of recipes derived from the Ranch. This would ensure that there was no possibility of a sannyasin, travelling between the different nodes of the European commune, ever having to eat lasagne over two consecutive days, however much they might wish to. Chefs would have to learn the new regimen, and the ordering department adapt their purchasing accordingly. It should, in theory, greatly improve efficiency – at the cost, perhaps, of spontaneity and gaiety. In fact, as Premo reminds me, the Ranch-derived portion control bore little relation to local appetites: *"We always had soooooo many leftovers!"*

All of this was swallowed down, more or less without demur. The only hint of rebellion came with the order to abolish toast. Surely this was an assault on the very essence of Englishness, on a fundamental bastion of individual freedom? Just so, Ma. Get over it, Swami.

I was kept busy in a variety of roles, not just in the kitchen. As Christmas – which was, to the immense disappointment of the kids, no longer to be observed – approached, I was part of the construction crew, spending the week in London renovating a large house in St John's Wood. That was fun:

easy camaraderie prevailed amongst the equal mix of men and women in the team, and I felt no pressure to pretend to a muscular physicality which I didn't possess. Back at Medina for the weekend, I attended a commune meeting at which it was announced that I was to be one of five people to be despatched to Freiburg, to help with the building program there, in just a couple of days' time. Where was Freiburg? I had little idea.

I spent Christmas day learning how to dowse: selecting a couple of copper rods from the Tools Store, bending them at a right angle, and then pacing a steady course over the lawns, registering the point at which the outstretched rods would suddenly swing together. We were attempting to plot the buried, and unrecorded, plumbing lines. Whether this resulted in a coherent, usable map I never discovered. Very early on Boxing Day my companions and I were driven down to Harwich, to take the ferry across to Hook of Holland. As we closed in on the dock, we passed a disconsolate crew of picketers gathered around their brazier, outliers in the desperate combat with the Unions that Mrs Thatcher had unleashed.

Did it cross my mind that there might be some correspondence between Margaret Thatcher and Ma Anand Sheela, both exemplars of a new feminist-derived empowerment? I feel sure that I was too bleary-eyed, too wrapped up in the astonishing adventure on which I had been consigned. For the next few years the travails of the United Kingdom under its intransigent dominatrix would be little more than a distant rumour, of riots and royal jamborees.

The Crunch

Bundling through Dutch border controls in the wee small hours: questions are being raised about our one-way tickets and our evident lack of supporting funds. I catch the word "Cult". This is evidently explanation enough.

Many hours later, our train arrives in Freiburg. We step out onto a very cold platform, flurries of snow blowing around our legs. We are expected, bade welcome.

The snow lay thick for several weeks. I had never been anywhere so cold. Fortunately, the block of flats which constituted our commune residence was well insulated and comfortable: the standard of living seemed far in advance of Britain. It was quite a different story at my designated place of work. There were around fifteen of us engaged in constructing a Spielhalle – an amusement arcade – in the city centre. All lay open to the elements, barely mitigated by the blasts of warmed air being blown onto us by the onsite heaters. Thickly encased in several layers of overalls, I did my best to perform my allotted tasks, making fumbling acquaintance with a range of useful tools. After a week or two, questions were raised about my suitability for the job; in particular, my eyesight was deemed to be not quite up to the mark.

One of the things which I had left behind me in Oxford, as I embarked on my adventures, was my pair of spectacles, worn since childhood. I had embraced the doctrine of "better eyesight without glasses" – the Bates method, as championed by Aldous Huxley. In retrospect, I can understand that this had served to disempower the rational aspect of my brain (the Old Nag!), whilst correspondingly enabling more holistic, impressionistic modes of perception. It had become easier to look into another's eyes, and to allow them in.

I was consigned to domestic duties: the unglamorous routine of the laundry, processing the steady throughput of the communal wardrobe. Sharing a collective clothing ethos – comfortable, but always red – made pooling of garments surprisingly unproblematic. Outward appearance had become so much less important as we concentrated on cultivating our inner being. Once worn, clothes were simply returned to the laundry and replacements sourced from Vimalkirti, the clothes bank. If you really wanted to cling to a particular item, this might be achieved by a safety-pinned label.

The laundry was steady and calming, but a little bit dull. Being posted to the cleaning department offered more opportunity for movement and exploration, getting to know the layout of my new home. We occupied most of a six-storey block of flats, accessed through two adjacent front doors. In the basement was a large car parking area, a grey zone of concrete and buttresses, with an automatic entry system redolent of James Bond. The building was impressively modern, and gloriously situated: in front, just over the road, the side of the valley rose steeply, neatly planted with vines to catch the sun; to the rear, a wide patio skirted the building, below which was a rapid stream, running freshly off the Black Forest hills – except now it lay deeply frozen, glinting.

Our day was structured from breakfast time at 7.30 until the end of supper twelve hours later, but it was by no means relentless activity. We didn't actually "work": our daily duties had been redefined as "worship", to be performed as if it were a meditation, with awareness and a sense of gratitude. The various departments to which we were allocated were known as Temples. It really is surprising what a terminological shift can effect. I wasn't cleaning toilets, that shameful occupation; I was worshipping in Raidas Temple, happily scrubbing under the rim and polishing the porcelain, for the benefit of my fellow beloveds. There was a sign above each loo, respectfully requesting swamis to pee sitting down, for the sake of hygiene and because "it is more relax". The sign was, of course, embellished with a big red heart. This was a very heart-filled environment.

In pairs, we visited each flat, home to about ten communards, who typically shared a room with two or three others. Personal space was restricted to a mattress with duvet, plus a small bedside cabinet, which might bear a picture of Bhagwan but no more than two books. The overall style was known as "Zen": promoting an atmosphere of clarity through clear lines, white walls, and absence of clutter. There was a strong emphasis on keeping everything clean and tidy. Each washroom received special attention, following a specified routine, being sure to use the appropriate coloured cloth.

At the appointed hour, we would break for tea, heading down to the canteen on the ground floor, taking our steaming mugs onto the patio. I was always surprised at how many commune members were smokers; they would gather in their designated "smoking temples", wreathed in aromatic fug.

Lunch was a splendid buffet, helping ourselves to an array of freshly prepared salads, tasty soup, neatly sliced bread and cheese. There would be a little time afterwards to relax with a special friend – maybe cuddled up in bed. Then back to worship until teatime, then through again till supper. It was an intense discipline, all conducted in a methodical, unhurried but diligent manner. It felt like love in action.

Should there still be surplus energy to burn, we could head into town, maybe using one of the commune bicycles, to visit the commune disco – the Far Out. This really was far out. It had been purpose built just a year or two previously, at the same time as the commune was established, and provided a good source of income for the 100-strong community. The style, in common with other "Far Outs" established in the larger German cities, had the same Zen aesthetic: light and clean, with an absence of dark corners. It was extremely popular, notably with the local squaddies, French soldiers based just across the border, who had their own style of synchronised dancing, forming disciplined lines on one side of the oval marble dancefloor, whilst the other side would be filled with wildly gyrating sannyasins.

After a few weeks of domestic worship, I was delighted to be assigned to Disco duties, which was essentially a night shift. This also coincided with Carnival time – the municipal festival common in Catholic Germany. We took part in the civic procession, an anarchic floatful of cavorting angels and devils amongst an endless stream of marching gnomes, witches, dangerous beasts, huntsmen – all the phantasmagoria of the Teutonic imagination. In the evening, everyone was ready to party. Kitted out in my devil's horns, I had a marvellous time running one of the several disco bars, caught up in the wild celebration.

Gradually, a change had set in. My sense of self was shifting: I was learning to set aside the embattled "I", wrapped in its protective cocoon, and allowing myself to dissolve in a wider identity – "Us". Here was an easy intimacy of hugs and smiles, and playful touch. Language had become secondary to feeling.

Although most commune members were German – apart from my fellow Brits, there was a smattering of Italians, plus some more exotic nationalities – our lingua franca was a very basic form of English, known as "Rajneesh English". This was certainly not a language for abstruse thought; my Oxford education counted for nothing. Should I ever launch into a sentence with *"I think . . ."* I would be immediately admonished: *"Swami, tell us what you feel . . ."*

Back in the house, I was set to worship in Magdalena, the kitchen temple. Each day began with the Gacchamis: kneeling on the floor, we performed a threefold ritual of submission: bowing to the master, to the teaching, and to the community. Then we got busy, each to their own task, co-ordinated by the kitchen mama: chopping, cooking, setting out the eating space, cleaning up. All was focussed on the end result: a meal imbued with Love. Magdalena, it was often said, was the Heart of the Commune.

I began to take notice of the "snacks mama", kneading the dough for sunflower bread, to be served at teatime. Soon we were hanging out together at teabreak each day. Her name was Kabira; we formed an attachment.

Ma Prem Kabira, with her daughter Devaki

Of all the many remarkable people I came to know in my commune days, Kabira was one of the few whose backstory was known to me, at least in part. She was old enough to have been married, raising two children with her Dutch husband in Brazil, where he worked for an international tobacco corporation. The marriage had then fallen apart, and she had returned with her children to Freiburg, where she had grown up. She started to attend meditation sessions, and had joined the fledgling commune not too long before I showed up. This much I gathered: sufficient to be impressed by her strength of will, in rejecting an unsatisfactory conventional lifestyle in favour of something radically different. Recently, she has provided me with a more nuanced account of her early days in the commune, for which I provide the following translation:

I was appointed Office Mama; I assumed it was part of my job to have an opinion about the commune income and outgoings – but Sakshi [the commune main man] didn't approve. I'd thought that the commune was supposed to be democratic.

There was a row, at the end of which I'd lost my Mama job and was appointed to washing-up duties.

That was the first shock, that burst my dream of an ideal world. I was riven by tears.

But somehow, despite this disappointment, I trusted that this might only strengthen my connection with Osho, since I didn't believe any more that the leader and most influential people in the commune were really "enlightened". I still thought that this was the right place for me to explore my self-awareness.

When I came into the washing-up kitchen there were mostly younger swamis, including a young Englander, Hafiz. All were good-humoured and fun to be with. Hafiz sat next to me often, while he waited for his tea to cool down to the right temperature, English style!

I came to realise that the Mama job, for all its apparent kudos, had only brought me stress, and that working on the washing-up was a much better way of enjoying being myself.

Later, though, when one of Sheela's aides came visiting, I complained that this job wasn't very fulfilling. That's when I became the afternoon snacks chef. This suited me very well, because I got a lot of appreciation. I was only surprised that the finance department gave me no spending guidelines for my ingredients – flour, butter, almonds, etc. So I had my little revenge, always buying top quality!

The ice had long since broken up in the rushing stream; spring had arrived, and I was beginning to appreciate what an interesting locality this was. Freiburg, nestling amid the wilderness of the Black Forest, was a special place: like Oxford, it was a famous seat of learning, except that it had been severely smashed up in the war. Most of the old centre had been obliterated: only the Munster, with its dramatic russet spire, had escaped damage. I was looking forward to exploring further.

My photo, taken in 2018, shows the centre of Freiburg, as seen from the heights of the Schloß-berg. The area around the Munster, which had been griev-ously damaged in the war, has been largely rebuilt in sympathetic style.

25 years ago this area was still beset with construction sites.

Sheela showed up, calling us all to a meeting in the disco. She didn't mince her words. We were all a disgrace to Bhagwan. In particular, Sakshi, who had set up the commune and built the disco, was the worst sort of disgrace. It was hard for me to grasp what was happening; it didn't match my experience at all. But it was soon clear what Sheela intended. The Frei-burg commune was to be disbanded, and all were to be dispatched to other nodes in the European commune. Only the disco, evidently a valuable money-spinner, was to escape this inferno: a small crew were going to stay on to keep it going, moving to a house in a local village.

In just a few days, so I was informed, I would be leaving for Berlin. Kabira, as my acknowledged partner, would be travelling with me on the train.

This was my fourth uprooting within a single year. I was becoming used to it – the discipline of fitting my entire belongings into a single small suitcase, with the confidence that all my needs would be duly met at my eventual destination. And what could be more exciting than moving to Berlin – "the city that never sleeps"?

Here was a strange anomaly, in which History had never quite resolved. Berlin was a walled enclave within a hostile socio-political system that had threatened ruin on Western civilisation throughout my whole life. Its designated role in the Cold War face-off was quite specifically as provoca-tion: an alluring shop window of consumer goods forever tantalisingly out of reach, for those whose parents had made the wrong choice back in 1961, when the Wall was erected. The shop windows stretched several kilometres along both sides of the Kurfürstendamm; and the Ku-damm was precisely where we were headed.

The Far Out Disco on Lehniner Platz might look a lot more shop-worn than its Freiburg counterpart, but it far surpassed it in popularity. It could indeed claim to be the city's number one nightspot – a key destination for any vagrant Ossi lucky enough to have wangled his way across the border, at least for one evening of precious freedom. Where else, at precisely 11 o'clock, would the guests be asked to clear the dance floor, to make way for the entire disco crew, all smartly attired in purple-grey uniforms (made in East Germany!), who would parade onto the marble, hands pressed together, and namaste to their guests? When the music started up again, the energy was redoubled. At the weekends it was normal for the party to continue until 5 am. It was so much fun.

Dörfchen residents filling the Dahlmannstraße balcony

Unlike in Freiburg, the commune itself was just a few minutes away, occupying most of the flats at Dahlmannstraße 9. This was a style of building common in metropolitan Germany: a central courtyard flanked by two parallel six-storey apartment blocks, linked at the base by a single-storey structure. At the back – the Hinterhof – was a small garden area. By the time I arrived there were more than 200 residents, twice as many as Freiburg. It was rather crowded.

Sheela's ongoing policy of closures and consolidation had resulted in a very international population. Alongside many faces familiar from Medina were representatives of a range of European nationalities, plus a selection of more exotic breeds: to my great delight, here was a small cohort of Brazilians, who had been encouraged by Sheela to abandon their homeland, trusting in the European welcome. I became aware that, however much I might consider myself a unique individual, I was indelibly stamped by my peculiar national characteristics: English were English, Italians Italian; while Brazilians, for all their variety of character, shared a special delight in life, a non-seriousness which provided the essential leaven to so much stolid Germany.

"Celebrate Everything!" was the over-riding ethos; it was no wonder that our disco was such a success. Life was a dance in which the ego could fall away. What was it that remained? Such was the great mystery we were all committed to exploring.

Bhagwan was our trusted guide on this adventure. We were so fortunate to have the gift of his teachings, of his diffused presence. Videos of his marathon discourses were screened regularly at the Institut, just a few hundred metres further down the Ku-damm. This was an impressive establishment, conveying an atmosphere at once both austere and bling, affluent and zen: clear white walls, marble and open space. In the basement

The Institut, towards the Restaurant area

was a large room for group meditations, and for watching video discourses. The Master had currently entered into Silence, but fortunately there was a substantial archive of his Poona lectures to immerse ourselves in.

Bhagwan's voice was remarkable, a measured flow of sibilance. Whatever he happened to be talking about, it was a mesmeric, spellbinding experience. Perhaps it didn't really matter what his ostensible subject was; as he explained: *"don't be distracted by the words, listen to the space between them"*. Slumped in front of the giant screen, more often than not we would fall fast asleep long before the two-hour discourse was done; or perhaps we would have drifted into a delicious dream of transcendence.

Sharing the space on the ground floor was Zorba the Buddha Restaurant, intended to convey the essence of Bhagwan's teaching through gastronomic pleasure. I felt very privileged and excited to be asked to help out with the cooking operation. The kitchen was certainly better equipped and designed than the rather makeshift commune facilities. This was my first experience of a commercial kitchen; I was curious how a wide range of dishes might be made available at short-order. Organisation, anticipation and effective preparation were evidently the key. There was a very large pot of cream sauce on the go, which might be used as the basis for various different dishes; could I just check the seasoning? As I brandished the salt container, I quipped that it would be a disaster if the lid were to fall off. The lid promptly plopped off into the pot, together with all of the contents. They never asked me back.

Magdalena, the commune's kitchen Temple, was much less exposed to the temptations of the ego. Fully engaged in chopping a vast bucket of onions, there was no need to consider its eventual destiny. The quiddity of existence (tathagat, in Buddhist parlance) lay in this very moment.

Just as in every room in the commune, a large photo of Bhagwan presided over our activities. The Magdalena image was adorned with an additional caption, well suited to the location: ***"I Am Cooking Something Else"***. What might that be? Bhagwan was the Master-Chef, and we had submitted to his guidance. This was a journey beyond the rational. No need to waste energy on mind-fuck; only trust, and all would be well.

There was growing excitement and anticipation about the forthcoming summer celebration in Oregon, to which the entire commune would be going. We would be in the presence of the Master: it was a thrilling prospect.

As if to stoke the process of impending transformation, our conditions of worship were suddenly reconfigured, with a further three hours added to our daily quota, three evenings per week. Taking our cue from the Ranch, all communes worldwide participated in this ramping up of energy: it was known as "The Crunch". Our tired bodies were asked to help in the construction project next door, by which what had been our difficult neighbour's flat was being transformed into a new meditation institute. We were doubtless too weary to speculate why this might be occurring. Ours not to reason why . . .

At last the day arrived: the whole commune filed through Tegel airport in a boisterous red-clad crocodile, Ranchward-bound, via a stopover in Texas – which was where I mislaid my carefully packed suitcase.

Arriving in Portland, I was assured that my suitcase would most likely turn up, sooner or later; for some distraction, I picked up a copy of the Oregonian newspaper. There was a special feature about the arms build-up at Rajneeshpuram: a meticulous breakdown of the Ranch's expanding arsenal.

There is much that I could say about the 1985 Summer Celebration in Rajneeshpuram. The recent Netflix documentary, Wild Wild Country, has brought this event, and its dramatic sequel, back into the public eye. In particular, the enigmatic relationship between Bhagwan and Sheela has been the subject of much speculation. But I shall restrict my own recollections to a single impression.

Lined up at the edge of a dusty metalled road, under the blazing midday sun, caught up in febrile exuberance, we wait for Bhagwan's Rolls Royce to draw slowly near. Here he is, with beaming smile, hands off the wheel, waving to us. It is a sweet moment. And then, following twenty yards behind, a second vehicle: a station wagon, in the back of which is a giant machine gun, prominently displayed. I can't help but feel that I have seen a Shadow; reflecting back on this, it occurs to me that this was absolutely the intention. Truly, here was a mystery on open display.

My suitcase was waiting for me at Portland airport. On the return flight I purchased a large bottle of Southern Comfort; I was seriously rattled.

Newly reassembled back in Dörfchen, the commune struggled to attain its former cohesion and shared sense of purpose. I certainly wasn't alone in being unnerved by my experience on the Ranch, without being able to say why. All had gone slack: the springiness, the overarching sense of fun, was gone.

One morning, just a few weeks later, I was busy in the basement scrubbing a well-cleaned skirting board, nursing an uncharacteristic hangover, when a rumour blew past: *"Sheela has left the Ranch"*. It was a heart-stopping moment.

Our bubble of belief, of faith, was pricked and burst. Over the next few days, an avalanche of revelations crashed against our dream palace. Bhagwan, talking once more, invited the world press onto the Ranch to witness the catastrophe. "Sheela and her Gang" were vilified as a fascist conspiracy. Witnesses were coming forward, sharing the stories they had been too afraid to utter. Had it all been a sham, a grotesque fraud? Where was the solid ground on which to step?

Many residents left, checking in their malas on the way out. Some sought refuge in the bottle. Me, I struggled to comprehend this calamity: I was struck by a resonance with Orwell's fable, Animal Farm. The animals in the farmyard had failed to notice how the rules were subtly rewritten, day by day, so that what had once asserted *"Two legs bad, four legs good"*, was suddenly proclaiming *"Four legs good, two legs better"*. Our vision of an ideal society had become a totalitarian nightmare. How could this have happened?

I needed to pay more attention.

The population of the commune thinned out, by half, and then still further. Just before Christmas I decided I too would depart. Sitting on the bus, heading into the shadow zone of East Germany, a song came to me, a distillation of this turbulent time. It was an evocation of strong resolve, and a recognition of the impermanence of outward appearance. It played through my mind as Germany slipped past; England drew ever closer.

House Burning Down

Existence is a house burning down
That's what Buddha said, and now he's dead
Burnt my fingers once or twice in this town
But the flesh don't heal till the soul gets real
So I tell you
Each day of my life I will be true
Each day of my life I will be true
Each day of my life . . .
Each day of my life . . .
Each day of my life I will be true

Life is a house on fire
See this tower fall, and that ain't all
My friend had a dream about fire
But it could not destroy all her love and joy
(So she tells me)
Each day of my life I will be true

> **Each day of my life I will be true**
> **Each day of my life . . .**
> **Each day of my life . . .**
> **Each day of my life I will be true**
>
> **Digging down deep in my dreams**
> **Day by day let them burn away**
> **But that clear spot is not what it seems**
> **Always something else, I gotta say**
> **Each day of my life I will be true**
> **Each day of my life I will be true**
> **Each day of my life . . .**
> **Each day of my life . . .**
> **Each day of my life I will be true**

Whatever I expected to find in England, I was quite mistaken: the dismal spirit of Thatcher lay over the land; all was cold and grey, uninviting. It didn't feel like home; so, once again, on Boxing Day I was on the train back to Berlin. From the station, I walked back along the Ku-damm through the slush, for want of two Marks' bus fare; arriving at Dörfchen, I humbly requested re-admittance, pleaded forgiveness from Kabira. It was good to be back home.

I lived in Dahlmannstraße for the next year and a half, along with around seventy fellow residents, some of whom were new to the commune. It was a time of slow adjustment, hesitantly feeling out the parameters of our new freedom. Red clothes and beads were first things to be abandoned; all rushed to purchase blue jeans. There was money in our pockets – pocket money, paid out by the still-flourishing disco – sufficient to support our new sense of individual identity. As the commune emptied out, so the urgent aspiration asserted itself, to possess a room of one's own, a door to close against the world. There were outbreaks of rivalry and bad feeling. Fortunately, through all of this drawn-out turmoil, Kabira was one of the few wise enough to retain her integrity. She offered a haven of stability.

We had more say in choosing our place of worship: I started to assert myself in the kitchen, taking on a variety of roles. Managing the stores was particularly satisfying. Cooking duties were also fun, now that the strict adherence to set menus had been abandoned. I can't say I have particular memories of this time in the kitchen; it was simply something I did.

It was a sort of fallow period, quite different from the intensity of Peak Commune. I taught myself German, explored Berlin, went to concerts, shopped for clothes. I was spending a lot more time in my own company, drawing away from Kabira. Life was tending towards normality, with all its frustrations and inadequacy. Were we still sannyasins? I know I wasn't the only one wondering what had happened to the spiritual adventure. This was all too safe, too dull.

I had heard Bhagwan tell of his own youthful questing, how he dared himself to dive into the centre of the river whirlpool, sensing that it was precisely there where a point of stillness might be found. Bhagwan was now re-established back in Poona; nobody spoke about the Ranch anymore. The rolling river had moved along, but it was still calling. I decided to head East.

The Centre of the Cyclone

Does it surprise you, dear reader, that I am making such a song and dance about this guru of dubious repute? Wasn't this supposed to be a book about a lovely café?

It's a fair point. Having just navigated, for your benefit, the shenanigans of the Sheela era – a veritable white knuckle ride – I am still aghast at the enormity of the Ranch debacle. Why on earth didn't I simply cut my losses, as so many did: shuffle back into place on the conveyor belt of normality?

Perhaps my best answer is that the account I have just provided has been written very largely in the voice of the intellect – she's good with words, that dear Old Nag, even if she doesn't always understand what's going on.

Something about that beardy chap with the questionable taste in robes had gripped my attention on quite a different level. I felt a compulsion to persevere with this relationship, however apparently nonsensical. I knew I could never forgive myself if I walked away at this point. Although I never felt able to lose myself in unquestioning devotion – unlike so many of my female colleagues – I was certainly hooked, fascinated.

Here was a real-life zen master, precisely the type that had excited my attention as a curious teenager, coming across the slim volume of koans, "Zen flesh, Zen bones", for the first time: a teacher who might recklessly overturn convention and decorum in order to provoke an over-earnest disciple into enlightenment – whacking them with a big stick, or even hurling them out of an open window. Encouraging the establishment of a model community, the summation of collective desires and dreams, then permitting it to self-destruct through its inherent contradictions: did this not display the essence of a Zen Master's practice?

I can feel the shock reverberating through me yet; I still feel deeply un-comfortable about the spate of poisonings which blighted the latter days of the Ranch, betraying the espoused principle of open-hearted welcome.

Should I share complicity? I had chosen to abdicate responsibility for my actions, to place trust in my designated pseudo-parents. I had certainly received a powerful lesson – but it wasn't the same as becoming enlightened.

Then again, the profound experience of community in which I had participated, in which I had pooled my best efforts, had sounded a deep chord, a resonance, a heart-connection. I simply loved the idea of a community that lived and broke bread together: here was a manifest alternative to the atomistic, dispersed society of individuals and small families, as championed by the likes of Mrs Thatcher. This, after all, was why I had returned to Dörfchen, despite the apparent hollowing-out of its spiritual mission. Now I was resolved to check in at ground zero.

Half-way across the world: the time of the Elephant Rains is just commencing. Our coach drives between airports through the torrential downpour, past an endless shabby shanty town. Another flight, and then we descend to our destination. I share a hotel room with a fellow pilgrim I'd only just met, and then take my bearings. The rickshaw drivers know where to take me: *"Ashram"*. Stepping through the "gateless gate" – actually a very security-conscious checkpoint – I present my AIDS test, and declare my wish to help out in the kitchen. Not interested in signing up for any expensive courses, Swami? Just so – I know that kitchen worship will be all the encounter group I need.

The Poona ashram had been more-or-less mothballed during the Ranch adventure. This photo dates from 1979, being used to promote the documentary film "Ashram in Poona", which shocked many by its portrayal of unfettered encounter group practice.

When I arrived, the orange robes were no longer apparent, and the prevailing atmosphere had become far less confrontational; otherwise, the built environment was substantially the same.

Our induction talk is given by Bhagwan's doctor Amrito. He shows us an apple: *"you need to consider that this fruit is covered in toilet paper"*. It's an important point he is making. In my first few days I occupy a room in a dingy tenement, and make the rookie's error of brushing my teeth in water from the tap. It takes a few days for my distressed tummy to sort itself out; thereafter I make a point of filling my water bottle only from the purified supply in the ashram.

I have come half way around the world, passing through teeming streets bearing witness to a very different culture, in which signs are written in indecipherable squiggles; now, in this bio-secure enclave of adventurous occidentalism, I am all set to put into practice all that I know about satisfying the Germanic palate. My skills are welcome.

The ashram kitchen comprises two quite separate operations. One, Miriam, concentrates on preparing meals for the ashram staff and workers, which is served in a canteen around the back of Buddha Hall. When I arrive, this is largely conducted by Indian disciples, producing spicy indigenous dishes. Visitors must purchase food vouchers, which can be exchanged for a selection of dishes prepared and served in Magdalena, situated on the other side of the small estate. There is a valiant effort to provide food that our predominantly European and American guests can recognise.

Magdalena has been entrusted to a voluble and strong-willed Italian, Swami Sarjano, fully intent on putting on a good show. He has had a new idea: a crêpe bar. *"You know how to make crêpes?"*, he asks me, daring me to display my ignorance. *"Sure – just give me the recipe"*, I answer. With barely withheld scorn, he obliges, and it is left to me to make this fantasy work. Short-order crêpes, with a variety of fillings: four food vouchers each.

It's the first of a series of challenges, as I grow more familiar with this slightly ramshackle system, improvising as best we can within the limits of what seems possible. There is a wonderful camaraderie amongst my fellow worshippers. Moving on from the crêperie, Sarjano institutes a system whereby various teams take responsibility for an individual plateful – perhaps fifty portions of each. I get to know a playful ma called Leela, who may have originally been English, teamed up with her wild-maned Bosnian partner. They have been living on the cliffs in Hawaii and on Goa beach, long-term hippie pioneers. She assembles beautiful composite dishes, with names like "the three treasures", "four principles", "the five elements". There is a very contained ma, Dolano, in red robe and long ginger hair, whose air of unassailability Sarjano does not dare to impugn. Many years later I discover that she has been recognised as enlightened – "the swan woman living in a hut by the river" – and has attracted her own disciples. There is a group of Germans who really don't know what they are doing, whose culinary imagination seems restricted to creating a toasted sandwich. And there is me, with maybe with an assistant or two, not always entirely successful in my intention (tip: never include walnuts in a stir-fry, they will turn the whole wok-ful black) but displaying sufficient competence to earn the boss's approbation: *"fa tutto"* – he does everything.

Sarjano himself devotes fullest attention to his pet project, a proper pizzeria, offering the genuine item to peckish punters after the evening discourse. Initially, the pizzas are assembled at the ashram and then rushed over to the local German Bakery for completion; eventually a proper pizza oven is somehow sourced, for the freshest, fragrant cheesey slices.

I work a five-hour shift, which is deemed quite enough in these steamy conditions. Not everybody is easy-going and relaxed: it's actually a highly charged environment, with psyches constantly being challenged by Bhagwan's forensic insights. He's pushing us hard, giving discourses twice daily. It can be difficult to stay focussed on the task in hand. One morning, I make the fundamental mistake of placing my finger inside the casing of an upright fan, as it whizzes around. The pain is immediate. What have I done?

I am worried about the consequences of being hospitalized in ill-equipped foreign parts, but fortunately there is no need to leave the ashram. There is an abundance of qualified medical personnel onsite, who today seem to be primarily busy with damaged digits – fingers and toes stripped of their protective nails. I will need to wear a fat bandage for a week or so, but otherwise there will be no serious consequences. Of course, I won't be able to cook for a while, but I am assured that my food pass will remain valid while I recover; in the interim I can make myself useful checking vouchers in the canteen. I feel valued, part of the team.

I live a couple of miles away, sharing a flat with other sannyasins in a very basic concrete block erected in the middle of a field. Most likely the owners have moved out to less salubrious accommodation, making the most of the tourist windfall. It's a useful base, but mostly I spend my time within the ashram bounds. I cycle in through the early morning, enjoying the stillness of the air, the dew-bedecked fields glinting beneath the rosy-fingered dawn.

Come lunchtime, with my dish of the day awaiting customer inspection on the café counter, I am just about done. The afternoon is mine to while away; I can look forward to attending the evening discourse.

The ashram occupied a single plot in what was, at least in part, quite an affluent suburb of Poona. For such a haven of tranquillity, it was in a constant state of development and reinvention. When I arrived, the large marble platform which constituted the principal auditorium – Buddha Hall – was in process of having its improvised roof of bamboo and canvas replaced by a soaring cantilevered canopy. Local construction workers scurried around amidst the sauntering outlanders. It was important to complete the project before the monsoon rains set in in earnest.

What had been the main building now housed a plethora of offices, session rooms, the visitors' canteen, plus a fancy boutique where all manner of pricey trinkets might be purchased. The area across to Buddha Hall was cordoned off, to allow the installation of an impressive water feature. Around the back of the main house an enclosure protected the Master's residence and garden from prying eyes. Adjacent to this were various legacy buildings incorporating the ashram workers' restaurant. All of these densely-packed structures were enclosed in a lush park-like environment: the abundant greenery of the sub-tropical monsoon season.

A relaxed babble of many languages filled the air. Old friends greeted one another in familiar sannyasin style, with hugs a-plenty. Patient queues formed to sign up for the latest groups and courses. An air of conscious spiritual endeavour prevailed. All these people were here for a definite purpose.

This was most apparent as time grew closer for the main event: participating in the presence of the Master. Lining up outside Buddha Hall, filing slowly past the sign, "shoes and minds to be left here", then passing between the gatekeepers diligently sniffing for undesirable odours, spreading out into the hall to choose the vantage point of choice: close to the musicians, not too many rows behind the Principal Disciples – there where the energy might be strongest. I carried a little cushion with me, to ease the discomfort of the hard marble floor. Nonetheless, it would be a marathon of endurance.

With the entire space jammed full and settled at last, stillness descends. The sound of an approaching engine is heard; the car halts, the door opens . . . and then Bhagwan appears around the side of the marble backdrop, always accompanied by his constant companion, Vivek. He greets us all, slowly turning in namaste, then gracefully settles into his comfy chair, places one leg over another, rests a small crib-sheet on his lap, and commences to speak. For the entirety of the discourse, he maintains the same position.

This was a very different experience from watching a video. All in that great gathering were devoting their fullest attention, gripped by the drama of spiritual elucidation. Should the proceedings ever risk becoming over-holy, Bhagwan might puncture such preconceptions with a smutty joke, consulting his notes before delivering the outrageous punchline with resounding aplomb.

When he considered that enough had been said, at least for today, he would signal to the musicians. The drum would thump, and the mood would shift into carefree celebration as Bhagwan rose from the chair, raising his arms in exhortation before disappearing back behind the marble screen. It was a bravura performance.

Trust that heartbeat better than emotion

Feel I'm drowning, but do I need saving?
Feel like I'm going down, ah don't let me drown
In my ears a rushing, like ocean raging
Listen to that sound, how it crashes and pounds
No time to argue or try to persuade me with reason
I can't see nobody gonna take me on the life raft that he's on
I just don't have a notion
But it's my heartbeat, and I trust it better than emotion
When I'm sinking in the depths of that deep dark ocean

Feel I'm dreaming, wishing I was waking
Waiting for the new day, for those dreams to fade away
For that sunrise bursting, that daylight breaking
Time just to play – nuts in May
And those shadows of the night hiding creatures of imagination
Are seen to be nothing more than hallucination
'Cause it's my heartbeat, and I trust it better than emotion
When I'm sinking in the depths of that deep dark ocean

Feel I'm spinning, beyond fear of falling
Arms swinging wide, sinking deep down inside
Down to that clear spot, hear the master calling
Nothing to hide . . .
And in the stillness at the centre of the cyclone that rages around me
I feel the pulsing of the heartbeat as protection and wrap it around me
To quiet all commotion
– That heartbeat, I trust it better than emotion
When I'm sinking in the depths of that deep dark ocean

Towards the end of that year – after I'd been at the ashram for several months – it was announced that Bhagwan needed to take a break. His health was increasingly fragile; there had been suggestions that unspecified indignities had been inflicted on him during his detention by the US prison service, from which he had never quite recovered. Discourses were to be suspended until further notice.

Many took this as their cue to head for Goa, or to seek some other means of distraction. The ashram was suddenly much quieter. I considered joining an expedition to Katmandu; for this purpose I had my photo taken at a studio on MG Road. I'm displaying a steady, serious gaze, together with some mystic facial hair. But what was the attraction of Katmandu? Raucous distraction and top quality hashish? I decided that it would be folly to abandon this place of wonders, even if the Master had gone into retreat.

The catering operation had been reconfigured, with the separate workers' kitchen being amalgamated with the principal cooking area – which freed up valuable space in the main house. I was asked to join the team preparing the workers' food, first of all on a morning shift, responsible for breakfast and lunch.

Breakfast centred around an enormous pot of pseudo-porridge, in which cracked wheat took the place of more difficult-to-source oats, plus sundry dried fruit and spices. My experience with the Munchies and Slurpies stood me in good stead. Something quite new to my experience was an order for several hundred hard-boiled eggs. The result, frankly, was a bit of a mess, in which the platonic ideal proved hard to recognise amidst a mass of blobby fragments.

My favourite component of breakfast was an exotic fruit compote, some compensation for the near-complete avoidance of uncooked ingredients, in view of the danger of infection. This was the special responsibility of Amareesh, a musician part-timing in the kitchen. He lived in the same block of flats as myself; some mornings I woke up to the sound of him practising his scales. Many years later I discovered that I had inadvertently purchased a recording of him duetting with Pandit Hariprasad Chaurasia, the acclaimed flautist.

Hariprasad was a noted friend and admirer of Bhagwan. While I was there, he and his colleague, tabla maestro Zakir Hussein, offered to play for us in Buddha Hall. What a marvellous concert! I realised that our daily practice in silent attention had established the ideal conditions for musical transmission, removing all the barriers between performer and listener, enabling a mutual transport of delight. It was an immersion in blessed limpidity such as I never experienced again – until I started to attend Oxford's Catweazle Club, justly fabled for its fierce discipline of listening.

The summit of my ashram cooking career came with my appointment to the afternoon crew, responsible for the main evening meal, sufficient for several hundred servings. This was a massive undertaking. Heading the team was another Italian, Paritosho, whom I had first met at Medina, a genial and practical manager. Our mainstay was a formidable powerhouse, Ayo, a sometime Royal Marine. With his partner Vayo, he had spent many years in Goa, wheeling and dealing. Now he was contributing an awesome degree of competence and drive to enable our daily miracle of manifestation.

Job done, we would load the massive pots onto a trolley and trundle it across the ashram. It would hold its heat for the next couple of hours. There would be time to clean up, put on some fresh clothes, and get in line for the evening discourse.

Bhagwan had commenced speaking again, albeit in a less demanding format. Discourses were now given in Chuang Tzu Auditorium, essentially a glorified veranda at the side of his residence. No need for all that malarkey with the limo! Here was just room for a couple of hundred faithful, squeezed together extremely tightly; it was a great privilege to be allocated tickets.

I became aware of how much of the time, sitting there in some discomfort, just a few yards away from the Master casting his spell, I was actually day-dreaming about exciting new clothes I might ask my East Street tailor to run up, from the colourful lunghis I had purchased. Of course, I needed to watch my spending now . . .

Had I plopped out of the vortex? Sometimes, in my afternoons off, I was quite bored. For all the easy friendships I enjoyed, I had formed no deeper attachments. It had started to feel as though life were on hold. And funds were running disconcertingly low; I had remained in India for far longer than originally intended. My original return flight ticket had been sold on – which involved travelling to Bombay with the purchaser, checking in, then ducking behind a pillar to hand over my boarding pass. I had managed to extend my visa, courtesy of Philip, the local Mr Fixit, who knew how to negotiate the complications of Indian bureaucracy: the essential lubricant was, of course, cash – preferably foreign currency. A couple of months further on, in that "time out of time", there seemed no escaping an impending financial crisis. I had trusted the sannyasin who flew back to London in my name to send me our agreed price on his arrival back home; I had found assurance of his good faith by looking into his eyes . . . but I was to wait for the promised money in vain. Now, as I turned away from the safe deposit office on the ashram, opening my requested envelope, my expression must have been easy to read. A voice beside me remarked: *"You look like someone staring at his last 100 Deutchmarks."*

A friend kindly bailed me out. I was able to buy a second hand ticket, travelling in tandem to Bombay to perform the shifty exchange. And then I was at Heathrow, in my light summer clothes, shivering in the chilly spring breeze. I had precisely a fiver in my pocket, the cost of a coach fare to Reading. I turned up at my mother's house, much to her surprise. Ah – those long-gone days before the mobile phone!

Questing

On my 30th birthday I had a vision of Death. I was sitting the Civil Service exam in Oxford's Examination Schools; my youthful trail of rebellion had apparently played itself out, and the prospect of developing a proper career was no longer to be dismissed out of hand.

Since returning from India, I'd quickly landed a temporary job fitting up a DIY warehouse in Reading – emblematic of the boom in home improvement which Thatcher's reforms had engineered. Then, back in Oxford, I found undemanding employment in the basement of the Inland Revenue offices: as part of the massive effort to shift record keeping into digital format, an immense amount of paper and cardboard documents needed to be sifted through, in order to remove any paper clips and similar awkward objects prior to shredding. With a small team of colleagues, we listened to Radio One and chatted inconsequentially while sifting through sack after sack. After this chore was successfully concluded, I was invited upstairs to be part of a proper office team, painstakingly transferring each item of data from paper to screen. It was my first experience of working with computers, and it seemed interminably dull. It may as well have been an exercise in spirit-crushing: I was rebuked for humming on duty, for disturbing the cloistered atmosphere of the office. It was a dismal routine broken only by the brief respite of tea break. I remember as a thrilling high point the occasion when I accidentally "deceased" someone from the records – but it all seemed quite detached from real life experience. Nonetheless, I was prepared to consider the possibility that the civil service might hold more exciting prospects, and my supervisor was happy to endorse my application form. She herself, with her partner, as was well known, lived only for the day when they could retire from their office-bound career and establish themselves in the cherished dream of their very own tea shop.

So there I was, half way through the exam. A break had been called, for those who required a nicotine boost. I'd been doing well with the set exercises, having been practising the art of problem solving over the past couple of weeks. Not being a smoker, I remained in my seat, set my pen down and observed the invigilator as he paced up and down, keeping an eye on his stop watch. His face was grey, his suit was creased and dusty, he had about him an air of dessication and decay . . . such, I realised, was the spirit that presided over my future.

Shocked, I found it hard to regain my concentration. I must have struggled through sufficient questions to merit an invitation to proceed on my supposed career path, but my mind was made up: this was not the life for me. Life was somewhere else.

Now in my lunch breaks I busied myself developing Plan B: studying Italian, with a view to heading south towards the sunshine. The previous Spring I'd been in the Tuscan countryside, spending an idyllic week as guest with a couple of German sannyasins. Maybe I could use my nascent kitchen skills to parlay myself a slice of paradise.

I hit the road again, rucksack on my shoulders, guitar in hand, sporting cool shades and a cheeky Chairman Mao hat. Thumb out, waiting by the roadside for serendipity to strike. Got a ride all the way through France, from the channel port to the Swiss border, with an eager young man in a hurry to hurl himself off the edge of the mountain with a hang-glider strapped to his back. He dropped me off some place in the Rhone valley, and I was fortunate enough to be put up for the night by a local couple who took pity on my lonesome figure. Hitching was a wonderful way to mainline the kindness of strangers – as long as you were prepared to wait, thumb out, by the side of a slip road, hour after hour . . .

Trying to get out of Menton, the very last town before the Italian border, proved particularly tricky. I wanted to get back onto the main highway, but there was no traffic heading out of town. After a long, frustrating wait, it eventually occurred to reframe my dilemma: I wasn't so much trapped in a corner, but looking in the wrong direction. If I turned myself around, then maybe the world would open up. And so it came to pass . . .

Once I'd walked across the frontier, I treated myself to a ride on Italy's excellent local rail network, busying myself en route puzzling out an Oggi magazine I'd picked up at the station. Stepping out into the warm midday sunshine at Cecina, I marvelled at the absence of people. At least I had a phone number to call, but so flimsy was my grip on Italian that it took a while to understand that the public phone required not one, but two tokens to make a conection. Perhaps you have forgotten how it was in those pre-mobile days. I'd come half way across Europe, without even announcing my intentions to anyone. I simply had a short list of possible destinations, not all of which I was sure actually existed.

My sannyasin friends had now managed to purchase a rural property, with a view to setting up a guest house. They weren't quite ready to take on any extra help, but they were willing to drop me off at a nearby hotel which was run by people I had come to know in the Berlin Commune. This turned out to be situated on the top of a hill, a long way from anywhere else. The staff, being all Italian, were, when I arrived, busily engaged in a massive row, in which my job interview – also in Italian – was subsumed. I felt distinctly out of my element.

I stopped off in Bologna, surprising a friend of a friend whom I'd last seen several years before, working together picking cabbages in the sodden Cornish fields. She rose to the challenge of my unexpected visit, whisking me through that picturesque city on the back of a moped, up into the hills for an alfresco rave. This was excellent and wonderful, but I was running out of long-term options in Italy. It seemed that I was doomed to head back North, up into Germany. At least I would be able to understand the language. I had a couple of maybe-contacts in Munich to check out.

A truck driver dropped me off close to the centre of München in the middle of the night, allowing me a few hours in which to explore before locating a bench at the railway station to fall asleep on. On being abruptly shaken awake and ordered to move on it took me a few moments to recollect where I was. But I did have a destination, and perhaps even a friendly break-fast venue, in mind: there was a sannyasin restaurant close by, one of the businesses hived off the commune that had also existed here until a year or so ago.

It was a swanky joint, in which I did not feel welcome. I must have been looking a bit rough by this stage, after a few days and nights on the road, and München was evidently not a place that looked kindly on wandering riff-raff. My bowl of muesli felt pretentious and over-priced. With the sense that I was running out of options, I played what seemed to be my last card: shortly before I'd left Poona, I'd befriended a Brazilian who had been working as a chef in Hamburg, at the Zorba the Buddha restaurant. I called them up: was there a job going? It must have been a good moment; they asked me to drop by.

I booked a ride with a lift share agency – a very civilised way to travel cheaply, without the hassle and uncertainty of hitching. By the end of the day I was taking grateful leave of my drivers, stepping out onto the plaza in front of Hamburg railway station. A man walked past, greeting me cheerfully: *"Herzlich willkommen in Hamburg"*. This was far more promising . . .

What was I doing, coming so far North? This hadn't been my intention, had it? On the other hand, or seen from a different perspective, perhaps it was a step well taken. There was, I instinctively knew, a deeper dimension to my reckless adventuring. I had thrown myself into the stream of circumstance for a purpose, which might best be expressed by the term Quest, that staple of medieval literature. There were, I sensed, dragons to be slain, a grail to be unearthed; and, dare I say it, there was a lady's heart to be won.

I had a phone number to call, someone I'd met in Oxford: Sasha, a fellow of eccentric ways, who'd made a big impression on my new friend Camilla, sufficient to persuade her to abandon her commitment to the narrow orbits of East Oxford, at least for a flying visit. So there was a happy prospect of seeing her again before too long.

It wasn't long before Sasha came to fetch me; he can't have been living too far away. Doubtless we walked through the very centre of the old city, past the palatial Rathaus, embodiment of independent Hamburg's wealth, power and influence, alongside prestige shopping arcades displaying all the stuff of affluence, past proud monuments, over canals and bridges, tracking all the while towards the most impressive of the soaring church towers dramatically piercing the skyline. I was to have plenty of time to explore all of this over the months to come; in that moment I was simply happy to have reached my destination, which turned out to be a crumbling late nineteenth century apartment block, one of the few buildings left standing in what was otherwise a large area of wasteland, the old street plan now delineated only by developers' hoardings. Evidently it wouldn't be long before Sasha's home would fall victim to the wrecking ball: stretched between the upstairs windows was a large banner proclaiming *"Senat fressen Strassen auf. Kein Abriss unter diese Nummer"*.

Sasha was exceedingly gracious, finding me some space on the floor of his cluttered apartment for a few days, while I got my bearings. I needed to move fast. My money was more or less all spent; I had staked all on one last throw of the dice.

Next day was my designated appointment with the Zorba the Buddha Restaurant collective, which turned out to be not too distant: a pleasant walk through Planten en Blomen, the delightful park that arced round the city centre, following the line of the former ramparts, then across a busy inner city ring road. The restaurant was a discreet establishment nestled in what was evidently a largely Turkish neighbourhood. If you weren't specifically looking for it you'd probably walk right on past. Those in the know passed through a gateway into a small garden courtyard, then into the Restaurant proper. Visible from the courtyard, on the flank of the apartment block rising up at one side, a large mural depicting two birds in flight indicated that this had been the location of Baile Rajneesh Neo-Sannyas Commune. Those flats would have housed a hundred or more sannyasins, living in more or less identical conditions to those I had experienced in Freiburg and Berlin. Now, unlike Berlin, this bustling, multi-national commune was gone; the Restaurant, however, remained as an independent business, as did the adjacent Meditation Institute and the Sauna, all open to members of the public, insofar as these might dare to broach the threshold of what was still very much an insiders' club.m

The Zorba collective had gathered for their weekly meeting: perhaps a dozen young people, equally male and female, seated around a set of tables pushed together. None were previously known to me, but all displayed that easy familiarity with one another which had pervaded commune life. All – at that time – were German, apart from a voluble, and hence slightly intimidating, Italian swami, who was, I soon realised, currently the principal chef. His voice evidently held some sway; but who was in charge?

Collectives, in my experience, are never as egalitarian as they might proclaim. There is always a power dynamic, founded largely on control of the finances, and generally framed by a reluctance to challenge the status quo. A principal function of the collective meeting, I came to appreciate, was the distribution of the tip money. There were equitable shares for all, according to the tally of hours worked. Nado, who had managed the restaurant finances since before the dissolution of the Commune, was the only one with proper business sense, who really understood the all-important magic of numbers. How many hours did he put in? As he explained on a later occasion: *"I swing a pendulum to see what feels right"*. I have no reason to believe that the pendulum was ever wrong. Without a steady hand at the tiller, this was a ship, crewed by enthusiastic amateurs, that could very easily run onto the rocks. I make this comment with all the benefit of hindsight! At the time, all that mattered to most of us was that we had each made a commitment to the sannyas adventure, sharing an understanding that life was play, together with a willingness to trust the Master's inverted logic: *"Leap before you Look!"*

When the agenda moved around to deciding on the portentous issue of appointing a new chef, I made my pitch. I'd worshipped in Magdalena over many years; I'd been a key team member in the Poona catering operation; I'd befriended their erstwhile colleague Nagarjuna. There was some sug-gestion that I might not fit so easily into a largely German-speaking set-up; *"aber ich spreche doch ganz fließend Deutsch"*, I insisted. Was I seen to be trying too hard? It was an uncertain moment – and then I was in.

I had a discipline to learn. Zorba's opened to customers in the early evening, seven days a week. As one of two principal chefs, I needed to show up in the early afternoon on three or four of those days. It could be a long, demanding shift, particularly at the weekend: everything had to be returned to a more or less pristine state before we left, so that it could be well after midnight by the time I got to cycle back home. I needed to know what I was doing, and I needed to be well-organised. The whole operation – the satisfaction of customers, and the respect of my colleagues – depended on my diligence and expertise.

I needed to gain mastery of the Zorba menu, the Card, which offered a choice of around two dozen dishes, all of which could be rustled up in short order from pre-prepared components. The early hours of the shift, before opening time, were devoted to ensuring that everything necessary lay readily to hand: there would be a range of vegetables to be steamed, sliced appropriately, and placed in a handy tub; several litres of basic sauces – bechamel and tomato – needed to be cooked, then held hot in a bain-marie; quantities of grain and pasta were prepared, ready for reheating as required. A large tub of pre-sliced onions was essential, as was garlic. It was a style of cooking by formula, demanding rapid production of the same result, night after night.

There was some opportunity for creativity: the chef's special of the day. I could tempt our customers with an attractive plateful of curry, rice and dal, all prepared in advance and assembled to order. Or I could use the all-important frying pan to rustle up something a little bit experimental: *"Bunte Tofu-Pfanne"*, for example, was a vivid fry-up of tofu and various vegetables, including steamed beetroot, in a rich cream sauce.

Cream featured heavily in many of the dishes, very often sizzled rapidly together with an equivalent quantity of white wine. Sometimes a dash of pesto added to the fun. Thus, generous cuts of oyster mushrooms would be sautéed in olive oil, then drenched in a cream, wine and pesto sauce, served on a bed of pasta: *Austernpilze à la Buddha*. It was all, I must say, a very German style of cooking; I would hesitate to call it cuisine.

More importantly, were we still "cooking from the heart", as we had learned to do in the days when the kitchen was at the heart of the Commune? I believe it did make a big difference, not knowing who was on the receiving end of each plate of food that left the kitchen. In the Commune, we were accustomed to referring to each other collectively as "Beloveds". We all ate from the same array of dishes, heaping our plates as we moved along the serving table; it was a communion. Could one have the same connection with someone who paid cash, hopefully with added tip? The relationship had certainly shifted.

Although we shared the aural environment, the kitchen felt quite separate from the dining room. I spent each evening in close collaboration with my colleague the salad chef, responding as required to the demands of our customers (always "Guests"), as relayed by the serving staff, but it was rare that I put my head around the door to survey the evening's clientele. So who were we cooking for?

Apart from the Far Out chain of discotheques, which had built a strong reputation throughout Germany as the best place to go for a fun night out, commune-operated businesses had tended to generate an invisible threshold, likely to discourage uninitiated customers. Perhaps there was some suggestion of Midwich Cuckoos, in the close, almost telepathic understanding between crew members, and their easy recourse to smiles and laughter. It wasn't quite normal, was it? In the transition to independently run enterprises some of this "clubhouse" air very likely remained. Still, sannyasins were by no means rare in a cosmopolitan, vibrant city such as Hamburg; moreover, their influence, friendships and connections dispersed into a much wider community, which might be grouped under the broad heading "Alternative". German culture was still noticeably engaged in a reactive swing from its catastrophic experiment with National Socialism, still haunted by that dark shadow. There was a widespread curiosity about new approaches to communal lifestyle, meditation, exploration of altered states of consciousness, techniques of physical and mental discipline, both innovative and ancient: all of which supported a rich smorgasbord of courses and weekend workshops, in which Zorba Restaurant, and the associated Meditation institute, provided a significant nodal point.

Here was a lot to explore, and I took to it with gusto. I found a pleasant place to live remarkably easily – first flat-sharing with a homeopathic doctor who practised Buddhist chanting, then with the drummer in a late-night rock band. I had a job I loved, which left me with lots of time, and money in my pocket, to enjoy all that Hamburg had to offer.

It was an open-hearted city: unlike Berlin, hiding its shadow behind an impenetrable wall, Hamburg had its wounds on open display. Its privileged position astride the Estuary of the Elbe, the portal connecting Northern Germany to the rest of the world, had made it wealthy, a hub for trade and industry. Until subsumed into the new Imperial Germany in 1871 it had been fiercely independent; it was still a separate state in the Federal Republic. Unusually for Germany, it still displayed a memorial to its heroic dead, fallen in the Great War: serried ranks marching to defend the fatherland, all around a great grey slab. The Nazis had erected this in 1936 as an invocation to self-less sacrifice. Then disaster had struck. In July 1943 the British Royal Air Force unleashed Operation Gomorrah. Immense firestorms engulfed much of the city, bringing to rack and ruin dockyards, factories, warehouses, offices, entire residential districts, together with much of the population. Many decades later, the city was still busy trying to make good. Hence Sasha's semi-derelict (but beloved) tenement block, presiding over an inner-city wasteland.

"*Deutschland muss leben / und wenn wir sterben müssen*" reads the disturbing motto engraved on the Dammtor War Memorial. "*Germany must live even if we die*". Thus the Nazis, in 1936, commemorated the sacrifice of life in the First World War.

A choice has been made to retain this monument, recontextualizing its sense and purpose, as part of a surrounding Peace Park.

Photo by Tim Tregenza, licensed via Creative Commons

Hence, also, the attraction of an "Alternative". The ready supply of damaged, low rental property enabled experimentation: out of the ashes had sprouted many exotic new growths. Once a week I made my way across town to run-down Ottensen, to participate in a dance meditation workshop in which there were no specific instructions, and no music, just an injunction to express oneself in motion – a technique originating in Indonesia. I attended sundry weekend seminars, being initiated into the practice of Reiki: there is energy flowing through your hands – who knew?; the mysteries of colour energy, which could be channelled by chanting the appropriate syllables; the arcane doctrine of Musicosophia, which aimed at unlocking the secrets enshrined in the forms of classical music by means of improvised movement; while, closer to home, there was the varied meditation programme offered by the Institute.

The range of innovative meditation techniques pioneered by Osho had recently been augmented by the "Mystic Rose": for three hours each day, for seven days, participants were enjoined just to laugh– however this might seem possible; then followed a week in which the instruction was simply to cry; during the final week those three hours would be devoted to sitting silently. This procedure was supposed to unleash all manner of psychic tensions, to tremendous beneficial effect.

I took part in this exercise twice. The first time happened to coincide with Camilla's promised visit to Sasha. I was busy supposedly crying, and finding this extremely difficult. I don't think a single genuine tear fell from my eye, that entire week. By contrast, when I came to visit Camilla and Sasha each evening, and to prepare a special supper, Camilla did little but weep. Her favourite song, endlessly repeated, was Julie London singing *"Cry me a River"*. I was captivated – but it felt as if there was a massive gulf somehow to be bridged. Here, I was a phony; she, the cry-baby, was the real deal.

Despite all that Hamburg had to offer – immersion in the sea of alternative possibilities; easy access to all sorts of live music, from sleazy late-night gigs on the Reeperbahn, often featuring living legends passing through, still paying their dues, to gorgeous productions at the State Opera; shaking my stuff once or twice a week at the Far Out disco; the delightful gardens of Planten en Blomen and the City Park; the open vistas of the Alster lake, around the shores of which so much of the city had spread; plus a couple of unsuccessful attempts at forming a relationship – I couldn't shake myself free of existential unease, my old companion. I longed for a connection that lay tantalisingly just beyond reach. There was a fateful abyss, and it was populated by dragons, growling and raging in the deep.

I made a good friend in the restaurant, a Brazilian swami named Ageya, who worked with me as salad chef. Like so many Brazilians I have come to know, his was a carefree, fun-loving character, the necessary antidote to too much German-ness. And his spirit had been set flying, for the moment at least, by a two-week stint at the Humaniversity, an institution I had already briefly visited, which had a reputation for no-holds-barred therapeutic mayhem. It was scary, but I knew this had to be my next port of call. I booked myself in for the two-week Tourist Programme.

The Phoenix Strikes Back

The attentive reader may recall that my teenaged self, back in 1975 or so, had chanced upon a report on the front page of an inky alternative news sheet, about a thrilling confrontative form of therapeutic process conducted by a commune of hairy naked Germans. It seems highly likely, in retrospect, that these were disciples of Bhagwan Shree Rajneesh, newly returned from Poona bearing tidings of exciting new methods of spiritual enquiry. Of course, it's hard to be certain that these were in fact orange people: even had the imprint been in colour, they weren't actually wearing any clothes.

Bhagwan, since the early 70s, had been attracting curious attention from many of the hard-hitters of the psychotherapy revolution: some would subsequently root themselves and their particular method at influential centres such as the Esalen Institute in California. They appreciated his willingness to abandon orthodox preconceptions of what spirituality – or psychotherapeutic enquiry – might entail. In turn, his teachings drew on the insights of Western post-Freudian analysis, matching them up with a wide range of Eastern esoteric disciplines. In particular, Wilhelm Reich's emphasis on the life force inherent in sexuality, and the destructive consequences of its suppression, found a strong correspondence in the vision of human potential espoused by Bhagwan. One of his earliest collections of public talks, "From Sex to Super-consciousness" created a sensation when it was first published in India at the end of the sixties, laying a sound foundation for his reputation as "the sex guru" which, with his keen eye for what made for good PR, he made no attempt to dispel, even while poking fun at the apparent trivialisation of his message.

It was out of this collision of profane and sacred, East and West, that a new style of therapy emerged, epitomised by the Encounter Group. The crux of this method was an understanding that the confrontations inevitably arising in human relationships might provide a powerful mirror into the individual psyche, if only one had the courage to allow them full expression in a controlled environment. It was a technique that demanded a high degree of skill and judgement from the group leader; there were immense forces that might be unleashed, a life-time of repression embodied in each participant, a festering dam of withheld vitality. At the Poona ashram, these therapists took their permission from the trust laid upon them by the Master, and took refuge from the peril of their own ego inflation in his uncanny ability to sound out their deeper motives. It was a mystery school, conducted away from prying eyes, a ground-breaking experiment to provoke a new sense of godliness.

Towards the end of the decade a decision was taken to launch the product on the world market. A prying eye was invited in and (so I understand, though accounts differ) a special session of an encounter group was conducted in front of an independent German film crew. Filming was also done in and around the ashram, attempting to capture the essence of this extraordinary institution. The resulting feature film, *Ashram in Poona*, was subtitled *Bhagwan's Experiment*.

There is no commentary. A succession of ashram activities is intercut with local bustling street scenes. We see vigorous meditation sessions in progress, ecstatic dancing, red-clad kids at play; careful attention being devoted to book production, mala construction, fabric weaving. There are revealing interviews with therapists and key workers. Bhagwan himself is marvellously represented, both in clips from discourses and with footage of intense darshan sessions: the drama is heightened by the sense of total engagement evident in the faces and bodies of his disciples, as a universe of wonder is unveiled. Plus, again and again we are cast into the throes of an encounter group going at it full throttle. Naked trauma is on open display.

Of course, it's the writhing mass of naked bodies, yelping and tumbling around on the padded floor, that left the strongest impression on the viewing public. It represents a challenge: will there be a shocked dismissal of such wilfully bestial behaviour, or might the existential truth be recognised, that this is a profound statement on the human condition? Energy demands expression, one way or another: *"fear is just anger turned in"*. As the group leader explains, the purpose is to look for what is in the way of achieving deep peace, to show people themselves more clearly, so that they might choose whether to continue or to change; that they might access a new dimension in their life.

We are not used to seeing vulnerability displayed so openly. Should we ourselves experience such moments, we tend to hide them away as objects of shame, to carry on as if nothing has occurred. But here is something truly wonderful: the trauma can be resolved. The same woman we witness utterly incoherent and distraught, we subsequently see transfigured, clarified, at ease with herself. You might even think *"I'll have some of what she's having"*. Overall, the film provides elegiac testimony to a powerful transformational process.

There were, of course, many who viewed it quite differently. There is a fine line between courting controversy and inviting a court summons. For whatever reason, the Encounter Group had evolved into something far more tame, by the time I signed up for a weekend of *"Absolute Freedom"* at Medina, early in my sannyas career. *"Absolute Boredom, more like"*, quipped our group leader, as she attempted to cajole us into some withheld animosity. I'm not saying it was a complete non-event, but I definitely felt short-changed.

There was, I learned, one place where the fierce tradition was still being celebrated. In the small, genteel town of Egmont aan See, nestling amidst the dunes that line the Dutch coastline, one Rajneesh therapy institute had staunchly resisted Sheela's attempt at world domination. The Humaniversity encapsulated Bhagwan's vision of transformation, as channelled by Veeresh Yuson, a truly remarkable  spirit who succeeded in combining independence of action with absolute devotion to his Master. It enjoyed a daunting reputation.

My fortnight on the Tourist Programme opened the door to a new chamber of treasures. Not everything was immediately accessible; here was no opportunity for a quick smash and grab. But the caskets were there, waiting to be unlocked; and the manner of opening, the intricate locksmithery, was a skill that might be learned.

At my reception interview I duly acquired a new name: perhaps responding to the long fringe now covering my eyes, I was dubbed *"Connection"*. What was it, apart from hair, which lay in the way of my contact with others? Learning to respond to this name, for the duration of my stay, provided repeated opportunity to ponder this presenting problem. It was an essential part of the tourist programme to be the target of constant challenges and provocation from the more long-term members of this therapeutic community. Well, it wasn't meant to be a holiday – but it might be possible to learn to have fun, in such a vibrant, constantly shifting group dynamic. There was a lot of dancing, physical activity, opportunities to socialise, expeditions to the beach; only hiding in a corner was out of bounds.

It was my good fortune that my visit happened to coincide with a special group event, on the final weekend of my stay, which had attracted many participants from the psychotherapeutic professions: Veeresh would be joined by his great friend and sometime colleague, Frank Natale, for *"The Phoenix Strikes Back"*. Both had been key participants in the Phoenix House drug rehabilitation program in New York, in the 1970s. Veeresh (as Danny Yuson) was initially there to combat his own heroin addiction, subsequently becoming staff member. The "hard love" treatments practised there had much in common with the methods explored in Poona, and Veeresh, freed from the incubus of addiction, had found it easy to fall in love with Bhagwan.

I found it easy to fall in love with Veeresh. Here was the very essence of "no bullshit" affirmation: no wafty hippy with an English public school accent (unlike so many of the Poona therapists); rather, a street-cool Puerto Rican, small and wiry, with an infectious sense of life's potential. The force of his presence was rooted in his own experience: he had succeeded in wrestling his own demons into submission, now he was driven by the urge to share this realisation. Just like they used to do at Phoenix House, he presented me with yet another new name: *"Misfit City Oxford"*.

But who was Frank Natale? Whereas Veeresh impressed primarily in a physical and emotional dimension, Frank's realm was the mind, with all its infinite possibilities. During the couple of sessions at his disposal, first of all he engaged our attention with a witty stand-up breakdown of the neuroses and hang-ups running through post-war culture like jam in a swiss roll. It wasn't just hilarious, it was full of startling insight. My mind, a backseat passenger for so much of my sannyas experience, sat up, started paying attention. Then we took a break, heading down into the basement for an opportunity to get high – this was Holland, after all! Reconvening, insight and engagement intensified. Using a pre-recorded soundtrack, he led us on a shamanic journey. As the insistent polyrhythms took hold of our dancing bodies, our minds followed his directions into a zone of wonders. Wow!

All too soon, it was time to head back to Hamburg. I had a lot to think about. I also had with me a small souvenir of Amsterdam, courtesy of the Mellow Yellow coffee-shop ("since 1967"), destined to diminish gradually over the coming weeks. My Hamburg lifestyle was put on notice: I determined to return to the Humaniversity for a full three months, just as soon as funds allowed.

Summer at the Humaniversity was dominated by a month-long megagroup, which that year was known as the Googooplex. Don't ask me why. I arrived six weeks in advance, time enough to soften up the psyche for full melt-down. I would join the therapeutic community, dividing my time between kitchen work and whatever crazy games Veeresh and his crew might devise to shake us out of our complacency. One way or another, he was determined that we ought to be enjoying ourselves. Just what was it that was standing in our way?

Veeresh loved to pump up the energy, to the point where the boundaries of individuality might simply drop away, where it was just too much effort to hang on to them. One sure-fire way to achieve this was through dance marathons, conducted either in the airy group rooms upstairs, or in the rather more constrained basement area, the Boozeria, which featured a bar. Boozeria sessions might also feature a live band: a hot-as-you-could-wish-for, tight rock and funk outfit sensitive to every whim of Veeresh's direction. First they would warm the room up, get us all moving; at a certain point – late – Veeresh would come on board, start to direct us in absurd, interactive games, changing partners constantly, mixing up the medicine; or lead us in

Veeresh and band raising the energy in Köln
Photo courtesy the Humaniversity

improvised chants to liberate the spirit. Are you having fun yet? If not, why not?

Early in the morning – very early – would be the AUM meditation, Veeresh's unique addition to Bhagwan's catalogue of dynamic meditation methods. Never one for restraint, he had bundled together aspects of a number of these to produce a ten-stage physical and emotional workout, lasting a full two and a quarter hours. Not only did this generate a powerful appetite for breakfast, but it also compressed an immense amount of experience into a short space, material enough to spend the rest of the day processing, one way or another.

More than a hundred participants were expected for the month-long extravaganza. A few days before, residents engaged in erecting a triple-storey complex of rabbit-hutches in the dormitory rooms. This was to be a very public melt-down – or perhaps a melting together. For all the ample space available in the house and grounds – conveniently distanced from neighbouring properties – this was unavoidably a sharing experience. Most of all, this was evident in the somewhat limited shared shower facilities. Shared also was a willingness to risk, trusting in Veeresh's special mode of practice, daring to display one's own particular brand of neurosis, and perhaps to recognise that, after all, it was possible to love oneself.

Again, we were each given a new name. *"What should we call you?"* they pondered. *"I'm sure you'll think of something horrible"*. *"Horrible. Yes, that's your new name"*. I had a friend called Slimy Bastard; another faced the ignominy of answering to Nice Guy.

A month of this went on for a long time. Each day kicked off with the AUM, and generally concluded with a session in the Boozeria. In between, there was some variety. Particularly intense were the weekend groups, which focussed in turn on the major fields of trauma – death, madness, sex

– shaking us up, breaking us down, putting us back together, perhaps in unaccustomed order. Dressing up and roleplay helped us to explore aspects of our identity we might normally keep under wraps. I recall a most satisfactory evening incarnated as the creature from the black lagoon, dressed in green tights, with face and arms painted to match; my consort was a wicked witch, with pointy hat and jet-black gown. In the morning I was obliged to accept responsibility for removing all traces of the green smears left on walls all around the building.

My madness, I discovered, involved facing up against everybody in turn, and then blowing them each to smithereens in my imagination. I was, at the time, costumed as the village idiot, incapable of coherent speech. Madness!

I had chosen to remain for a couple of weeks after most everybody had left; I wondered why. I was tempted to stage an escape, but where to? It would be better to leave in good order, with a sense of purpose. Frank Natale, I learned, was due to start a series of trainings in Amsterdam, now his home base. There was my purpose! Instead of running off without rendering proper thanks, I marked my exit with a ritual pudding – a large tray of tiramisu, the luscious dessert which was a staple on the Zorba the Buddha menu.

Frank was keen to disseminate his Life Skills courses, five separate modules intended as tools for personal empowerment. It had occurred to me that both he and Veeresh, in their engagement with dependency of one sort or another, had recognised that one of the most subtle and seductive addictions might be self-identification as a "spiritual person". The master-disciple dynamic was a minefield full of displaced egos – *"my guru is more enlightened than yours"* – and vicarious holiness. Under the guise of serving a sacred mission, all sense of personal responsibility might be wilfully abandoned. I know I wasn't the only sannyasin who was checking in with Frank – and Veeresh – on the rebound from the Ranch debacle.

Bhagwan, in his role as Zen master, had emphasized the need to drop the mind, to cultivate watchful awareness. Now here was Frank, affirming the mind as a crucial player in a manifesting universe. If this was tantamount to heresy, I was ready to listen. Spiritual endeavour and self-determination were not necessarily in opposition; rather, they could be complementaries.

The mind, so Frank taught, is essentially an organ of creation, participating in the Incomprehensible Collective Mind (no less!) which some might choose to call God. Thought, projected upon the world with sufficient willpower, has the capacity to shape destiny. It was by no means an original observation, but I was impressed by how he presented it. "New thought" – the doctrine that ideas are active agents – was a mainstay of Scientology, and underpinned the dismal visions of self-entitlement propounded by Ayn Rand, so influential in forwarding the neo-liberalism agenda. "The Power of Positive Thinking" by Norman Vincent Peale had made a strong impression on Richard Nixon; later, Donald Trump was to be a regular attendee at the church where Peale officiated as pastor, effectively bestowing on himself divine powers of infallibility. Clearly there are immense dangers here; all depends on the purity of intention. But mind and heart need not necessarily be at odds. I liked the sound of that. Simply, I found Frank Natale trustworthy.

Anything is Possible

Exercise: Imagine if your life could be any way at all. How are you willing to have it? To do this, separate what you are willing to have from what you believe is possible. Accept that your current perception of reality is limited by old beliefs that may not serve you. After reading each of the following, close your eyes, give yourself a minute and imagine that anything is possible.

1. Allow yourself to imagine your life exactly the way you choose it to be.

2. Focus now on your relationships and how you choose them to be.

3. Focus now on your work or career.

4. Focus now on your health.

5. Focus now on your physical surroundings.

6. Focus now on your inner states of consciousness.

7. Focus now on any other area of your life that you choose.

8. Focus on how you are willing to have your life now.

When you open your eyes, return to normal consciousness and make a few notes in your journal. If working with a partner or group, you may share your experience.

Frank Natale's Results Course provides practical step-by step instructions on how to identify and manifest "anything you want"

from "Results: the Willingness to Create" by Frank Natale

He drew my attention to the distinction between the mind and rational thinking. Rationality was merely a useful subset of the mental process, a means by which experiments might be conducted within a specified framework of logic. So much of our mental universe transcends such boundaries. Was it all just stuff and nonsense, a wilderness of monsters? The enlightenment thinkers who had championed the rationalist cause treated the wealth of mythology inherited from the classical world with a suspicion bordering on contempt. Now I began to understand that mythology was tremendously important, as a means of rendering the intimations of the spirit accessible to less elevated consciousness. We could learn much, advised Frank, by studying the writings of Joseph Campbell: his explorations of global mythology, and the way the mythological approach might provide a guide for everyday life.

I devoured these texts eagerly – the four-part Masks of God, The Hero with a Thousand Faces. I was, I recognized, embarked upon my own Hero's Journey, the archetypal adventure of the soul for which Campbell had provided such an illuminating map. I had chased after challenges, faced trials and dangers, sought guidance from those who had gone before; now, it occurred to me, was the point at which I might request the boon, the prize with which I might return to my homeland.

"Be bold! Be courageous! Anything is Possible!" Such was Frank Natale's message. Now it was time to pose my question as ardently, as sincerely, as possible: what was it that I wanted?

Something to do with a Restaurant, maybe?

Mystery School

What a treat, to be able to settle in Amsterdam, at least for a while. I felt I deserved a break, after the rigours of the Humaniversity. Now I was free to shape my own agenda, day by day, in a city oriented to the satisfaction of whim and desire.

I'd hit town to coincide with Frank Natale's seminar on Self Esteem, which was held at the (recently rebranded) Osho meditation centre, the Mystery School. I rented a room in the adjoining commune over this period, and was able to find a more permanent residence without much trouble: a room in a sannyasin shared house not too far away, on the edge of Vondel Park. It was known as the Vondelpalast, perhaps with the same sense of irony that had inspired Preston's Palace Hotel. The accommodation was quite basic – a mattress on the floor, perhaps with a chair for postural variety – but I had become used to this, and my housemates were friendly, although there were no shared meals. It was certainly a great location: not only was access to the park literally out the back gate, but within short walking distance were three wonderful art galleries – the Rijksmuseum, the Van Gogh gallery, and – my favourite – the Stedelijk museum of modern art, with whole roomfuls of works by Malevich and Mondrian, amongst so many other iconic pieces. Also close by was the Amsterdam Conservatory, offering the opportunity to sit in on performances by apprentice musicians, while the renowned Concertgebouw, for full orchestral blowouts, was just down the road. A brief stroll down a leafy lane led to the Singelgracht, the outermost of the semi-circle of canals that girdled the old city. There was so much to explore.

I'm not in a hurry, just sauntering along, following the line of a canal as it pursues its curve. Houseboats line the banks, bedecked with carefully tended miniature gardens. Cyclists wobble past along the cobbled street, beneath a stately progression of handsome buildings, tall and narrow, topped with elaborate finials, each proclaiming *"success"*. Cross over a bridge, lined with parked bicycles and more flowers, pass on to the next canal ring, circling closer to the centre. What could lie at the heart of this marvellous city? I stop off at a coffeeshop for refreshment, fill up a little pipe and study the map I've just purchased. How marvellous this city plan! It's a cobweb, to snare the curious, or half a target, for those with half an aim. There are four or five concentric half-rings, and there at the centre, the original source of its mystique,

two near parallel canals are pinched together to form a sort of vulva shape. This is the famous red light district, de Wallen, temptation on open offer. Oddly, the oldest building in the city, the Old Church (de Oude Kerk), presides magisterially over all this shamelessness. Just around the corner is Dam Square, littered with phallic bollards, and dominated by the royal palace, the former Town Hall, where all business dealings were conducted back in the day. Seagoing ships would have been offloading their cargo directly onto the Damrak wharves. But it's been a while now since salt water ran in the veins of Amsterdam: in the twentieth century the Zuiderzee, the shallow bay giving access to the North Sea, was drained and converted to polder, reclaimed land, turning Amsterdam into an inland city, its canals briny no more. I wondered how this transfusion might have affected the local psycho-geography. Was I being too fanciful?

The remarkable city plan, its canal rings advancing progressively outwards from the central core, densely bordered by high-rise business houses, was testimony to the steady accrual of wealth by a merchant elite. Amsterdam had grown rich on worldwide trade: from the 17th century onwards the Vereenigde Oostindische Compagnie (VOC) had been phenomenally successful in servicing the European demand for high value luxury goods: exotic spices, silk and porcelain. The VOC was a pioneer of capitalist enterprise, successfully harnessing the power of pooled resources to create a far-flung empire of trading bases and territorial control, centred on the colony of Batavia, the archipelago now known as Indonesia. This was an imperial history that had much in common with that of its rival, Great Britain – except that the Dutch appear to have made a much greater effort to come to terms with its more shameful aspects. I learned much from an exhibition at the Tropenmuseum, *"Wit over Swart"* (white over black), which examined how underlying assumptions of racial supremacy had permeated deeply into the Dutch culture and psyche, framing and characterising even the most trivial of day to day ephemera. Here was a nation unafraid of encountering its own shadow. Perhaps this explained the overall relaxed, chilled, nature of this city. Or was it more a consequence of the ready availability of cannabis?

As for me, sure, I was enjoying the sudden absence of pressure, but I was resolved not to slip into a rut of self-indulgence. I had been fired up by Frank Natale's trainings, made aware of how my own expectations determine my life results. Rather than being content to drift with the prevailing current, I was cultivating a rigorous practice of taking responsibility for my actions. A key strategy was making a daily list: things I choose to achieve this day. No need to be too grandiose – world peace is likely to be some time in coming along. Don't be afraid of including the apparently trivial, was the suggestion. Accordingly, onto my list went: have breakfast, brush teeth, talk to someone I haven't met before . . . it was okay to work up. Some days I wrote: go busking in the street; on others: don't get stoned. At the end of the day check how many of these results have been achieved, enjoy the sense of empowerment this brings. If some results remain unticked, don't beat yourself up; just ask yourself if maybe you were standing in your own way.

Self Esteem, Frank had taught, was chiefly generated in two life arenas: the experience of supportive, creative relationships, and through passionate productive work. Here was plenty for me to concentrate on. It was no good just imagining myself a better, more fulfilled person: I needed to share my vision with the world, to enlist its creative power. Ultimately, what ought to be driving the vision was not mere selfish aggrandisement, but the desire to attune oneself with what might benefit one's fellow humans, and the planet of which we were an integral part. Brushing my teeth was just the beginning.

There were, I supposed, many vegetarian restaurants in Amsterdam in need of an enthusiastic chef. I had interviews in three such establishments, each of them an attractive venue, but nothing went click. Maybe they didn't get where I was coming from – but more likely is, that none of them corresponded to what I really wanted. I had been hanging out in Amsterdam for about three months when the ideal job fell into my lap.

On those days when I'd resolved to make a new friend, the best place to achieve this was at the Osho Stad bar, in the commune where I'd already briefly stayed. This not only provided the default evening entertainment for residents, but also served as a meeting place for the wider sannyasin community. I developed a taste for the local tipple – Kriek, a cherry beer – and practised the social skills I'd learnt at the Humaniversity. Here was an easy welcome, based on shared understanding and life experience. Most of those lounging on sofas or propped up on barstools would be Dutch, with a smattering of other nationalities, but conversations were like as not conducted in English,

Sightseeing with friends.
Photo by Vijen

or could easily flip into English if required. I really liked being here; it was an Amsterdam iteration of communal living: a society of individuals taking pleasure in each other's company, hanging out and having fun. I got talking with the current kitchen coordinator, who was keen to move on as soon as possible. He suggested I put myself forward for the job. There was no salary, but it was exactly what I wanted to do.

There was one important proviso: in order to qualify for the crucial trial shift, I needed to supply a recent AIDS test. This had been a regular three-monthly procedure in all of my commune experience, but it was some time since my last test. The only option was to hightail it to the Humaniversity, where short-notice AIDS tests were standard practice. The atmosphere at the Hum was intense, thick, like plunging into bioenergetic soup: I had arrived in the middle of an AUM intensive, with no fewer than four AUM meditations being conducted every day. It was a relief to escape out into a more normal world. On the bus back to Amsterdam, clutching the boogie-box I'd managed to retrieve from the Humaniversity kitchen, I was chatted up by a couple of girls who wanted to know what my favourite hip-hop group was.

Having creditably demonstrated my kitchen abilities, the final stage of my induction was an interview with the residents' committee. They were happy to offer me a room rent-free, as a special case. But they would like some reassurance as to my commitment to Osho's vision. Was I, perhaps, simply pursuing my own interests? It felt like a low blow; my immediate reaction was to storm out of the room – how dare they impugn my sincerity? It took a minute or two for me to calm down. Just tell them what they want to hear; I know my aim is true. And then all was well. I was once again a commune member, but at a further turn of the circle – or of the coiled spring.

This was the deal: as kitchen co-ordinator I was pledged to 32 working hours per week, responsible for providing three meals a day for whomever of the commune's seventy to eighty residents had purchased meal tickets. I needed to make sure that the stores were well topped up and that purchasing ran smoothly. Crucially, I was given a budget by which I could measure expenses against income. I would have a staff of two or three helpers, plus I would need to organise a residents' helpers rota: all communards (including myself) were obliged to devote two hours a week to tasks such as washing-up or vegetable chopping. This meant that everyone had some stake in the orderly conduct of the kitchen operation; also that I got to meet each of them in a work environment. It has been my experience that working together on a shared project, such as getting a meal out on time, can be a great way of getting to know one another. It was up to me to find the ideal balance between relaxed friendliness and effective creativity; to tune the kitchen to a harmonious pitch. It was a challenge I relished: if I was successful, then all would be able to taste the result, in meals that had that special quality that only comes from food prepared with love.

The role of kitchen coordinator brought both responsibility and status. Each Wednesday morning I was expected to participate in the commune Board Meeting, which might last two hours or more. I'm not generally a big fan of meetings, but these were certainly engrossing. Hitherto, the inner workings of commune organisation had been a mystery I hadn't particularly concerned myself with; now I could appreciate just how much effort went into keeping this ocean liner afloat. There were always at least a dozen items for consideration – including the kitchen coordinator's report – and I came to realise that this magnificent structure, apparently sailing so serenely over the waves, was suffering serious structural problems, was in fact plagued with rusty machinery and leaks below the waterline. Most threatening was an impending court case, by which the building's owner, avid to maximise profit, was seeking to prove that the commune breached terms of contract in mixing business and residential use. This was not without legal merit, since much of the property was in fact devoted to the Mystery School, the activities of the meditation institute, which was a significant source of funds. It's worth bearing in mind that the Oregon commune had endured a long-drawn-out legal confrontation regarding zoning restrictions, which had ultimately proved fatal. Idealism can so often fall victim to the bureaucratic niceties which uphold our consensus reality.

Money – again, something I had paid little heed to over the past several years – was also a pressing concern. It was made clear how important it was to keep a grip on kitchen expenditure. Such items as out-of-season organic tomatoes (generally unripe) were amongst the first things to be struck off the purchasing list I'd inherited from my predecessor. Thenceforth I gave much careful attention to perusing our various orders – from the wholefood suppliers, the cash-and-carry wholesalers, and the vegetable market. I was learning how to adapt my knowledge of German to the peculiar sounds of the Dutch language, so that what arrived on the doorstep was precisely what I was expecting. I was also developing a sense of how much stuff we got through each week: a rough rule of thumb was to allow a box and a half of (assorted) vegetables per meal. That would allow for a degree of improvisation, as long as there was a reliable store of basic ingredients.

Perhaps we could learn to adapt to the ways of the world. A business consultant, intrigued by our remarkable experiment in communal living, offered to provide a training seminar. He had a name well suited to someone of an enquiring mind: it sounded just like *"Qu'est ce que c'est?"* – Kees Kesej, perhaps. We had a unique product, he assured us; we just needed to lower the threshold discouraging potential customers. Our insistence on provision of an AIDS test to participate in Mystery School activities was clearly a major problem. But at least we could allow the public into our dining room, to enjoy our delicious food. My kitchen – Magdalena – was to be rebranded as Zorba Restaurant. Menus were to be displayed daily in the Mystery School, to draw visitors further into our web of enticement. I began to give more thought to defining the meals we were offering, to add a note of adventure into my description: "A Night in Tunisia"; "Tuscan Romance"; "Ashram

Special"; "Take me to the Casbah"; "Olé!" – each supper became a special event, an evocation of the exotic.

After a month or two, the impact of sustained high standards and efficient systems were clearly apparent – most of all in the general happiness of those queueing up to enjoy the service. There was always a rich variety of dishes, attractively presented, buffet style – soup and salads at lunchtime, main dish with appropriate accompaniments, followed by dessert, in the evenings. On those days when I was the principal chef I was enjoying trying out new ideas, expanding my repertoire. I was thrilled to be immersed in creative process; It felt good to be appreciated.

This was the back entrance to the Osho Stad commune, which occupied the site of a former convent. Following the adverse court decision, the commune was obliged to let go the larger part of the property, continuing as a smaller entity named "Mevlana".

I had a room all to myself, with ample space to stretch out in. A large window opened up over the central courtyard, from which I could watch my colleagues come and go, or gather in friendly groups on the lawn. I felt free to contribute the sound of my favourite music to the lively buzz of chatter; the bell of the church next door chimed the passing hours; early each morning our resident rooster proudly asserted its pre-eminence over the henhouse. It was a happy time – but I was also a bit lonely. Each of these rooms were large enough for two: a set of wooden steps rose up from the centre to access separate mezzanine platforms. Quite likely at some point I'd be obliged to share. Would that be so much fun?

I suppose I was wary of entering into a relationship. I'd realised, during my frenzy of self-examination at the Humaniversity, that I'd treated Kabira rather badly in Berlin, as I attempted to shift a stale dynamic. We'd been close, had looked after one another in a difficult time – and I'd tossed our relationship away like a used hankie. Now I had the grace to get back in touch, and our connection sparked up once again. She came to stay for a week, and we had a lovely time; in the following weeks many fond letters and poems were exchanged. It was enough to shake me out of my solitude, to abandon my reservations about sharing a room. My new roomie was an engaging, gregarious young woman; I enjoyed her company. But her sociable lifestyle was keeping me awake at nights: the only way to get some sleep was to take my duvet with me to bunk down in the laundry. She was kind enough to recognise the problem, and moved out to another room. I had the space to myself again.

Here Comes Trouble . . .

On the edge of the city there's a rumour hits the streets
And the rumour starts running just like ice in the heat
Some are fetching guitars, some go for their guns
'Cause here comes trouble and his brother fun
Here comes trouble, here comes fun
Here comes trouble, here comes fun

Old Mister Trouble he's a family man
He don't play for peanuts in a one man band
In the big parade they'll be banging on the drum
And calling here comes trouble and his brother fun
Here comes trouble, here comes fun
Here comes trouble, here comes fun

Down the road they're coming, the air is filled with sound
Everybody's clapping, my blood begins to pound
I got to burst out singing, this ain't no time to run
'Cause here comes trouble and his brother fun
Here comes trouble, here comes fun
Here comes trouble, here comes fun

Up and down the town they'll be shouting for joy
The dogs and cats are playing with the girls and the boys
Everyone's behaving like their life's just begun
'Cause here comes trouble and his brother fun
Here comes trouble, here comes fun
Here comes trouble, here comes fun

I had arranged with Kabira to pay her a return visit in Berlin, professing great excitement at the prospect. But long distance love can be a fragile thing, prone to disruption by the unexpected cosmic event. One afternoon, as I treated myself to a cappuccino in the Mystery School coffee bar, I fell into a clinch with a young woman who had just arrived back from Poona. My breathing, my heartbeat, fell into synchronicity with hers, time stopped . . . we were in deep space.

Her name was P—. It might as well have been Pandora – a door opening into infinite possibility, an ineffable promise of annihilation in glory, a consummation forever out of reach. I tremble at the recollection.

Discovering the dubious powers of patronage, I made sure she got a job on the kitchen team. It wasn't long before P— was my new room-mate. I recorded this development in a letter to my mother: *"My present room-mate, P—, is a very pretty woman with whom I am conducting a wonderfully difficult romance. She also likes to work in the kitchen, is in my eyes hopelessly religious and I am afraid quite bananas. She has stars in her eyes and some of them she says are for me . . . How delicate the plot now becomes. Next week I will go for a week's holiday to Berlin . . ."* Goodness knows what my mother made of this.

In my letter to Kabira, written just a week or so before, I had been rather more graphic: *"This last week I've simply been pushing myself too much, I'm totally stressed . . . what's happening to me? Others have been asking me that too. Why, for example, did I wake up the whole house in the middle of the night? My friends had to drag me out of my room, just as I stood on the bitter edge of fury and violence. I don't think I've ever in my life been so enraged. The very next day, in the middle of a peaceful cookshift, I suddenly sprang upon a certain woman, I wanted to beat her up . . ."* It doesn't look good, does it? *"The Space-Cake remains on her plate, under the glass bell, unconsumed, an inviting delicacy. I struggle against the ancient wisdom regarding space-cakes, that they can't be both eaten and possessed. This is truly a crazy, confusing passion, and I'm falling right into it – if I want to. Somehow it is also a game, and I enjoy the drama – but not the stress."* (my original letter was in German, so the translation is a bit approximate)

No doubt this was a two-sided game we were playing, but its effects were being felt all through the commune. So much drama was disastrous for the steady, measured process of cooking. My emotional instability was finding its way into the food. I was turning into an irresponsible monster.

Was I kidding myself, that I somehow had a choice in all of this? On my birthday, I made my way to the residents' committee to demand a new room all for myself, insisting that they couldn't refuse my birthday wish. I duly removed all of my stuff while P— was otherwise engaged, installing myself in a tiny but delightful space in the furthest corner of the building. Later that afternoon I became aware of howls of anguish emanating from my former room. This bird had flown.

"She has no power over me", I declared to myself again and again, like a mantra – but it just wasn't true: how can you deny magnetic attraction? We continued to meet each other in the kitchen – all over the place, in fact – and sparks continued to fly. One morning, over breakfast, I overheard a couple of friends discussing an imminent ten-day meditation retreat in France. I immediately signed myself up, arranging to accompany my friends on the train to Paris – and beyond.

The course would be led by S. N. Goenka, well known for his rigorous approach to Vipassana Insight Meditation. My surrender to the teaching was hamstrung from the start by my recollection of Osho's damning putdown: *"Goenka is an idiot"*. Nonetheless, I signed an undertaking to stay for the full ten-day retreat, and to submit to the various instructions as the course unfolded. The procedure involved a lot of sitting still, maintaining an upright posture whilst concentrating the mind in specific ways. I'd never mastered an efficient sitting posture, such as lotus position, so this was hard going. At least there was a wonderful vegetarian buffet to enjoy during the meal breaks. In the evening Goenka himself would give a discourse, guiding us along the path. I found it difficult to attune myself to his teaching: the voice was simply wrong. The only thing that stuck in my mind was his reassurance that if we persisted in this technique, after a few lifetimes we might well attain enlightenment. Pie in the sky, in short . . .

During the pause between sitting sessions, I attempted a few yoga poses, to ease my aching muscles. I was spotted by one of the course assistants, who demanded that I desist. Something snapped: my submission to the discipline, in fact. I was overcome by a fit of hysterical laughter, much to the bemusement of my fellow meditators. Next morning, I announced that I would be leaving. My offer of payment, to my surprise, was rejected: I had chosen to reject the teaching, so it wouldn't be appropriate. Thoughtfully provided with a picnic lunch, I was driven to the nearest main road. I was at liberty to go wherever I wanted, with an unexpected supply of cash in my pocket. I stuck out my thumb; a truck stopped, heading towards Auxerre, through which I had passed some years before. Along the way we passed through the most beautiful village I could imagine; when I arrived in Auxerre it just didn't feel right. I hitched right back to the beautiful village.

I checked in at a small hotel and went for a walk, coming to rest on a bench by the small lake facing towards the village, which clustered on the side of a small hill, crowned by a medieval church. My mind was clear, open to the beauty and wonder of the world. I felt transfigured. And I felt free. I had walked away from the rigours of spiritual commitment, and it felt so right. Was this what the old teaching meant: *"If you meet Buddha on the path, cut off his head"*?

For the next several days I rejoiced in my unaccustomed purity of spirit and mental clarity, exploring the local countryside, writing down the stream of thoughts provoked by my footsteps, avoiding anything which might sully my vision, like coffee or alcohol. At night I was active witness to a succession of delightful dreams: an aquamarine vision of dolphins at play; and then a curious episode in which the Prince of Wales explained how happy he was in his marriage to Lady Diana.

The time came to head back towards Paris, and thence to Amsterdam. Close to home, as I reviewed my notebook, it occurred to me that not once had I mentioned P—.

My thoughts and emotions seemed to have settled, coalesced into a vision. I was filled with excitement at the prospect of returning to England to manifest my dream – of a place that might foster the spirit of community, acting as a hub for friendship and creativity. I knew just the place where this was needed – East Oxford's Cowley Road. I realised I had been gathering the necessary skills and experience to make this possible; only one crucial piece of the puzzle had yet to fall into place. All depended on one last, bold throw. Camilla had accepted an invitation to come stay for a few days, and I had high hopes of success.

I met her off the plane at Schiphol airport. It was by now high summer, and very hot. We walked all around the city I had come to love so much, and we talked, and talked. About my adventures since last we'd met, the Humaniversity, Frank Natale, Joseph Campbell . . . about our various hopes and dreams. It was an enchanted time, in all that heat; then at last the storm, impending for so long, broke. Rain lashed against the skylight, lightening flashed, thunder rolled; inside, all was at it should be, an oasis of delight. Next morning, breakfast was served in bed . . . and then it was time for Camilla to head on back to the airport.

My time at Osho Stad was drawing to a close – and it was evident that the days of the commune itself were also numbered. The court case had been irretrievably lost; the largest part of the property would have to be relinquished. Uncertainty and insecurity stalked the commune: one woman lost her grip on sanity; one man fell from the side of the building as he conducted external repairs; he survived, as did the troubled teenager who attempted suicide by hurling himself off the roof. The sultry, stormy weather persisted, fierce gales blowing open any loose window fixings, broken glass strewing the city streets. Throughout it all I drifted in a glorious happy haze, my love compounded every other day by a phone call, or a letter written on flimsy magenta wrapping paper, from my beloved Camilla.

My letters are similarly enraptured, full of strangeness and charm: *"One night I step out onto the roof and P— is there. We haven't spoken for weeks, but still she takes my hand and shows me the moon, shining big and bright. I look into her eyes and see it reflected back, mystic, wonderful – and we hug, a deep silent falling into forgetfulness. It's nice, but that's as far as it goes . . ."* Somehow I have broken my dangerous addiction – or its object has shifted, to something more practical and fulfilling – and more full of promise.

Reflecting back, after so many years, on this pivotal episode, I am tempted to draw a connection between my yearning for spiritual revelation and my doomed desire for Lady P—. My choice to abandon the quest for enlightenment in some imaginary future lifetime was tantamount to embracing the creative potential of this very life, with all the skills, insight and perceptions I had garnered in the course of my adventures. Now it was up to me to find the right place to manifest my dream, and to identify the best support to make it happen.

The time for departure, and my return to Oxford, drew near. There was one last gathering of the whole community to attend: an occasion for sad farewells, but also an opportunity for a bold statement of intention: I would be creating my own restaurant on the Cowley Road, and it would be called *"The Magic Munchroom"*.

The collectively-run Keyno restaurant in Munich made a policy of exploring a wide variety of national cuisines: each Monday a different destination would be announced, so that guests might experience something quite unexpected. This struck me as an excellent idea, playful and fun. I had started to attempt something similar in the Mystery School kitchen, and would continue this gastronomic globetrotting in my subsequent catering career. This cookbook would be a useful source of ideas.

This was a gift from Kabira when I was in Amsterdam; inside the cover, alongside a photo of Osho, she has inscribed "For the Master-cook". Does she mean me, or Osho?

Recalibrating

The summer of 1990 was drawing to a close when I returned to Oxford, fired up with sense of mission. It would yet be a full seven years before the consummation of that vision, with the establishment of the Magic Café on Magdalen Road. Curiously enough, this correlates remarkably closely with the time lag between Margaret Thatcher's downfall and the onset of Tony Blair's hegemony. Sometimes historical process demands a little time to work its way through the system.

Nonetheless, historical process had not been idle while I had been off on my adventures. I felt like I was checking in from a different planet: I'd missed the gradual, insidious redefinition of British social and political culture, cumulatively amounting to a fundamental change. During her decade in power, Margaret Thatcher, with remarkable tenacity, had been re-engineering the very essence of Britishness: imposing a new model of civilisation, no less, all the while insisting that all she was doing was standing up for common-sense values. As I was debriefing Camilla on all the strangeness of my commune experience, nothing seemed stranger than her insistence that Mrs T really had claimed: *"There is no such thing as society, only individuals and their families"*. What a preposterous, insane idea! Yet this was the bedrock foundation of her policy.

It would, of course, be a mistake to identify this programme solely with one politician, however rebarbative. Her achievement drew on deep roots, ideas that had been brewing for decades, whether formulated in the economic theories of Milton Friedman or the pseudo-philosophical fictions of Ayn Rand. The capitalist model of human destiny had always had a problem with that awkward, intangible object, the individual soul. What possible purpose could it serve, if it were not engaged in the measurable cycles of consumption and profit? All that mattered was economic functionality.

This dismal vision was boldly, relentlessly expressed, as if it were an irresistible force, like Arnold Schwarzenegger's Terminator: ***"There Is No Alternative"***. Objections would simply be over-ridden, blasted into submission like the hapless Argies in the Falklands War; the striking miners struck down by a militarized police; the Peace Convoy corralled into a field and systematically brutalized, their homes destroyed; protest movements, such as the women of Greenham Common, infiltrated, discredited and sidelined.

Money was now the universal signifier, the essential cultural lubricant. The customer – or guest, as we had learned to say in the commune – was now a client, a consumer of product. This might be a very attractive, well imagined and tightly organised product, such as the Womad or Glastonbury festivals, but could these really be an equivalent to the anarchic solstice celebrations at Stonehenge, wild and free? The pathway to empowerment was now via the personal computer, each year freshly reconfigured, demanding a constant upgrade. Confronted by such a dazzling conveyor belt of consumer goods, the very idea of fixing a faulty product, or of buying last year's model second hand, seemed ludicrous. The junk shop, hitherto the principal agent of recycling, vanished from the streets. One of the very last, Steptoes on Magdalen Road, would soon be forced out of business in a police crackdown on the black economy: this would, as we shall see, have significant consequences.

Culture – all those vocations concerned with exploring and sharing the ineffable mystery of being – was diminished and defiled: the value of an old master now solely to be measured by its realisation price at auction, something to be purchased as an investment, or to be vicariously consumed via a souvenir selfie. Rebel music, which had led the charge in the counter-cultural moment, was just another commodity, neatly packaged in the latest digital format, another source of profit for the multinational corporation. And the artists, the musicians, had become mere functionaries: "creatives", cogs in the cash machine, or else obliged to busk for spare change.

Where was truth, love and beauty in all of this? And if society had been officially declared non-existent, where did that leave community?

The scale, the purpose, of my ambition stood out in stark profile. Here was a veritable mountain to climb. I was striking out against the sick spirit of the age – but I needed to recognize that I was a long way yet from base camp.

First of all, the mere foothills of my endeavour, there were all manner of practical challenges to be mastered.

Top of the list was a formal name change: establishing my brand, if you like. I'd given some thought to this, during my wanderings in the French countryside. I'd long since moved on from my given name; it carried difficult, disempowering connotations for me. The exotic nature of my sannyas name might serve me well, suggesting a magical persona, an evocation of otherness. It was the name I had learned to respond to over the last seven years. I settled on Hafiz Robert Ladell. Robert was there to uphold my father's input, just in case his spirit was miffed. Ladell was my mother's family name – and, of course, my Uncle Bill's.

Armed with my new identity, I headed to the bank to open an account. They didn't want anything to do with me, some mysterious vagrant – until I produced a cheque with a small number of zeros, my share of a family legacy. Good old Uncle Bill! During my last hectic day in Amsterdam I'd failed to check through a pile of stuff for significant items; only when I reached Oxford did I realise I'd inadvertently left this cheque behind. Luckily, a diligent friend posted it on – with a mild scolding for my messiness. I'd left behind my mala, too – but that was quite intentional.

It wasn't possible for me to move in directly with Camilla. Instead, I accepted the offer of a room from a fellow sannyasin, S——, the mother of an old college friend. Both had also trained with Frank Natale. Whilst attending his Results seminar, S—— had identified becoming a foster parent as her Significant Life Result, but was daunted by the financial implications. How much money might she need? It was suggested that she write down a figure, so she entered her six-digit phone number on the page, and shared her wishes with fellow participants. Shortly afterwards, she was informed that this very amount, conveniently expressed in pounds sterling, had been deposited in her bank account by a fellow course participant. It happened to correspond very closely with the price of a substantial house in North Oxford, the ideal base for her future foster family. This was a magnificent corroboration of the Frank Natale method; but it didn't take too long to realise that living in someone else's Result was not an automatic pathway to achieving my own. Apart from anything else, it was simply the wrong end of town.

I had more luck with my next house share, joining up with Pradeep to sign a year's lease for a house in Jericho. Like myself, Pradeep was a refugee from the commune: still busy processing the catastrophe of the Oregon Ranch, in which his cherished dream of idyllic communal coexistence had collapsed in scandal and shame. Now his intention was to set himself up in independent practice as psychotherapist – so we were both attempting to adapt the skills we had learned in a very specific closed environment to the more circumspect mores of the wider world. I was grateful for his supportive friendship, and for his crucial insight: the best way to make connections is to construct a network with yourself at the centre. This was, of course, still pre-internet: a quasi-palaeolithic age of paper, scissors, and paste. Pradeep, soon to be Philip, did have a new-fangled Apple computer, with which he compiled, designed and published an A3 information sheet called Green Events. It provided a calendar of activities which might interest a certain sort of person – precisely those who might be interested in relationship therapy, Philip's designated field of expertise. There was always a prominent mention for his ManWoman Centre; and in return for distributing the sheet at selected venues throughout the city, there would also be a small advert for Magic Feasts Vegetarian Celebration Catering.

In the absence of my own premises, catering seemed the best way to bring my project forward. All I needed was a suitable kitchen, lots of specialist equipment, a means of transport . . . actually, I had none of these. Philip helped me convert some of Uncle Bill's funds into a (not very reliable) second hand car, then provided some coaching towards passing the driving test. I'd never learned as a teenager: my father's insistence in continuing to drive in the wake of a debilitating stroke had left me nervous of propelling a large chunk of metal at speed. Four attempts later, I was at last a certified master of the road. Moving stuff around is the *sine qua non* of catering; delivering on a promise, from here to there at the appointed time, its very essence. I needed to develop a clear understanding of logistics: how much, how many, how long, simply how . . .

Most important of all, the question: how might I spread the message of what I might be capable of? Once again, Philip came up with an excellent idea: the Networking Dinner. What better way to make friends and influence people than to share a convivial meal together? Tickets were sold via Green

Events. We had just about enough space in our central room to squeeze in twenty chairs – which I managed to borrow from an amenable community centre. I prepared a sumptuous vegetarian feast in our rather basic kitchen; we sat down together, shared our stories, made friends. Philip had designed some communication exercises, to allow us a chance to state our core message. We did this several times; I would adjudge these evenings a great success, inasmuch as they laid the foundations for many enduring friendships and creative endeavours. The Barefoot Boogie was one such project. They also provided good practice in cultivating the professional standard of catering I was aiming for.

As the joyous experience of running the Osho Stad kitchen, emperor of my own domain, slipped into a distant realm of memory, I had begun to appreciate the extent of my culinary ignorance. I'd never actually had any formal training; I'd simply been fortunate in the peculiar range of my opportunities, gained in the most tolerant of circumstances. If I'd perpetrated my share of disasters, these had all been filed in that blessed plot labelled "learning experiences". How might this measure against a more orthodox process? I was desirous of improving my baking technique, so signed up for a couple of modules at the local tech college. Our teacher had evidently learned his trade in the army; he had an unfortunate habit of referring to over-baked biscuits as "Bob Marleys". My colleagues were mostly school leavers, though I do remember one woman there to further her career in guesthouse management: she disdainfully described an earlier course in which a whole session had been devoted to sticking a cherry in the middle of a halved grapefruit. I had to conclude that no great mysteries were likely to be revealed. At the end of each session we were permitted to purchase samples of the class produce to take home: these failed the all-important Camilla Test. I aspired to cook from the heart; what this school was teaching was industrial technique.

I was also conscious of my ignorance of business practice. This was something the government of the time was eager to foster, as a crucial foundation for the dynamic enterprise culture they had called into being. Their policies over the past decade had succeeded in rotting out much of Britain's manufacturing and industrial sector, resulting in daunting levels of unemployment. These numbers might look a lot less incriminating by inviting willing would-be entrepreneurs to substitute their dole payment for a quasi-wage termed Enterprise Allowance. Training courses were offered; results were expected to blossom forth after a certain period of subsidised product development. It wasn't a bad idea, but it turned out I was a little late at this particular feast: government funds had been swallowed up by middle management and consultants, leaving nothing left for the intended recipients. Oh well, I needed to learn to be self-reliant: I didn't want to be sucking on this particular momma.

What I did want – badly – was a place to cook, ideally one that could satisfy the stringent demands of the Environmental Health Department. Camilla's house, now at last my home, was a delightful domicile, but its kitchen was tiny and not exactly squeaky clean. I asked around, checking out various possibilities. My good friend Supi had started teaching yoga at the Asian Community Centre, just off Cowley Road; she suggested I check this out.

When I first arrived in Oxford in the mid 70s and started exploring its Wild East – Cowley Road and its environs – the area between East Avenue and Divinity Road was occupied by the Cowley Road Hospital, part of the NHS estate. Despite its impressive Victorian facade, there was something dismal and forbidding about its aspect. For those with deeper roots in Oxford, that was well understandable. It had been purpose built in the mid 1860s as a Workhouse, an institution intended to address the problems of indigency, poverty and beggary by drawing impoverished unfortunates away from the

prestigious streets of central Oxford. Up until its closure after the second world war, it offered a mean-spirited home for the derelict, as well as an overnight hostel for tramps passing through on their restless migrations. At the beginning of the eighties this large estate had all been demolished – apart from the chapel. By the end of that decade this sturdy building had been incorporated into a brand new establishment, the Asian Cultural Centre.

The Asian Cultural Centre in 2020

This was, I imagine, the product of fervid brainstorming at the Town Hall, intended to curry political favour amongst the incoming cosmopolitan populations of East Oxford – rather than being the result of grassroots demand and input. How else to explain the bogus concept of "the Asian Community", as if there were not a host of cultural differences between the various groups of South Asian origin, many of these fraught with conflict? The largest of these communities, currently congregating in makeshift mosques while waiting for funds to accumulate for something more permanent, were Muslim. What sense was there in a business plan centred around bar takings? And had nobody been consulted about the most appropriate kitchen fittings for large-scale Asian catering? All of these failures of imagination were to prove greatly to my benefit.

Tasked with making this venture work was Mr Jawaid Malik, a most engaging man, both genial and practical. Evidently his primary concern was to generate an income for this handsome but not entirely culturally appropriate venue. When I described what I had in mind – a vegetarian community café – he suggested that I offer this on two lunchtimes each week, maybe Thursday and Friday, and see what happened. He'd set an easy rent, at least to begin with. He couldn't have been more supportive; *"just don't mention it to the Board"*.

Here was a spacious, fully equipped kitchen, with a mighty eight-burner gas oven, an appropriate range of sink units, fridges and freezer – plus a lockable storage cupboard which I was welcome to use. Directly adjacent, across a small corridor, was the lounge area, redundantly fitted out as a bar, which would make an ideal café space. This was a wonderful result. The only down side was that it lay somewhat off the beaten track, several hundred yards distant from Cowley Road. Somehow I would have to persuade people to make that jump.

Let's see how this all looks from the perspective of my good friend and constant support, Jon Bowen.

I came to Oxford in 1989 after realising that my incipient career in science had been a mistake. I was hoping to meet interesting creative people, and I wasn't disappointed. Oxford at that time was alive with "alternative" culture: poetry groups, art groups, magical ritual groups, self-help therapy groups, dance groups, drama groups, meditation groups. Whatever weird and wacky philosophy you might have been into, it was happening somewhere in Oxford.

In 1991 I spent 5 months away, helping to nurse my beloved grand-mother as she declined into death from cancer. When I returned there were adverts pasted on all the lamp-posts along the Cowley and Botley Roads: "Barefoot Boogie – booze-free, smoke-free, shoe-free dancing". This sounded like a great way to let out some of that pent-up grief and frustration – and it was!

Over the years I had been banned from a number of dance venues for various reasons, ranging from dancing with other men to being "dangerously wild". The Barefoot Boogie was quite different: I was by no means the most wild dancer there, and whatever you needed to do, you could do without judgement from others, as long as you were respectful to other dancers and their own processes. It was brilliant.

After a few months word got around that people were needed to help manage the Barefoot Boogie. I had some time on my hands, it seemed like a great opportunity to meet new and interesting people, so I put myself forward.

I don't remember much about the first management committee meeting beyond a friendly chap with a bright smile by the name of Hafiz. He was full of energy, and bouncing off the walls with excite-ment about his new venture: "The Magic Café".

Thrusting a hand-drawn flyer into my hand offering a free cup of something, he urged me to "Come along, come along, Asian Cultural Centre just off the Cowley Road, Thursday and Friday lunchtimes."

I immediately liked Hafiz, his relentless optimism was instant therapy for the depression that plagued me in those days, so I went along.

I had never visited the Asian Cultural Centre before. Set back off the Cowley Road between a stretch of waste ground and a new housing estate, the modern urban architecture blended in seamlessly with housing association flats and didn't appear remotely Asian. Nor did the receptionist, a beautiful young, very non-Asian woman in sexy fluorescent hot-pants who directed me to "the bar" if I wanted the café. A bar? In a centre predominantly aimed at the local Muslim population? Curiouser and curiouser.

My first taste of the café was a joy: several of my friends were already there, amongst many other people who would become my friends in the years ahead. The food was brilliant, and Hafiz's wonderful salads – each one a vegetarian platter in itself – rapidly cured me of a lifelong suspicion of raw vegetables. As for the legendary chocolate brownies, anything that wasn't chocolate was coffee, providing a caffeine hit that I'd never experienced before – so intense that I wondered if there might be some secret hallucinogenic ingredient . . .

At that time in my life I was making a lot of decorative art, mostly paintings, and was looking for possible places to exhibit my work. I don't remember whether this struck me on my first visit to the café, or if the idea grew by degrees, but at some point there was a moment of enlightenment: the expansive brilliant white walls of "the bar" would look a lot better covered in brightly-coloured art.

After the café was closed, I spoke to Hafiz about the idea of putting up paintings in the café and he was thoroughly enthusiastic: his vision of a community café could expand to include a community exhibition space, so he suggested I talk to the receptionist. It turned out that she was herself a trained artist, also looking for exhibition opportunities, so she enthusiastically took up the idea. We decided the first step would be to put up a picture rail in the "bar"; she said she would raise the idea with the centre manager. I distinctly recall her saying: "I'll put my hot-pants on for work tomorrow, Jawaid always gives me what I want when I'm wearing them."

The hot-pants worked and the picture rail went up, and over the next few weeks three or four other local artists started to join us in regular planning meetings. Soon we had planned a six-month programme of exhibitions, workshops, skill-share days and performances, and thus "Magic Arts" was born.

There were magnificent highs and embarrassing lows. On the "high" side I made my first ever sales of my paintings from those walls, and had the privilege of performing alongside some fantastic movement artists.

On the downside, I remember when we exhibited art by a friend of a friend from Sheffield: he put so much into the exhibition, hiring a van to bring his paintings and spending days hanging them just right. On the night of the private view the gods threw down torrents of rain, while lightning graced the skies and thunder filled our ears. Nobody came and no paintings were sold. Neither the artist nor my friend ever spoke to me again, so profound was their disappointment. Never mind.

That little artists' co-operative didn't last long. We met every week to talk about our dreams: our day dreams and our night dreams, looking further and further ahead in our lives, and deeper and deeper into our souls. After about 9 months it became clear that "being artists" was simply a stepping-stone to another place for each of us. One of us decided that her true priority was to have babies; another was called to teach; another went on to study architecture; and I myself was drawn to organise ritual events . . .

Over the five years of its part-time existence, the Magic Café at the Asian Cultural Centre slowly built up its clientele, from no more than half a dozen or so loyal supporters to a regular and reliable turnout of fifty to sixty, all of whom had made a special effort to seek out this special place. These were the people I wanted to reach, to connect with, and to enable new connections to spark up, take root and grow. I noticed something interesting: all the tables available were of the trestle variety, with space for six to eight sitters. If you arrived with a friend or two, most likely you'd be drawn into the conversation at the other end of the table: by the end of lunch, you might have doubled your friendship count.

Liveliness was unleashed. This was most apparent in the junior constituency. I had recognised that, if community were to mean anything, then it must embrace the family. Above all, there needed to be a fond welcome for mothers with their infant children: a safe space for them to hold their babes to their breast without any hint of disapproval. It was a shock to realise how rare this was, how "normal" it might be to be refused entrance to a café with the admonishment: *"you're not bringing that [i.e. the baby] in here."* Lactating mothers had in fact been amongst the first to discover the Magic Café, their attention drawn to this interesting new venue whilst attending prenatal classes at the local health clinic. Doctors and nurses would come along too, attracted by the healthy food on offer.

What had initially resembled a clubhouse, where those in the know might be sure to bump into each another once or twice a week, was slowly evolving into a zone of serendipity, somewhere where the anticipated agreeable lunchtime might be augmented by an encounter with the entirely unexpected. In short, the Magic Café, just as I had imagined it could be, was in full process of manifestation.

Was it not simply enough, that wherever I laid out my wonderful spread, there would be the Magic Café? I had been accepting all manner of catering commissions, from stalls at local fairs, to residential trainings and full-scale wedding blowouts. Most of these had their own agenda: sometimes it was simply required that I offload the food, arrange it nicely, pick up my cheque and leave. Nonetheless, there were occasions when I felt it appropriate to advertise my presence with a handsome banner which I had run up with the sewing machine – Camilla must have helped me out with the fiddly bits. One event in particular offered the opportunity to manifest the Magic Café properly, a chance to unfurl my banner with pride.

The Oxford Dance Camp, held at Spring Hill Farm in 1995 and 1996, was inspired by a vision entirely congruent with my own: to generate a communal spirit of celebration, where family groups and friends could share their stories, their food, their music – and their passion for dancing.

Happily, there was a well-equipped kitchen onsite where I could work efficiently and hygienically, sufficient to provide a similar service to my normal Magic Café offer. The first lunchtime proved a great disappointment. Hardly anyone showed up: everyone had organised their own lunch around their own family campfire. What was the point of me being there? Shortly afterwards, I was able to make my feelings clear at the afternoon camp gathering. Here was a tremendous opportunity, not to be missed, to come together as a community, to enjoy the same food, to break out of the closed family groups. Why not make lunchtime a shared experience?

And so it came to pass: lunch was to be enjoyed in public; the evening meal a more private affair. The days were blessed by blazing sunshine, filled with joyous collaborative celebration; in the evenings the shared hot tub, a masterpiece of improvised outdoor plumbing, provided the ideal place to relax: under the stars, close up and bare naked in the warm and murky water. Clothes were stripped off, barriers fell away; the portal of possibility had swung open . . .

The Magic Feast

My childhood was graced by an epic adventure, the tale of little people unexpectedly swept up in a cosmic struggle between the forces of light and darkness. I'm referring to JRR Tolkien's Lord of the Rings – perhaps you guessed.

It concerns an expedition fraught with incident and danger, towards an uncertain end. Joseph Campbell would have had no problem identifying the classic motif of the Hero's Journey. Maybe you're already racing along that well-remembered narrative, halfway to the very Crack of Doom. Let me call you back; press pause, rewind. Our friends have barely left their home patch, the familiar fields and hedgerows of their extended youth. And yet they have made that leap into the realm of enchantment. Uncertainty and peril snaps at their heels. An air of sudden dread is just as suddenly banished by a faery tinkling – "like mingled song and laughter". Their paths have crossed with a roving band of Elven folk, the elder race, purveyors of inscrutable wisdom and mystery. These are hurrying along through the glimmering twilight, moving purposefully towards some appointed rendezvous. A clearing opens up under the forest canopy: here we are – and its suppertime!

It's a marvellous feast, such food and drink as our ingenue heroes have never tasted, can scarcely relate to previous experience – and such fascinating, delightful company, at once respectful and kind, yet engaged in some ineffable drama beyond comprehension. Nourishment is duly delivered; there is the pleasure of repletion and relaxed enjoyment; some inkling that this drama may extend to embrace their own affairs; and then, in the morning, the elves are gone . . .

A meal can be far more than simply a necessary pitstop. There is always the possibility of a sharing, perhaps with some unexpected stranger or guest. At the feast of Pesach – Passover – Jews link themselves to ancient tradition, commemorating their liberation from bondage. An extra place at the table is always set, just in case Elijah (another such purveyor of inscrutable wisdom) happens to drop by. And who knows who might come knocking at the door, in need of revival and good company?

Back in my hitching days I was travelling through France with a rucksack and empty pocket, hoping to reach my friend in Valencia, Spain. I'd made the mistake of arriving in France on Mayday, a date on which the entire country comes to a halt. No traffic was progressing along the main routes; such lifts as I was offered – little kindnesses – took me ever deeper into a countryside of small towns and villages. By nightfall I had no choice but to unroll my sleeping bag underneath a trailer park caravan. The following day progressed in similar manner: slowly, intermittently, hardly any further towards my distant goal. Towards dusk I stood disconsolate on a rural lane, hungry, weary, thumb upheld . . . and a car stopped for me, whisked me away . . .

My benefactors were on their way back home, to finish their preparations for a celebratory meal. Perhaps it was a birthday, or some other special anniversary. I was invited to participate; offered the use of a shower, encouraged to change my grubby travelling clothes for something more festive. It was past dark when the party commenced. I took my place at the table, along with around a dozen others. I was made welcome; my rudimentary French was complimented; a mood of bonhomie prevailed, reinforced with each successive delicacy arriving at the table. I have no recollection of whatever might have been served. Did I insist on being vegetarian? I really couldn't say. Wine was, of course, passed around, repeatedly, to the point where song was called for: each of us to contribute a performance. I offered my best rendition of *"On Ilkley Moor Baht 'At"*, in proper north country fashion. It's a tale of consequences: what happens when you're ill equipped for the elements. Essentially, you'll die, and the ducks will eat you up, and we'll eat the ducks; *"then we shall all have etten thee"*. Was this an appropriate song for such a feast? Or was it simply an acknowledgement of the circularity of existence? At five in the morning, champagne was uncorked, and quaffed with all due ceremony. A comfy bed was then provided, and I slept a blessed sleep.

Next day, I was driven out to the main highway, dropped at a sensible hitching station. I have no idea who these generous souls were, but I still remember them with gratitude, and the hope that I might one day have the big heartedness to do something comparable. As it happens, I never made it to my friend in Valencia, being turned back from the frontier for being penniless riff-raff – but that's a story for another time.

All of this was on my mind as I chose the name for my fledgling business: Magic Feasts Vegetarian Celebration Catering. Magic was my brand, the touchstone for transformational process. The word is closely related to imagination. With each client I would endeavour to fully understand what the meaning, the purpose of the proposed meal might be, and to design a menu that best supported that intent. Was there a particular symbolism that was important, perhaps a culinary style to be referenced? What manner of guests was expected? I understood that the food in itself was subsidiary, a means of exciting and satisfying the senses, opening up the channels to the delights of social intercourse. Camilla had some useful advice, as I considered my culinary compositional style: make sure the food is sexy, a turn-on. Colour, shape, taste, texture: all should be on offer, inviting exploration.

Exploration, of course, is a matter of picking and choosing, between a cornucopia of temptations, all styled to seduce. Desire cannot be marshalled into measured portions, cut one-size-fits-all; it will strike each appetite at a different angle. So my preference has always been for self-service, lining up, plate in hand, just as I had been accustomed to do in the commune buffet. Those towards the end of the line need to feel assured that there will be sufficient of everything they might fancy, to banish the looming spectre of disappointment. "Sufficient" needs to be presented in such a manner as equates with "Abundance".

Garden Party

Focaccia
Sesame Crackers

Salsa
Spicy Lentil Paté
Apricot Chutney
Tzatziki

Bean and Walnut Balls
Aubergine and Tomato Borek
Samosas

Pizza Hafizza
Spinach and Ricotta Quiche
Seitan Bourguignone
Lasagne

Exotic Rice Salad
Marinated Vegetable Salad
Mixed Green Salad

Mango & Cashewnut Trifle
Mousse au Chocolat Orange
Fresh Fruit Salad
Cream

A plate is only so big; but what's the hurry? Repeated voyages of discovery may be made, as the meal unfolds in stately progression: from the first encounters with a range of hors d'oeuvres set ready on each table, nibbles and dips to waken the tastebuds, to share with neighbours, to stimulate conversation; then appetite will have arisen, and must be satisfied with a fuller plate, each corresponding to individual desire; perhaps then there is a pause, an opportunity for a different type of stimulation, for music, for speeches, for poetry; following which, dessert will be a consummation, fabulous and fulfilling; at the last, should satiation yet be held at bay, there is still the possibility of some final tasty morsels, to accompany a reviving cup of coffee – or one last fizzing glass of champagne.

Big Wedding Blow-Out

Starters

Breadbasket: Organic Rolls & Poppyseed Baps
served with a selection of seasonal delicacies:
Celeriac Remoulade
Dilled Cucumber in Yogurt
Bean and Walnut Paté
Stilton Pears
Sweet and Sour Red cabbage

Main Course
Ratatouille
Baked Potatoes
Baked Parsnips
Leek and Mushroom Pie
Blue Cheese and Broccoli Quiche
Millet and Carrot Salad
Green Salad

Dessert
Apple and Hazelnut Crumble
Dried Fruit Compote   Sherry Trifle
Mousse au Chocolat Orange.   Cream

Supper
Sunflower Seed Bread
Ryebread
Cheese and Mustard Fingers
Tomato Salad
Apricot Chutney
Caponata

Should all go well, the event will be remembered long after the details of the dishes served – as a general sense of well-being, of convivial conversation, new friendships fostered, expectations exceeded. The twinkling eyes at the close of the evening are a magical result: a mood has transformed, a new idea has taken root, a romance has kindled. The feast itself, the progression of dishes so artfully presented, will have served its purpose.

As I recall the process of preparing those fabulous feasts, and examine some of the more elaborate layouts, I find myself perplexed as to how I can have achieved so much in the time available. To be sure, some items may have been prepared a day or two in advance; some use may have been made of the freezer. Nonetheless, I was committing myself to a highly complex process, involving not merely the creation of as many as two dozen menu items, but also their delivery to a specified location, the establishment of an on-site cooking operation in an unfamiliar kitchen, preparing the dining hall, spreading the tablecloths, laying out the place settings, setting the hors d'oeuvres ready on the tables, preparing the food line for the main course and dessert selection, supplying the necessary cutlery and crockery, clearing and cleaning these when appropriate, all the while supervising and motivating my small team of helpers, doing my utmost to keep this juggernaut running smoothly on its well-imagined track.

In my most troubled dreams I find myself in a loop of mis-achievement, in which the parameters of location constantly shift, recipes refuse to resolve, intentions take a sudden spin, collapsing into chaos and frustration.

Fortunately, the waking creative moment is not like that. I am reminded of a phrase used by Osho: one should be like a hollow bamboo, a channel for the melody carried on the wind. When all goes well, if a state of inner calm is maintained amidst the maelstrom of activity, that's how it can feel. But this blessed state is not something attainable without  careful preparation or constant practice. Those musicians I admire most owe their moments of soaring inspiration to hours of daily practice, diligently repeating scales and phrases until music simply pours through their fingers in a giddy stream. I may not have been the Jimi Hendrix of catering, but I had gotten good. Over the seven years in which I plied my trade as Magic Feasts I had earned the right to consider myself a professional, a master of my art. As someone dedicated to "the way of the heart" – an amateur – this might prove problematic.

I'd always set my prices deliberately low – reasonable, as my Café flyers insisted. The pursuit of money as an end in itself had never really interested me, although it was nice to be acknowledged for my skills. I could have charged more, I suppose – others certainly might have. But a cheque seemed such a flimsy, flyaway reward for all that heartfelt effort. Ah well, I always maintained that money wasn't the main thing: somehow there was a satisfaction to be gained from not being greedy, from enabling magic to take its course.

My most enjoyable jobs tended to be those in which I was providing for a residential group, people who had come together for a common purpose, to learn a new skill, or to deepen their awareness. Over the duration of the course, whether this be a weekend or a fortnight, a group identity would emerge from the crucible of shared

> ### *Small Wedding Party*
>
> *Focaccia*
> *Organic Rolls*
> *Poppyseed Crackers*
>
> *Tzatziki*
> *Hummus bi Tahin*
> *Guacamole*
> *Salsa*
>
> *Marinaded Olives*
> *Apricot Chutney*
> *Onion Bhajis*
>
> *Eggah Chequerboard*
> *Spinach Filo Triangles*
> *Aubergine Borek*
>
> *Exotic Rice Salad*
> *Tomato Salad*
> *Green Salad*
>
> *Pinwheel Cookies*
> *Honey Jumbles*
> *Ginger Stars*

endeavour. The boundaries of individuality would shift, as each grew responsive to the contours of the other, and new friendships would burgeon over the suppertime table.

It would be an opportunity for me, too, to participate the collective journey of discovery. Away from home, immersed in the daily rhythm of the group, I could be sensitive to what might best support this adventure: waking early, for example, to greet the breakfasters with the irresistible scent of freshly baked spiced fruit bread. I particularly savoured those weekends working at the Abbey in Sutton Courtenay. This is a tranquil retreat house, maintained by the sort of Christian community in which a statue of the Buddha holds an honoured place at the kitchen window. Here there was no need to play music while I busied myself cooking: the stillness of that ancient place flowed through me; or sometimes I would burst into spontaneous song.

My food was well received, much appreciated. As the weekend drew to a close, I would be beset by requests for particular recipes, writing these down again and again on proffered envelopes and torn-off notepaper. It occurred to me that I could make this a lot easier by compiling these recipes in advance. Thus was conceived the first series of my Magic Cookbook – Seasons to Taste.

I resolved to produce four booklets, at three-monthly intervals over the course of the year 1995, roughly corresponding to the seasonal progression. As a set, it's a handy collation of my repertoire of that time. It's also an exhortation to the joy of cooking, and an invitation to stretch the frontiers of one's imagination in the pursuit of shared delight. I've done my best to explain my recipes as clearly as possible, and Camilla has contributed some marvellous illustrations, drawing on her gift for rhythmic patternings and decoration. Plus, there are framing texts intended to blow the mind – just a bit.

Birthday Feast

Olive Bowl
Cheese and Mustard Straws
Sesame Crackers

Bean and Herb Paté
Salsa (Spicy Tomato Dip)
Sweet and Sour Red Cabbage
Marinaded Mushrooms
Apricot Chutney

Exotic Rice Salad
Mixed Green Salad
Spinach Filo Triangles
Leek and Mushroom Quiche
Blue Cheese and Broccoli Quiche

Ginger Stars
Honey Jumbles
Caramel Shortcake
Chocolate Hazelnut Clusters
Fruit & Nut Truffles

"Welcome to the Magic Feast"

Just imagine. Every Thursday evening across small-town America – perhaps even throughout the whole world – diligent and respectable citizens retreat into the privacy of their studies and devote an hour or two of quality time to the magical practice of visualization, in accordance with instructions received mail-order from the Ancient and Mystical Order of the Rose Cross.

Lighting a candle, maybe an incense stick or two, they close their eyes and, focussing with their inner sight, imagine for themselves a matchbox, turning it every which way in their minds, opening and closing the box, maybe even removing a match or two to perform devious imaginary tricks.

They have entered, so they are assured, upon the paths of initiation; no doubt with perseverance the very secrets of the universe will be theirs to command – and with that, the power and ability to shape the world of matter.

Mind accordingly expanded, our enthusiast draws in his awareness, checks his breathing, becomes conscious of the clothes against his body, and glances at his watch. Ah-ha – just about supper time. Wonder what's for dinner tonight ?

And – it's a surprise !

A special charm inhabits these booklets. They are the product of a vanished age, in which the marvels of desktop publishing had yet to be made widely available. The text had originally been written on an Amstrad computer – my first encounter with such advanced technology. A cloak and dagger expedition to the computer room at Brookes University gained us access to the cutting edge of software, by which text could be formatted in a choice of fonts – such a revelation! Clutching our precious printouts, away we scurried.

Back home, on the desktop, real scissors, proper paste, were employed to position Camilla's pictures on the page. Sometimes she drew directly onto the text.

Our local printshop cultivated a guerrilla attitude: rebels against convention, guardians of the mystery of generating a pdf document from my carefully collated sheets, custodians of the technology which might transform this, in a marvellous feat of creative conjuring, into a small stack of booklets. Spring was here at last!

It wasn't long before I invested in my first Apple computer.

Metamorphosis

A desire unfulfilled is a nagging itch; a result unachieved a constant rebuke.

I had arrived back in Oxford in 1990 with high hopes, feeling unstoppable. I had been remarkably successful, within the parameters of a small community open to experimentation and rapid turnarounds, in shaping the commune kitchen into an efficient and popular operation. All was well and good: I was providing what was generally desired, in accordance with the wishes of the governing body. The basics were already in place: a well-equipped kitchen, protocols of practice, and, not least, a large client base disinclined to look any further for culinary satisfaction than within their own familiar boundaries.

How different the big world! For all that I had learnt to draw sustenance from existing friendship networks and to actively cultivate new ones, I was now essentially a lone actor, a sole trader, unaffiliated to, and wary of committing to, organised collective endeavour. True, I had, as the magnitude of my task became apparent, asked Kabira to place an advert in a German sannyasin magazine, offering partnership in an exciting new project, but there had been no nibbles on the line. I'd even, as I became aware that the Amsterdam commune was on the brink of closing down, made enquiries about purchasing the kitchen equipment – though heaven knows how I might have managed the practicalities of moving and storing such substantial hardware. Perhaps this was simply nostalgia, clutching after a familiar, safe existence that had already slipped out of reach. I had made my choice: it was one freighted with challenge.

So many years on, I had achieved much: accumulated a substantial amount of useful equipment, upgraded my wheels to a handy little white van, developed my culinary skills to an impressively high standard, built up a sound reputation for imaginative vegetarian catering, and cultivated a loyal clientele for my twice-weekly pop-up café. And yet, all of this seemed provisional, as if I were endlessly in the waiting room of existence. Already it was many years since I had first made my bold declaration of intent, and begun to make a practice of backing up my promises with the confident assertion: *"you will see"*.

One afternoon, as I enjoyed the company of my friends in the aftermath of a successful Magic Café lunchtime, it was proposed that we each make a commitment to doubling our income over the next twelve months. Each of us had chosen to evade the strait-jacket of salaried employment, valuing freedom of self-expression over financial security: it was a choice that defined out identity. Were we ready to tweak the balance between these polarities?

Me, I didn't want to get drawn into a commitment based on numbers on my end-of-year spreadsheet. I needed to jump to another level. Twelve months on from now, I declared, I would be opening the Magic Café full-time, in my very own premises. We each wrote our results on scraps of paper, following which, so I understand, these were ritually burnt. That was in Summer 1996; as far as I was concerned, the pressure was now on.

The Asian Cultural Centre had been good to me. In particular, Mr Malik had been unfailing in his support – I'm sure he appreciated the wide variety of customers drawn to the café, all of whom might be tempted into otherwise using the premises. Nonetheless, in important ways it was far from ideal.

The isolated location, as it turned out, hadn't been such a problem. Gradually, over time, word had spread that something distinctive, unique even, was available, just a short distance from the main drag. I had sought to manifest something that I myself might hope to discover: a venue that offered a warm welcome and a chance to foster friendship, in a nourishing environment defined by good, freshly prepared food, agreeable music, and congenial company. I had never come across such a place – not in Oxford, at least. It was encouraging to discover that I wasn't the only one with such an expectation.

Magic Arts had been a brilliant innovation, helping to reframe the space, adding a shifting range of colour and image to the otherwise drab institutional furnishings and blank white walls. Jon, in his affectionate account of the art exhibitions he initiated, alludes to the limited public such events were likely to attract, on display for just two lunchtimes each week. Just as musicians have a need to be heard, so artists are compelled to share their unique distillation of vision. He is too gracious to mention the uncomfortable fact that, on one of those days when the café wasn't open, one of his own paintings was removed from the wall – never to be seen in public again. I'm sure it upsets him still – one of his babies forever absent without leave.

This was a borrowed space, shared with various other users – some of them not even human. As an experiment, I instituted Friday evening openings, offering candlelit dinners: a choice of two distinct platefuls, plus dessert. This of course meant a greatly extended day's work for me – often it was after midnight before all was cleared up and tidied away – and a much greater risk of ending up with leftover food. Still, I wanted to extend my range, attempt something new; I knew that it might take a while to build up custom. Then a rat was spotted scurrying around in the lounge; the environmental health was called in, and the lounge was placed out of bounds. Traps and poison were laid, to no avail. For the following fortnight, Ratty could be observed through the windows, looking resilient if not particularly well. As one of my customers suggested, why hadn't they just introduced a cat? Meanwhile, I was obliged to offer my candlelit suppers in the far less suitable upstairs hall; my assistant obliged to scurry up and down the stairs, while the suppers were despatched up the (well-named) dumb waiter, each plateful suffering an icy blast in transit. This really wouldn't do.

What I most disliked, though, about my part-time café was the unavoidable daily chore of construction and demolition. The set-up might have been rudimentary – opening out the trestle tables, placing the chairs, assembling a cunningly constructed sneeze-screen to protect the food, writing out that day's menu, setting out the crockery and cutlery, arranging a display of communicative flyers, plugging in the boogie box – but it all needed returning to base at the end of each session. Anything left in the lounge might not be there next day. It was a constant reminder that this was not my space.

At the beginning of 1997 plans were afoot to reconfigure the centre, moving the office into what had been the lounge. I would have to relocate my café into the Activities Room – attractive enough, in a bland sort of way, but at some remove from the kitchen. By this stage attendances had grown considerably – which was of course great – necessitating frequent trundling of encumbered trolleys through the passageways. I had begun making it known that I was keen to locate my own premises, to go fulltime. I was even putting out feelers for potential collaborators, as the daunting nature of my quest became apparent.

In a file labelled "Newsletter" I discover the following document:

Many Happy Returns

Recently, my brothers and I have been sifting through suitcases full of family memorabilia, and one thing that came to light was a small photo of a little boy – me – standing at the end of the garden drive, on the threshold of the big world. It's my first day at school, so I am wearing an unfamiliar cap and blazer, satchel strapped across my shoulder, and feeling very nervous. It was, I recall, a difficult day.

On February 13 1997 the Magic Café will be five years old; can you believe it? If cafés were little boys it too would be facing that terrible transition, full of wonder and trepidation. Still, if little boys were cafés, can you imagine what sort of a sticky mayhem that might be? Clearly, there are limits to the analogy, but the fact remains that it does feel like about time that our dear Magic Café began to make its way into the wider world. I feel rather like an anxious parent, reluctant to let go sole responsibility for my child, but also looking forward to a time when not everything has to be undertaken by myself.

I am full of plans and best wishes for my offspring. I am sure there will be a place for him in Oxford – perhaps even on the prestigious Cowley Road. I will do my best helping with the homework, but I recognise that I need to enlist the help of others, with skills and talents I do not possess, to draw out our prodigy's still latent capabilities.

It is time, I believe, to start sharing our fantasies.

I really couldn't say for sure whether this bulletin was ever printed up and distributed. One way or another, though, the message had seeped out, so that various suggestions started to come my way, more or less impractical. At last, word reached me, perhaps via the staff at the Inner Bookshop on

Magdalen Road, that the premises next door were soon to become vacant. This was Steptoes, a shabby secondhand emporium – in short, a junkshop, its contents spilling out onto the forecourt, the debris of our consumer civilisation. Word was, the proprietor had been advised by the local police to cease trading, on the grounds that not everything on sale might have been legitimately acquired.

I spent an afternoon sitting on the wall outside the bookshop, intent on measuring the footfall along Magdalen Road – as I'd been advised on my business training course. There was not much to report: it was a quiet backstreet, with a few local residents making their way to somewhere more interesting. Across the way, an old-style ironmonger, Silvesters, faced onto a scruffy neighbourhood pub, The Eagle, still displaying out front a litter of broken glass from the weekend revelries. Next door to Steptoes was a very discreet business, reticent as to its true nature; only much later did I realise this was actually a purveyor of gold for Asian weddings. All in all, it seemed a sleepy, unpretentious neighbourhood. Maybe this was all to the good: rents were high along Cowley Road, likely to be much more affordable here; and, after all, people had been happy to make their way down Manzil Way to discover the delights in store at the Asian Cultural Centre. The Inner Bookshop, which had initially started out on the Cowley Road, had become well-established in its new location. I reckoned that if something were special enough, people would be happy to make a small effort to get there. Or maybe, for many prospective customers, this was exactly the right place, just in the middle of a residential area. Was it not good sense to place the community living room close by the bedrooms?

There was, as I considered the way forward, a considerable hurdle in my path: the city planning department. Nothing could happen without their permission. My whole future depended on the grant of an A3 certificate, enabling use of premises for purposes of catering. There were forms to fill in – and forms about forms. It was a world of bureaucracy I instinctively rebelled against. In Charles Dickens' novel Little Dorrit he describes a government institution the very purpose of which was to stifle initiative, to grind down creative impetus by lumpen plodding process geared towards the ultimate goal of saying **"no"**. With his special gift for naming, he dubbed this the Circumlocution Office.

I answered all the questions on all of the forms, jumped through all the hoops as best I could, used my clever computer to draw suitable plans and diagrams, and did my best to point out what a blessing the Magic Café might be to the City of Oxford. I submitted my package of documents with fingers well crossed, trusting in the judicious wisdom of the city planning department.

Meanwhile, to forestall the possibility of the property being snapped up by some other interested party, I made a deal with "Mr Steptoe". In effect, I would be employing him to mind the store while I waited for my permission. He seemed confident of a successful outcome, lurking in the shadowy interior, now largely cleared of clutter, drinking mugs of tea and playing chess with whomsoever happened to drop by.

The property, 110 Magdalen Road, was owned by Mr Mohammed Alyas, an electrical engineer who had run a second hand TV shop there before relocating to more constricted premises around the back. I liked Mohammed; obviously he needed to look after the interests of his family, and he was a little apprehensive about how viable the café might be, but it seemed likely that we could reach an agreement on terms of lease without too much unseemly wrangling. A provisional lease was duly signed, pending a more formal document formatted in proper legal style. I had made a commitment for the next ten years, and I felt fine.

By curious coincidence, my personal life was also moving onto another level. I was engaged to be married, to Camilla of course, my constant companion for the previous seven years. The wedding had been arranged for high summer – now just a few weeks away. Change was in the air. The Café at the Culture Centre would be closing up, so that full attention might be given to the process of transition.

On the morning of my very last session, as I was busy in the kitchen preparing lunch, I was visited by Craig and Elise, whom I had come to know as regulars at the Café. They were, I knew, intensely engaged with Green politics, and passionate about stimulating green initiatives in the community.

I liked them a lot, and welcomed their insight into the corridors of local power. They had some awkward news. The planning department, in their judicious wisdom, had recommended rejection of my proposal. The council were sure to act on this – unless I immediately proposed to appeal this decision in front of the council's Planning Committee. This procedure would allow me a scant five minutes to state my case. It was a moment of high jeopardy; my carefully laid plans stood on the brink of ruin.

My friend Raga had prepared a small, surprise ceremony to mark my departure from the Culture Centre. As I stepped up to accept a large colourful thank you card, apparently the product of a classful of busy little fingers, I found it hard to stay in the moment; I barely glanced at the card. Now, as I examine it closely for the first time, I can see that each of the individual fold-out cards contain messages and good wishes from my regular customers. All this I had been much too upset to take on board, and too much in shock to explain why.

It was time to rebuild my sense of unstoppability. First I had to understand how my application had failed: I requested a meeting with the planning officer concerned. Ushered into a sparsely appointed office, I sat down opposite this arbiter of destiny. What could be the problem? The bureaucratic mind unrolled its template.

The proposed café was simply in the wrong place. Cafés belonged on the Cowley Road: that was the zone for cafés.

The neighbourhood stood to lose a valued amenity. She was, of course, referring to a junkshop of dubious repute.

Her killer argument, though, related to Car Parking Standards TR10, as determined in the Local Plan Review. This prescribed a strict ratio between likely customers and available parking spaces. Parking on Magdalen Road was limited. QED – café not possible.

It amounted to a staggering failure of vision. Did this person live in a box? Had she ever even been to East Oxford?

Could TR10 really be an immoveable object? After all, elected officials might see things rather differently. It had come to my attention that the Planning Department had recently made a serious blunder in granting A3 status (food preparation and sale) to a property on Walton Street, under the impression that this was intended as a neighbourhood chippie. Perhaps by some sleight of hand, the eventual occupant turned out to the upmarket celebrity chef Raymond Blanc, with an attractive new bistro venture. This had provoked a sudden parking crisis in the locality, as gourmets flooded in from across the region. How embarrassing! However popular the Magic Café might turn out to be, I couldn't imagine my customers being similarly transported. How might bicycles and feet relate to Policy TR10?

This seemed like a point worth framing my argument around, as I prepared my case for the Planning Committee members. These were all city councillors, necessarily responsive to the concerns of their electorate. Each received from me a well-reasoned manifest designed to provoke that nigh-unheard-of thing, a rethink of the planner's recommendation.

Satisfied that everything possible had been done, I got on with the important business of getting married. This was to be the best Magic Feast ever: I made sure that the caterer received special commendation in my groom's speech. Then my new wife and I went on holiday. The Planning Committee hearing was scheduled for a week or so after our return.

On the morning of the hearing I woke from a dream in which Frank Natale had appeared in his Grand Wizard persona, pointed hat and all. It seemed an auspicious sign.

Touch of magic for modest man

By JO HILLIER

CAFE owner Hafiz Ladell appealed to councillors to let him set up business in Oxford by saying: "I'm not Raymond Blanc."

He was given the green light to open his Magic Cafe in Magdalen Road, east Oxford, despite city council officers recommending that his planning application for change of use from a shop be turned down. They feared the cafe would bring too many cars into the already congested area.

But Mr Ladell told a planning committee meeting: "My contention is that parking is a bit of a red herring. As you can see I'm not Raymond Blanc and I'm not asking people to come from all over southern England to eat my food."

City councillor Patrick Stannard, who supported the proposal, said: "Magdalen Road is almost a city in itself. There is a theatre, three pubs and a bingo hall which cause most of the traffic problems

but the roads are not blocked."

Head of planning Linda Wride said the officers were concerned that if permission was given, bigger names like top chef Raymond Blanc could move in at some point.

But John Tanner, vice-chairman of the planning committee, said: "The chances of McDonalds or Raymond Blanc coming in there are not great, therefore it's an acceptable risk to take. The shop could remain empty and become an eyesore."

Report in the Oxford Mail

The adjudication took place at the Town Hall, in a room fitted out like an old-fashioned courtroom. Five minutes had been allotted to me; I chose to give half of these to local councillor Pat Stannard, who had kindly offered to speak on my behalf. Since the members had doubtless considered my submission with care – so I flattered – all that remained was to present my best optimistic, generous nature. Surveying the platter of dry biscuits on display, I regretted not being able to bring any delicious cakes; then I made the obvious point that I was not Raymond Blanc.

Pat Stannard made an excellent case, pointing out the fantastic diversity of Magdalen Road, practically a city in itself: a theatre, several churches, two pubs, three grocers, some wonderful specialist businesses – all it lacked was a café.

What sealed the deal, though, was little Alfie Bowen, barely four months old, present with his parents Dolly and Jon to offer moral support. Chairperson Maureen Christian, in declaring herself ineligible to vote by virtue of her position, pointed out that, had she been eligible, she would vote with the baby. The vote was duly carried. The way ahead was clear! It was a moment to savour.

Photo: Paul Freestone

With the wind blowing strongly in our sails, it felt like time for a party, to celebrate taking possession of our new premises. Actually, these weren't entirely vacant – there was still a fair amount of clutter to be removed, not least from the basement, still heaped high with a litter of ancient televisions and builder's debris – but Mr Steptoe was gone, his pocket stuffed with just reward. It was time to raise a glass or two to the future, in company with our friends and supporters. Time, too, to imagine what the new Magic Café might be.

I'd been doing plenty of thinking already, using my computer to draw up a proposed new layout, and had asked my dear friend Rob Valentine, fresh from his best man duties, to provide his assessment of what needed to be done to bring my dream to fruition. Quite a lot – in brief; then, meticulously itemised, a schedule of actions to be performed, in precise order, each stage, after the manner of Lewis Carroll's Hunting of the Snark, denoted a Fit: thus, "Fit the First: Demolition".

Rob was brilliant, a master of many disciplines, a woodworker of repute and wielder of incisive intellect and wit. Thanks to the clarity of his imagining, by which all necessary materials, down to the precise number of tacks and screws, had been calculated and costed, I was able to have a clear idea of the likely cost of my dreams. Briefly: a lot. Where was this money to come from?

Our wedding, despite the caterer having offered his good services for love, had made a substantial raid on our savings. In those days, money was far from cheap. The man at the bank in the sharp suit had offered us a loan to match those savings – at a cost; having signed us up to this, he then, in best mafia style, imposed a little extra "protection" – the infamous PPI: *"you wouldn't want anything to happen to you before you'd paid up in full, would you?"*

By way of contrast, loans offered by friends came with built-in kindness and good wishes. In total, it was just about enough.

D-day arrived: Fit the First – Demolition. Rob had engaged the services of a musclebound hulk, the marvellously named Mr Toad. He, like most of the fabulous crew working on the renovation, were denizens of the river and canal, prototypes of Philip Pullman's Gyptians, creative free spirits from the city margins – not so much a pool of talent as a creative stream diverted into this landlocked locale. Toad got busy swinging his mighty sledgehammer. There were various internal walls to remove; for a week or two all was rubble and dust. I kept myself out of the way, apart from schlepping sackfuls of debris to the city dump. Fit the Second would see new walls being laid, all according to my carefully delineated instructions. At this point, certain departures from the plan began to emerge, with straight lines being compromised, sinuous curves snaking unforeseen, all suggestive of nonlinear organic process. These features would be somehow be assimilated into the structure, forever to be known as "Toadisms".

Rob, Chief of Works, with the Mighty Mr Toad

Toad hopped away; new talents stepped into the breach, skilled operators all. Mike, Mike, Vic, Steve, Dave, Darren . . . every day bore witness to steady progress, initiative, innovation, improvisation. Step by step, fit by fit, the café lineaments emerged from the dust.

Down in the basement – how I love basements! – there was much to be done, rather more than had been foreseen. Here I'd envisaged my storeroom, and a staff-only loo. Ideally, I would like this all handsomely appointed, but this was never going to be a public space – the Fire Safety Officer had made that clear. Rob was concerned that we needed to stay focussed on the main project if we were to remain on budget. Precisely at this point a man I'd never met before came into the premises, asking for me. According to his horoscope, so he said, this was a propitious time to invest in a community café. Would I be interested? Magic, or what?

The scant nine weeks allotted for our transformation process slipped by, in fits and starts. I was determined to open up before Christmas. Infrastructure was laid in place: electric cables and copper pipelines for water and gas, cunningly inset or discreetly tucked away. Walls were smoothed and rendered; in the new kitchen I observed the plasterer produce a pristine silky finish, his body all the while a-tremble, presumably a means to balance his un-

Rob Valentine at work. **Photo: Paul Freestone**

failingly steady hand. Carpenter's benches appeared, devoted to shaping the serving counter, creating fairground-style boxing for the electricity fusebox, and a railing for the basement stairs featuring a procession of diamond cutaways. It was a hive of focussed creativity – such a contrast to the rushed and perfunctory work of the roofing contractors whom I'd engaged to fix the flat roof and skylights at the back of the shop.

Furniture had begun to appear, as yet stacked up, as much as possible out of the way. I'd been scouring the second hand markets for tables and chairs, on the lookout especially for the larger tables which might encourage new friendships, as I'd noticed at the Asian Cultural Centre. A somewhat scruffy, but invitingly comfy sofa was contributed by my friend Andrew, together with a magnificent oak banqueting table, seating up to a dozen, destined to be a special feature of the café. A disparate collection of chairs was gradually accumulating. The overall style was shabby chic – a happy consequence of

133

our limited funds.

I had left the choice of paint to Camilla, trusting in her mastery of colour combination. Her selection at first seemed surprising: bright sunflower yellow for the walls, topped with cinnamon brown; a deep blue ceiling, matching the carpet tiles decking the floor; and a detail of poppy red for the dado rail running high around the wall. In one final frenzied fit of dedicated decoration, making the most of the last few days before opening, the premises were transformed. The overall effect was tremendous, splendid: at once harmonious and uplifting.

Camilla applied her skills to reproducing her meticulous calligraphy on the external signboard: a jolly assertion of identity, flowing with graceful precision, vibrant yellow over crimson background. It was a proud moment, witnessing this fixed in place above the shop window. The Magic Café had arrived.

Job done! – Rob, Mike, Steve, Me, Carrie, Camilla, Jenny, Dave

Community

And so we come to the heart of the matter – the stage of fulfilment, the vision become manifest. We discover that the Café is indeed filled, not necessarily all of the time, a constant stream of business, but rather an ebb and flow; there is a tidal rhythm. And that pulsing element, entering and departing through the front door, is that marvellous, protean being, a community.

Was it there already, a disparate potentiality just waiting for the right venue to contain its strange and mutual attraction? East Oxford, as I had long been aware, is home to many extraordinary people, with myriad interests and talents, diverse activities and associations. There are many places to meet, to socialise. The bookshop next door has played host to many a whispered greeting. Many a conversation has been misunderstood against the blaring background noise of a busy public house. There are certain cafés beloved of a particular coterie, their regular custom well respected by the management. In this particular city the annual influx of students – a massive youthful surge – is catered for by an equally massive industry geared towards a steady turnover of custom and clientele. There are open spaces a-plenty, where, should the weather permit, mothers with infant children can spend time together, without the pressure of having to conform to social decorum – as long as, you know, they don't do that disgraceful – and yet so entirely natural and full of grace – act of feeding their infant child in public.

I make no claim to have invented the local community. It has simply been my delight, over ten years and more, to provide a welcoming environment for it to discover itself in a state of relaxation and enjoyment – if not to come together, then at least to leave together, having discovered, through mutual sharing of interests and experience, that the world is a greater, more multi-facetted, and less lonely place than they may have imagined.

Over ten years and more I have been the presiding spirit of this place,

Photo: Gerald Garcia

visible through the hatchway next to the coffee machine in my characteristic position, gazing out from the kitchen, observing the arrivals and departures, the gravitation towards certain corners, the aggregations, and the intimate tête-à-têtes. All the while my fingers keep busy: shaping the bread rolls, rubbing fat into flour, or composing yet another bowlful of Passion Cake. Meanwhile, with my detached attention, I am weaving a spell. Each of these people present are here as my guests, whether they are aware of this or not; it is my chosen duty to provide a place of refreshment, of enlivenment – a function not merely of the delicious food and drinks on offer, but also of the very guests themselves, as they discover a more complete identity under the pleasant stimulus of an easeful environment, and consequently a desire to share this with the persons sitting close by.

Many of these good people are known to me already, some as friends of many years' standing, some more by reputation, as significant beacons in the local cultural landscape. There are families, and groups of friends, who make regular appearances, laying claim, if possible, to the same privileged table; individuals who can be relied upon to appear at a set time each day, for their special treat, a toasted teacake, or the famous choc-fudge brownie. Some I will come to know by name, and perhaps discover some background to their life stories; many more will recognise my face for many years afterwards, as "the man who used to run the Magic Café". Over the course of a decade, many hundreds, thousands, will pass through that jolly red door, confident of a restorative half hour – or longer. How could one encompass the cumulative result?

Parents bring their children, in the sure knowledge that this will be a popular choice. *"Mum, can we go to the Magic? . . . and afterwards can we go to the Goldfish Bowl?"*. The Goldfish Bowl – an emporium of exotic fish – is for many the local zoo. It's possible to spend a whole afternoon on Magdalen Road. First, though, is the opportunity to cuddle a big fluffy elephant, or to tip out a large box of toys, scattering brightly coloured plastic across the floor. Boys will seize control of the pull-along truck; little girls will immerse themselves in the social etiquette of the big pink dolls' house. Camilla discovers a couple of sisters playing at cookery class, loading a saucepan with an unlikely ingredient: *"but you're cooking Sooty!"*, she exclaims. The children settle into their chosen corner, absorbed in the universe of imagination. Meanwhile, perhaps equally important, their parents can swap stories, exchange their inconsequential banter, offloading the pressures and strains of family life.

I gain greatest satisfaction from the appearance of a group of young mothers, generally mid-morning when the café is otherwise quite tranquil. They rearrange the furniture at the front of the shop, so they can sit round in a circle, each with their infant in their lap, sharing the adventure and challenges of child-raising, unselfconsciously opening their blouses to their hungry infant, safe, empowered, and nourished.

The Magic Café

A clash of prams at the door
Boobs hanging out on every sofa
The warm milk of companionship
Smells of nourishing and inviting foods
   Each morsel inspired and pampered
      By the whirling dervish of the kitchen
      – Mr Hafiz !
The colours of Tibet
The music of life
The art at the heart of East Oxford
Thank you, Hafiz, your crew and wife
We raise a toast to a thousand more years of the Magic Café!

Alexandra Lewis, December 2007

Alexandra Lewis, 2007
Photo: Kate Raworth

Maybe it's not everybody's cup of tea. The Oxford Mail dispatched its restaurant critic to check us out, then sent a photographer to capture an image of me holding the remains of a cherry pie. The resulting article wasn't something I'd want to frame in the window. Evidently it wasn't their scene, not their idea of nourishment. The soymeat lasagne didn't go down too well, the bread rolls not what they expected . . . the reviewer clearly found it difficult to relax. Everywhere, mothers with frisky children, spoiling their lunch. Oh well . . .

Being adjacent to the Inner Bookshop was ideal for both businesses. Ruth and Anthony, the owners, had been very supportive of us setting up the Café. Their specialism was the cornucopia of spiritual endeavour: tightly packed, if somewhat dusty, shelves carried all manner of possible truths. Browsing can be thirsty work; a quick trip next door the essential restorative. Or, the object of search at last attained, what better reward than settling into the sofa, coffee close at hand, to explore those musty pages?

East Oxford being what it is, the café was frequented by a goodly number of authors, quite often hanging out together at the big round table. I recall Hugh Warwick being introduced to me as *"the hedgehog correspondent of the Daily Telegraph"*. I'm glad to say that he had long since broadened his media profile, whilst deepening his expertise in the fascinating field of hedgehog studies. He is now widely known as Hedgehog Hugh.

I used to love to come into the café and read and work – I got to meet some wonderful people just by being there. But then it would turn into a crèche and there were kids running around and (this was

Photo by Zoe Broughton

before noise cancelling head- phones) it was impossible to work and I would leave. And then I had kids and I went back in and found out what was so special – it was a space where the kids could be themselves (up to a point) – and there were books and toys and you could sit your sleep-deprived body down for a while in the company of other parents who looked just as rough as you.

If you choose your spot carefully, it might be possible to keep disturbance to a minimum. Even better, if you were an adept at projecting an aura of imperturbability. Such a man was Francis Cameron, frequently to be seen at the small table tucked away in the alcove next to the basement stairs. With his long, straggly white hair and beard he might well be taken for the resident wizard – and perhaps he was. He was certainly a man of extra-ordinary accomplishments. In the course of his long, varied career he had attained distinction in many varied fields, as professional organist, academic, linguist, anthropologist; most recently, he had embraced the esoteric spiritual path of wicca. He would be deeply immersed in writing – or else he would be equally deeply engaged in conversation, discoursing on the mystery of the embodied soul.

Francis Cameron presiding on Broad Street, 2005.
Photo courtesy Liz Steele

No doubt there were many books composed – in part at least – in the Café. One certainly made an international impression: The Mascot, by Mark Kurzem. Of slight, ascetic appearance, with close-cropped hair, well-trimmed goatee, and the round glasses of an intellectual, Mark was a café regular, happy discussing favourite films with his friends; he was also a man with a mission, which kept him tapping away on his laptop over many an hour. He was, he told me, writing about someone who had spent their childhood under an assumed identity, constantly in peril of discovery. As I learnt more, reading his book when eventually published, I discovered the full, scarcely credible story: that person was his father, Alex Kurzem. Alex had been a small boy, just six years old, when his infant understanding was ripped apart by the irruption of the second world war. His home village in Belarus was overrun by the Nazi invasion, and all Jews, including his parents, were slaughtered. Terrified, the boy had fled into the forest, eventually falling in with an SS brigade imposing its authority on the district. Something about this

THE
MASCOT
The extraordinary story of a Jewish boy and an SS extermination squad

MARK KURZEM

little, evidently Jewish boy inspired compassion, even love, in these har-dened soldiers: they adopted him as their mascot, appointing him to their regiment, with his very own tailored uniform . . .

Alex had maintained absolute secrecy about this dreadful experience. Mark's diligent research, and the award-winning documentary he made, had allowed him at last to reclaim his suppressed identity, which jarred so uncomfortably with his assumed lifestyle in suburban Australia.

It was a reminder of the precarity of life, of the dark shadows which may lurk behind the veneer of civilisation; of the potential catastrophe of social collapse, should the bonds of community come asunder. Alex came to England, proud of his son's achievement; he was a guest on Women's Hour; and he visited the Magic Café. Tragically, shortly afterwards, Mark himself fell victim to a degenerative wasting disease, dying in 2010. But his remarkable book persists – as does his film, now available to view on the internet.

Magical Senses

Melodic sounds playing wrap around you as you enter
As do the sounds of coffee making machines and cups clattering

Smells of food mingle with the smells of coffee and chocolate
Which stimulate the senses and makes your mouth water

The warm Mediterranean yellows warm your cold bones
And you can almost hear the sighs as people relax to the melodic tones

Jayne Allsop, March 2005

I practise the art of holding the space, of shaping its atmosphere. Chief amongst my tools is the choice of music, selecting the soundtrack that best suits the moment. I've always enjoyed this, not so much to assert my excellent and wide-ranging taste, as to subtly engage with the collective energy, to nudge it towards fulfilment, whatever that might be. As the day progresses, so the soundtrack shifts. Mozart seems the best choice for the morning, establishing a sense of disciplined creativity and invention not only for the lone coffee drinker carefully perusing the Guardian, but also for the kitchen chefs, steadily assembling the lunchtime menu. Lunchtime arrives to a cheery fanfare, a shifting of tempo, music to accompany the rattle of cutlery against plates and the busy gurgling of the coffee machine. It tootles away in merry accompaniment to banter and chat, pitches punchlines into joyous crescendo, resolves complexity into unexpected harmony. My favourite picks: Thelonious Monk interpreting Duke Ellington; the Modern Jazz Quartet playing Gershwin. After lunch, the mood may lighten, take flight, perhaps to some exotic destination: to Brazil, Cap Verde, or Timbuktu. There will be time too, in the later afternoon, for the art of song: music to cheer the tea-time gatherings and speed the chore of washing up – Eva Cassidy, Madeleine Peyroux, Burt Bacharach, the Mamas and the Papas. One last change of gear comes on the threshold of 6 o'clock. It's time for our guests to move on, and for the well-practised procedures of closedown to unfurl: in the kitchen, all has to be cleaned and put away, all surfaces swabbed down, the floor swept and mopped; in the café, the tables are cleared and wiped clean, chairs stacked up, and Henry Hoover unleashed for his daily exercise, gobbling up all the scattered cakecrumbs. Skanking makes it easy, singing along with Bob Marley and the Wailers.

I liked to work with people with whom I felt in harmony, who shared a sense of what I wanted to achieve. Chris Jardine was evidently one such:

I started working at the Magic Café in April 2000 and worked there for about eight months in total. I'd just finished a DPhil in Chemistry, but I was looking to get a job in a more environmental field. Trouble was – those jobs didn't really exist back then, so it was a bit of a slow process to find anything. My old supervisor took pity on me for not finding anything and lined up an admin job for me in one of the colleges, starting in one week. I couldn't imagine anything I'd rather do less, so I needed a better job fast! I'd got an interest in food production and cooking, so I went into the Magic Café to try and blag a job.

I was a bit surprised to be taken on, to be honest, mainly because I did eat meat! My interest in food was very much from the organic production side of things rather than cutting meat out of the diet. So when the "are you a vegetarian?" question came up in a mini-interview with Hafiz, I thought that was it, and I'd end up having to do this terrible admin job. Fortunately, Hafiz offered me a shift that Saturday. And the rest is history.

I absolutely loved my time at the Magic Café – and I learned so much while I was there. I still cook Magic Café recipes for myself even today. Most customers might not realise how much attention went into each dish and salad to get them just right. It was a real eye-opener for me to learn how to create attractive dishes. All salads had to feature a range of colours, so they are visually appealing. Hafiz was very particular about the size and shape that each vegetable was cut to. At first, it seemed a little bit control-freaky (sorry, Hafiz!), but then you learned that if some stuff is too small, it sinks to the bottom of the bowl as a mush. A bit like a pack of cornflakes. And then it all made sense.

Hafiz was equally particular about the type of vinegar used in each salad – white wine for this one, cider vinegar for this one, balsamic for this one. Again, it seemed over-fussy – but it was absolutely right. Choosing the right vinegar really does make a difference to the taste of the dish. My kitchen still has a full range of six or seven types of vinegar.

It was this attention to detail that stuck out for me. Not only that – but the constant attention to detail over years and years ensured that

Chris checking the solar panel installation on our roof, 2009

standards stayed supremely high. I'm sure it was a major factor in the Magic Café's continued success. You see so many restaurants that get sloppy over time or try to take shortcuts to cut costs. Not under Hafiz's watch! Twenty years later, and now running my own business, I'm continually aware of the need to maintain standards on each and every job. You're only as good as your last piece of work, as they say, and I definitely learned that working under Hafiz at the Magic Café.

I remember that summer as a particularly carefree time in my life, with a really nice rhythm to it. In at 9 to open up, set the tables out, and defrost the cakes (you can freeze cake – who knew!). Then onto salad prep 10-12, whilst serving the odd customer coffee and break-fast. Then a crazy rush 12-2 over lunchtime. 2-5 was washing up and cake-making, then floor mopping and shut down until 6. Nothing was particularly hard, but there was a variety of things that needed to be done to keep the operation running. And we got a couple of 15-min-ute breaks, morning and afternoon, for a latte and a cake. God, I loved those millionaire's shortbreads! I must have had at least one a day all the time I was at the café. I definitely put on weight!

The special thing about the Magic Café was the way it embedded itself as a kind of community focus. This was before there was a real café/coffee shop culture in the UK, so the space was pretty unique at the time. Ground-breaking, even. There were regulars through the morning and a bunch of familiar faces every lunchtime. And always the same couple of people sneaking in for last orders at about 4:45. Afternoons was mums and kids time – which I remember as a bit of a mixed blessing. Great for custom, but the mess, noise, crumbs, half-eaten cakes and tantrums were a bit much sometimes. But looking back now – where else was there for mums to go with their toddlers? Certainly not the dreadful Eagle Pub over the road. The Magic Café must have served such a vital role in those days.

Part of the appeal of the café was Hafiz's carefully curated record collection, which brought its own ambience to the café. There were about 20 CDs on repeat – Mamas and the Papas, Emmylou Harris, and kora playing by Toumani Diabate and Ballake Sissoko all spring to mind. I do remember Thursday afternoons, when Hafiz would be off doing the weekly shop for the café, gave the junior staff a couple of hours to change the mood by sneaking in our own CDs. It was all in keeping with the downtempo, world music vibe, but perhaps shall we say a little more beats-oriented! We nearly got busted when customers came to the counter to ask what we'd been playing yesterday. A quick "err, not sure . . ." in front of Hafiz, followed by a whispered "We weren't meant to be playing that – it was the Afro Celt Sound System by the way . . ." when we were cleaning their tables later. Good times!

That wasn't the only mayhem that occurred when Hafiz was

out. One day, left with responsibility for making cakes, I managed to concoct a full two trays worth of chocolate brownies without any flour in them. They came out thin as a biscuit. Whilst I hid the offending mess out of sight in the outdoor bins, Zoë Bicat, bless her, ran to the Coop to buy a brand new set of ingredients. Between us, we managed to make a new set and dispose of the giveaway off-brand food wrappers before Hafiz came back. I don't know why we worried so much; he'd have probably laughed his head off.

All in all, I loved my time at the Magic Café. I learned a huge amount about food, catering, and about running a small business and making it a success. It was a special time and one which I remember very fondly.

Poplar Wood, silk painting by Cassandra Wall

The vibrant sunflower yellow of the café walls proved to be an ideal background for art exhibitions; each month saw a fresh display, a new set of windows leading through into the land of vision. The artists were themselves generally Magic Café regulars. For them, it was a valued opportunity to communicate, to demonstrate the force of their sensibility – and also to sell their work.

Most successful, certainly from the latter point of view, was Cassandra Wall:

It was my first solo exhibition at the Magic Café, and my colourful silk paintings and textile collages married well with the deep yellow walls. It was amazingly successful as I sold I think something like £1500. It was a huge encouragement to keep going with my art as it had obviously made sense to other people who wanted it on their walls. I was on local Oxford TV, as it was then – also publicising the café. It was part of Artweeks, on the East Oxford trail. . . I organised many meetings of various friends and groups of friends, including an opening lunch gathering – it was great! Such a confirmation – and here I am many years later as a professional *artist, in a top gallery in Oxford, with my own agent.*

It was a wonderful interaction with the community and nice to be lurking there, home from home, as I made up more cards to sell while the lunches went on around me.

Various friends generally used to say: "Shall we meet at the Café?" – no need to specify which one!

Cait Sweeney recalls exhibiting her work at the Magic, at a time when she was helping out on the Café team. It was a varied selection of work: some ceramics – pregnant belly candle holders, some paintings (pregnant bellies again), plus an intriguing composite creation, "Shrine", featuring chicken wire, red velvet curtain, candles, and a range of obscured images of the artist herself, semi-naked. Sad to relate, Shrine ended up in a neglected corner of the café basement, but otherwise, the exhibition was a great success:

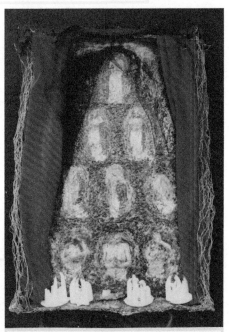

Shrine, mixed media, by Cait Sweeney

I sold all the ceramic pieces – there were 9 of them, plus a painting of a pregnant nude to some bloke who was in the area and had popped into the café; he asked at the counter who to see about buying one of the paintings, so it was good to say, "that will be me." He told me which one he was interested in, saying he'd need to consult his wife first, and then left. He came back about half an hour later with the cash saying: "as it's nearly Christmas I thought you could probably use the money now. I'll come and collect the painting in the New Year when the exhibition is over." He'd decided that he wouldn't consult his wife, but give it to her as a Christmas present. It's always great to sell a painting, but there's something extra special about selling one to a complete stranger! Don't know who he was and no idea where the painting is now . . .

Not everyone who identifies as an artist, of whatever description, can make it pay; sometimes they need a day job to keep the wolf from the door.

I was very happy to offer employment to someone of creative disposition – this was always a plus point when I sat down with someone asking after a job. Working on the first novel? – sounds interesting, Walter; performance poet? – yes please, Stephen; flamenco dancer? – olé, Deborah; juggler and jester? – that sounds fun, Justin; butoh dancer? – what's that, Ruth? As for musicians, I was always delighted to share the kitchen with such gifted and generous people: Zoë, Rom, Lilia, Colin, Sharron, Josie, Andy, Dorota, Jamji, Renan . . . it was a great thrill for me, and a privilege to provide some sort of income while the act came together.

Magic Music

Music to munch to...Saturdays 1-2 pm *(-ish)*
@ The Magic Café, Magdalen Rd, Oxford

4th Nov	Simon Stafford
	Acoustic duo play an eclectic mix
11th Nov	Dave Noble & Jali Fily Cissokho
	Guitar and kora in delicate interplay
18th Nov	Jude Mann
	The mystery of the celtic harp
25th Nov	Nag Champers
	Playing ragas
2nd Dec	Pete Galpin
	Chill out with swell soul jazz
9th Dec	Mark Bosley
	Ambient guitar and bazouki
16th Dec	Jane Griffiths & Colin Fletcher
	Fast tunes played slowly on fiddle and guitar
23rd Dec	Maeve
	Gentle ballads and feisty blues

Saturday was always special for me, and not just because it was the last day of my working week. The café followed a different rhythm, one centred around the live music session running from one until two o'clock. First, though, I would have had a very hectic morning. In contrast to the normal slow morning trade, fried Saturday morning breakfasts were a popular draw, so that as many as twenty special platefuls needed to be prepared at short order, all in the middle of the regular lunch preparation. Memorably, most of these would be enjoyed by a large group of bizarrely attired actorly folk, evidently some sort of role-playing club: Vikings and sorcerers all sitting around the long table in a jolly hubbub.

Tracey Collins: music to munch to

From 12 noon lunch would be served, and very likely a queue would develop, snaking down the café. Saturday lunchtime could get very busy! By one o'clock, all being well, things would be sufficiently under control to permit my well-earned break. First I needed to make sure that the musicians had all they needed. Mostly, this didn't involve an electricity connection. These gigs were, by and large, all acoustic; I was anxious to avoid the competitive ramping up of noise levels that often mars pub performances. At least the carpeting served to dampen the ambient noise.

A fantastic variety of performers were featured, in a programme compiled every two months, first of all by Tracey, who coined the slogan "music to munch to", then, when she moved North, by my good friend Maeve. Most of these musicians were local residents; there was a considerable crossover with the Catweazle Club. Unlike Catweazle, with its strict injunction to maintain silence during performances, musicians needed to accept that not everyone might be ready to listen – a great shame, really, because I for one was keen to give total attention. I collected my lunch and found a seat as close nearby as possible. It was always a treat, and occasionally there would be something utterly outstanding: such as, a couple of exotically dressed Congolese musicians – Bernard Kabanda and Samuel Bakkabulindi – stopping by on the way to Womad, or – my absolute favourite – locally based West African kora player Jali Fily Cissokho, jamming along with the wonderful Dave Noble, aka Natureboy.

Abbie Lathe and friends

If there was a CD on offer – and often there was – I tended to pick one up as a souvenir, and encourage others to do the same. Turn the page – see my collection! Otherwise, I didn't feel able to pay out much more than a tenner each, plus a free meal. Was I colluding in the general practice of taking musicians for granted? Still, there was generally the reward of a warm reception – except on these unfortunate dates in the heat of the summer, when it was just possible that the café might be virtually empty.

Amongst my collection of CDs acquired from café performers, one that received frequent plays was Samantha Twigg Johnson's collection of self-compositions, Organ of Habit. Great voice, wonderful songs – and a lovely person too. I'd heard her perform at the Catweazle; how great to welcome her to the Café. Here's what she recalls:

Playing at The Magic Café was an utter delight. I remember giving out handbills before the show and feeling excited, proud and nervous. I don't have clear

Samantha Twigg Johnson: 'Peggy Lee meets PJ Harvey'

147

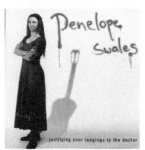

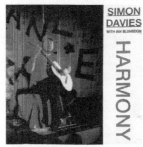

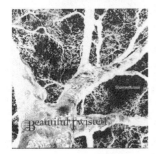

149

memories of the experience of singing – I often tune out a bit – but I do recall scarfing down my vegetarian feast with relish, and being made to feel utterly welcome and at home. I had admired (and still admire!) the music of Sharron Kraus, so the fact that she worked there gave the place an added sparkle. I also loved the notice board, crammed with information on workshops, opportunities, and gatherings. It gave me a sense of such cultural abundance, and posting my gig notices there gave me a sense of achievement and belonging.

With all this surging creativity and warm feeling generated, I like to think that the Café was a good place to fall in love. So here's a sweet story offered by Elaine. She served on the Café crew, too:

When I came to work at the Magic in 2000 I had been unemployed for a while after a life in education as a nursery headteacher and erstwhile education lecturer. My health had recently suffered and I was at a turning point in my life seeking more spiritual and personal fulfilment. The therapy of the magical community of the café and the wonderful food, drinks and conversations encouraged by long communal tables were just what I needed. I made new wonderful friends there and found new networks, interests and even housemates from the amazing Magic Noticeboard.

A true love story with the café had also begun when my new boyfriend Graham, whom I met on a Greek island, as you do, arrived at the Magic, invited by me to join our Saturday music and lunch session. He walked in with his hat, long hair and beads, came over to the counter, a tall figure with piercing blue eyes and greeted Hafiz with, "Nice café, man!" From henceforth he was embraced by our friendship group there, and at the Elsfield commune we frequented, and he continually described Hafiz's establishment as "the BEST CAFÉ IN THE WORLD!" Sadly, some few months later Graham was diagnosed with

motor neurone disease and could no longer walk. However, in true style he found a super 'Four Wheel Drive Buggy', with which he made a grand entrance to his beloved Magic Café. The friends he had met there were with us until the end when he finally let go of his amazing life-force. I will always be so grateful to the Magic Café for enabling him to be so happy and supported on the way towards his next magical journey!

It would be hard to celebrate Elaine without invoking her great friend Maeve Bayton. I first saw Maeve onstage, as a member of the legendary feminist punk band, the Mistakes – that was in the late 70s, at the Mayfly festival on Oxpens meadow. They were a bit shambolic – it was perhaps their second-ever gig – but nonetheless inspiring. Her career subsequently took a side-step – becoming an academic at Ruskin College, achieving a doctorate in legendary punk feminist musicians, no less. How fabulous to have her organising the music for our Saturday gigs! She took the opportunity to squeeze in the odd show for herself:

I fell in love with the Magic Café from the first time I encountered it, at the Asian Community Centre. From then on it became a sort of cosy club where I would look forward to meeting my friends every Saturday lunchtime. I don't remember ever going there without knowing at least a couple of people. It was such a safe and friendly place. I loved the community aspect of it. The various groups: people working NGOs, Green Party activists, etc. And the notice board was a real treat.

I started doing music there when Tracey Collins encouraged me to play with her. I was scared initially but after a couple of times I began to enjoy it and, when Tracey left for pastures new, I took over organising it. It was fun being able to invite musicians to play every Saturday in return for a delicious magic lunch and 10 quid. They were guaranteed an audience who, although chatting and eating, always made a point of showing their appreciation by clapping. It was a great time and I thoroughly enjoyed myself.

Some particular memories:

Tracey's wonderful covers of 'Seize the Day'; Kath Tait playing 'Bastard' to an astonished audience; Colin Fletcher and Jane Griffiths moving me to tears with their slow Celtic tunes. There are just too many people to mention.

Regarding my personal performances, it certainly sharpened me up and made me more confident. I've always said, "if you could play the Magic you could play anywhere". For instance, I shall never forget the occasion when, in the middle of a ballad, an eccentric (and possibly drunken) Scotsman in a kilt came right up to me, his face barely six inches from mine, and yelled "do you wanna buy a guitar?!"

At other times I found myself playing with small children happily attached to both my legs.

You had to just carry on playing, whatever . . . !

There was also the time when the café was absolutely full of Buddhist monks and they sat there not eating because they assumed it was disrespectful to have lunch whilst I was playing! I soon disabused them of that notion.

Such happy times. Unforgettable.

Maeve is a great aficionado of the blues – in particular of dynamic women such as Ida Cox and Bessie Smith – but she has also written many fine songs in other genres. I was delighted when she suggested composing a song specially for the Magic Café. We sat down for a chat, while she took notes, and then worked it up, together with Colin Edwards (also a veteran of the Magic team), into a rousing anthem. "Feed your Heart at the Magic Café" – precisely.

It's a catchy tune, although, sadly, Colin's intricate ragtime figures, thumb cunningly picking out the bass line, have always proved way beyond my own capabilities.

Feed Your Heart

(Colin Edwards & Maeve Bayton)

Got a wooden spoon and a nine inch knife
This how I choose to spend my life
Working at the stove I'm feeling good
There's lots of love going into this food

We've got tables and we've got chairs
A second-hand sofa from the woman upstairs
Sun on the carpet, toys on the floor
Children smiling round my kitchen door
Chorus
If you've got the appetite, I've got a menu
Here's what we could do
Let's get together at a colourful venue
This Magic Café was made for you

Over in the corner talking in whispers
Sharing a secret, a couple of sisters
People in jumpers, cold outside
All hand knitted and worn with pride

There's a man in a kilt gone a bit too far
Trying to flog me an old guitar
Man with a lap-top tapping the keys
Sipping a coffee, feeling at ease
Chorus
If you've got the appetite, I've got a menu
Here's what we could do
Let's get together at a colourful venue
This Magic Café was made for you – so you can
Refrain
Feed your heart – at the Magic Café   x4

Continues over >>

Spinach quiche, a green mandala
Cinnamon and coriander
Fresh-ground coffee, frothing milk
Origami and patchwork quilt

Cappuccino intervention
Singers competing for attention
Cakes of passion and of cheese
Saffron robes and dungarees
Chorus
If you've got an appetite, . . .

Nursing mother, eating for two
Magic Café welcomes you
There's no need to eat alone
Pull up a chair and make yourself at home

Friday night and we're full of beans
Can't get a seat 'cos there's too many Greens
Candle on the table, lights down low
Maharani's cheesecake, with Cointreau (mmm!)
Chorus
If you've got an appetite, . . .
. . . for you – so you can
Feed your heart – at the Magic Café . . . x6

"Business is Important, but . . ."

"You're famous, you are!" So my neighbour greeted me as I returned home in the evening. I'd been on the BBC 6 o'clock news, offering my testimony to the changing times. In fact, the BBC outside broadcast team had spent the entire morning in and around the Magic Café, drawing their van into the back alley, setting up a satellite dish, and faffing around with their microphones and cameras in the kitchen while Justin and I did out best not to trip over these alien devices.

They are here to celebrate a breakthrough moment in UK politics. The election for the European Parliament on June 10 1999 – the first in the UK to feature proportional representation – had returned a Green Party candidate for the first time: Caroline Lucas, sometime Oxfordshire County Councillor, now to represent South East England in Brussels. I'd had a phone call from the BBC news office, who had somehow decided that the Magic Café was the ideal location for this story. Evidently it was considered the hub of the Green movement. I was, of course, tremendously flattered.

12 noon approaches, the unyielding lunchtime deadline: only the green salad remains to be finished. The cameras zoom in on a final flurry of flying lettuce – but the director isn't quite happy. Could we please do that again? *"No"* is my brusque reply. Don't they understand deadlines?

But with lunch duly out on the counter, and the first customers collecting their satisfying platefuls, the pressure is off. I'm ready for my close-up. Just a short interview, in which I acknowledge the significance of the moment, and seek to explain why I believe it's important. In the event, they clip down my contribution to one brief soundbite, but I'm happy with the result.

"Business is important," I opine, *"but it's not the main thing . . ."*

Perhaps there just wasn't time, with the cameras running, to expand on that observation. How might I have continued? And what **was** the main thing?

I had at least owned up to being a businessman, something about which

I couldn't help but feel some ambivalence. The hippie mindset had always downplayed the importance of money, insisting that such vital commodities as music, love and dope ought to be Free. Surely this was the key message of the Woodstock generation? I'd been intrigued by the yippie manifesto proclaimed in Abbie Hoffman's "Steal this Book". Of course, I had paid 50p for my copy in a second hand store; and I had subsequently learnt the truth that there is no such thing as a free T-shirt, even from Woolworths. I'd lived in a commune without any cash to call my own, but this had been strictly dependant on a very efficient collective enterprise, the Far Out disco. When we started to distribute pocket money for private spending, I realised that this was in fact a magic pass to the emporium of abundance. Money is an essential lubricant in the system of commodity distribution, even if, should you consider its philosophical underpinnings, it is rooted in that mystical forest garden, the collective imaginary.

If I wanted to manifest my vision, as something more attractive than a free food kitchen offering spit-and-flour chapatis, I must become an adept in the mystery of pounds shillings and pence – good old £sd, as we used to say in the old days.

When I started the Magic Café at the Asian Cultural Centre, I began to keep careful records of numbers of chocolate brownies sold, and carefully calculate expenditure against cash received. It was all written out, longhand, as were the end of year breakdowns, by which I satisfied the demands of the Inland Revenue for its due share of my hard-won income. I made a habit of placing business receipts in my left-hand back pocket – something I still instinctively do. Orderly, painstaking record-keeping became second nature, however intrinsically dull this might be. Acquiring a computer proved to be a great step forward, at least from the point of view of efficiently zipping up a column of figures. I went through a brief period of making exploded pie charts, as I explored the fun possibilities of this new technology. Now I discover that these early forays into financial analysis have disappeared into the netherworld of obsolete file formats.

In short, I trained myself to adopt a business sense. Part of the transition process towards a full-time café had been the elaboration, for the benefit of potential investors, of a cash-flow chart. This had, for the first time, drawn my attention to the consequences of VAT registration: so much of that money sitting in the bank, apparently yours, must, once every three months, be surrendered to the government, on pain of severe consequences. All is not as it seems on the surface. Business is a suitcase of worries, to carry in with you to work each and every day.

But it is not the most important thing – so I must constantly reaffirm.

On that particular occasion, for the benefit of the BBC interviewer, I could have pointed to the subject of their broadcast, the acknowledgement of the Green perspective as something worthy of note. I'd been very happy to have been colonised by the local Green party – *"can't get a seat 'cos there's too many Greens"*, as Maeve's song wittily suggests. They had been hiring the café for evening gatherings, always respecting the space and leaving it pristine when they left. I wasn't (yet) a party member, but, being someone who thought a lot about the particular demands of our changing times, I was glad that there was an organised political movement to address the rapidly approaching ecological crisis. East Oxford was indeed a Green Party bastion, much of its electoral success due to the tireless efforts of Craig and Elise. These two lived just over the road; Craig's ecological consultancy business (Best Foot Forward) had its office just a couple of doors away; the Café was practically home from home.

Elise and Craig at the Elder Stubbs Festival 2019, sporting civic regalia. Both were to serve as Lord Mayor of Oxford: that year it was Craig's turn.

Then again, the Labour party, perennial masters of the City Hall and, come election time, bitter foes of the Greens, could just as easily claim credit as supporters and sponsors of the Magic Café. Pat Stannard, the local Labour councillor, had been invaluable in speaking up at the planning adjudication. I imagine that, in terms of political orientation, most of the Magic Café regulars would be content to describe themselves as "anti-Thatcherite". In short, what the Magic Café represented to them was, that there **was** such a thing as society. In coming through that jolly red door, they were making it plain that they were a part of a community – one that was richly diverse, but

157

that held in common a certain civilizational attitude. It was an affirmation of a selfhood that took pleasure in sharing.

This was most apparent in that extraordinary phenomenon, the Magic Café noticeboard. In designing the café interior, I had instructed my chief of works, Rob Valentine, to produce the largest possible pinboard, and to place it in the central position, so that everyone would be sure to see it as they made their way from the entrance to the counter. It would be a public forum, a distillation of significant information, and available for any posting without charge. Local events, matters of concern, cultural communication, classes and workshops, business services: all was welcome. There was no apparent organizational principle – no "yoga zone" or "parents' corner". Nonetheless, it was far from being a chaotic jumble – although so it may have appeared on initial inspection. It was important that everything was visible, even if it had to be searched for. The very act of searching, so I believed, might well provoke a serendipitous encounter. From time to time – perhaps on a quiet Saturday afternoon – I would remove everything from the board, sifting out anything that might be out of date, and removing items that seemed inappropriate. Then I would create a brand-new collage, juxtaposing colours, ideas, and shapes, just as if it were a Magic Café salad. Items relating to a person's livelihood, such as a business card, needed to be properly visible: these I tended to place on the wooden boundary frame, where there was less likelihood of being covered over.

Anything notice larger than A4 tended to be a more professional production, most likely advertising some cultural event or upcoming gig. Oxford is not short of such attractions – and there are many places where these may be promoted. I exercised my judgement in choosing which to favour, either on grounds of intrinsic interest, or simply because I liked the poster design. For these favoured few there might be space on the wall adjacent the noticeboard – but certainly not crowding out, or shouting down, the community conversation.

"Feed your Heart, at the Magic Café": thus the refrain of Maeve and Colin's song. The lesson I had drawn from my various adventures in community living, and from elaborating the concept of the Magic Feast, is that nourishment is a many-tiered cake, of which the nutritional content of the food is merely the base layer. A perfectly presented dish, constructed from the finest ingredients, may fail absolutely in its mission to please if consumed in stressful circumstances. First of all, as a palate cleanser, what's required is an unburdening of the spirit. That, for me, was the essential purpose of the Magic Café.

> ## Magic Café Notice Board
>
> **I'm sorry if you get bored**
> **But think where's this notice board . . .**
> **There's always room for something more**
> **Anti hunt and anti war**
> **Non-violent communication**
> **Yoga, Buddhist meditation**
> **Dance the 5 Rhythms**
> **Drum the stress**
> **There's always room, I'll name the rest**
> **Tai Chi**
> **Alchemy**
> **Emotional or Aroma therapy**
> **Or is it the**
> **Philosophy or**
> **Reflexology with**
> **Osteopathy? Does**
> **Gestalts counselling with**
> **Fusion life drawing**
> **Require**
> **Reiki treatment**
> **Darshan or Shiatsu?**
> **There's always room for something new**
> **I hope you're not bored**
> **Can you name the notice board?**
>
> *Anon*

The interior of the café – the comfy sofa and chairs at the entrance, the vibrant, harmonious colours, the choice of music, the unpretentious,

159

idiosyncratic furnishings – was all directed towards provoking a sense of ease, of participation and belonging.

Some might cavil, that the food displayed at the counter might not correspond to a strict dietary regime, or be worthily proclaimed as exclusively vegan, or 100% organic. The menu, in all its daily changing variety, was, rather, composed as an exercise in inclusivity – and of fun. Veganism was acknowledged and honoured; but so was the deliciousness of cheese. Personally, I never saw the point of a worthy cake. As for the secret ingredient in the chocolate brownie: this was not, as Jon Bowen hypothesizes, hallucinogenic, but simply an awful lot of sugar. In retrospect, perhaps it was far too much sugar – but I'm still being badgered for the recipe.

To clarify: the ingredients were in large part organic, delivered every few weeks by the wholefood supplier, but for the daily groceries I relied on the local supermarket, making a speedy tour of the aisles on my way to work. It was an efficient system, ensuring that veggies used were always fresh, and that the fridges weren't clogged up with unused goods.

I'm naturally reticent about bigging up my cooking skills, so I'm grateful to Chris Jardine's fulsome account of our regular kitchen practice. This was indeed food prepared with love – that is, with a particular recipient in mind, the honoured guest at the counter. As one of our regulars observes: *"it was one of the few places where you could taste the barakat in the food."* I had to look this up: it's an Arabic word meaning "blessings". Just so.

Service at the counter was speedy and efficient. I always encouraged my staff to be present for our guests, to be themselves, friendly but not fawning. The transaction becomes more than just food for cash; there are good feelings attached: a smile, or a joke, on both sides of the bargain.

Have you ever been served a coffee prepared by someone who does nothing else throughout their whole shift, back turned on the customers, lost in a wilderness of froth and steam? I feel sorry for these functionaries, and find it difficult to enjoy the result. I had such lovely people working with me: Magic Café staff, in all their variety, were wonderful and full of life – the real secret ingredient.

It all amounts to a collaborative project: here is a shared space – and a space to share whatever needs to be shared. Look over there: someone sitting at the table, fingers dabbing at the last few cake crumbs, contemplating the cocoa sprinkles on their cappuccino froth; there is an air of repletion, and of spirit loosening up, unfurling like a rosebud, fragrant. Across the table, there is a sudden glint, an eye-sparkle, with a smile that quickens into conversation . . . It is a point of embarkation – who knows where it may lead?

This is what fed my heart, day after day, as I observed the myriad social interactions, catching fragments of conversation, sudden irruptions of merriment, subtle dynamic transformations . . .

Such is the ethos of an amateur. Could this really be sustained, year after year, forever carrying my briefcase of worries? Would all of this intangible sweetness of experience be sufficient to balance the scales, when set against all of the stress and exertion, the weariness of body and mind as I counted the pennies from the till at closing time?

Hanging behind the serving
counter: an octagonal mandala
by Ruth Russell.

The Elastic Limit

Those two long-haired gentlemen have been sitting at the table for hours, their ebullient conversation fuelled by cup after cup of hot black liquor. Boyle in particular is well pumped up, steam practically coming out of his ears. His imagination apparently knows no bounds, expanding and contracting, springing dramatically from one topic to another: optical devices that might enable sight across vast distances, or examination of the minutest of dimensions, special suits to allow exploration of the ocean bed, the elasticity of biological boundaries, carriages that might traverse the very heavens, the manipulation of consciousness by means of potent *druggs*, the ability to dispense with sleep . . .

His increasingly wild gesticulations send a cup crashing towards the floor . . .

"Whoops! Never mind – fancy another, Bob?" He holds out a couple of penny pieces to the ever-patient management.

"Not sure the old ticker can take it, old chap . . . heartbeat's off the scale . . . what the heck, I will if you will . . ."

Hooke has pulled his favourite toy from his pocket, stretching it out like a squeezebox, letting it spring back together – again and again, it's so diverting. He has a sudden idea: *"What if we could stretch time itself? What do you think, Bob?"* Out comes his pocket watch, and he attaches it to one end of the coil, holding the other end between his fingers. The timepiece plunges directly downwards, held by the twisted wire, then comes to a sudden rest just a couple of inches above the table. *"Hm, fascinating . . ."*; he swings the watch gently, like a pendulum, observing how it settles at exactly the same point; *"I was talking to Newton just the other day . . . and maybe there's some link between time and relative dimensions in space . . ."* His eye is drawn to the large chronometer adorning the coffee house fireplace . . .

Vaulting unsteadily upright, his lurching limbs sending the chair toppling in equal and opposite motion, he reaches for the clock. Before the management has time to protest, he's found a hook at the back on which to attach his spring. It's a bold experiment – too bold, as it happens.

The wire pulls out, as far as it can go – then snaps. The clock hurtles downwards, crashing onto the flagstones and spilling an intricate array of cogs and levers.

The proprietor, ever tolerant, merely raises his eyebrows, folds his arms across his chest, and calls for a skivvy to fetch a broom.

Hooke's Law: the extension is proportionate to the load – provided the elastic limit is not exceeded.

A couple of years after I let the café go, and finding myself somewhat at a loose end, searching as ever for meaning and purpose, I was persuaded to stand in the City Council election for East Oxford's St Clement's ward, representing the Green Party. This was Caroline Lucas' sometime pitch, so I felt honoured – even more so when she contributed a supportive comment to my election flyer. As I worked the streets, knocking at all the doors, it was heartening to be so well recognised. I had high hopes of success, as someone with a reputation for getting things done.

The Labour Party had other ideas: word reached me that a rumour was spreading up and down Divinity Road. It was being put about that, whilst running the Magic Café, I had actually gone quite crazy.

Regardless of the reason, I was pipped at the post; perhaps it was a lucky escape. But it did leave me wondering: did I really go a bit nuts?

It's not as if I hadn't foreseen the risk. Here it is, clearly stated in the Business Plan with which I hoped to impress potential investors:

"The principal danger in starting up a new venture is, I believe, to attempt to achieve everything all at once, thus over-extending one's resources. Conversion of the premises at 110 Magdalen Road to the new Magic Café offers all sorts of possibilities, but it is my intention to take a gradual approach towards developing the business. Initially I intend to build on proven

strengths, exploring other possibilities as and when I believe that the business can support them."

Then again:

"employing helpers can be expensive, if expected custom fails to materialize. Wasting money on unproductive labour could be a disastrous drain on revenue during the early stages of the business. I would seek as much as possible to capitalize on my own skills and efficient methods of working; in the early months I would expect to undertake most of the cooking myself. Extra help could be drafted in as and when required, and in this way a small pool of trained cooks could gradually be built up."

Wise words . . . but then again, also foolish. I was committing myself to relentless, wearying activity, in the hope that somehow things would come good before my energy ran out.

I'd convinced myself, through careful calculation, that the Café would need to be open on one evening in the week, on top of the regular openings from 10 until 6 from Monday to Saturday. Friday nights would have to be a double shift – at least for me. I'd done that before at the Asian Cultural Centre, hadn't I? At least for a few months, anyway, before Ratty called time – and then I'd had the rest of the week in which to recover.

It was somehow my expectation that someone just like me would turn up, looking for a gig. After a while, I learned to acknowledge the wonderful variety of people attracted to helping out in the Magic Café kitchen. More than anything else, working with so many special, unique individuals was the greatest possible gift. Apart from anything else, I got to do a lot of unwrapping.

As I've discovered from checking through my old accounts spreadsheets, a grand total of 182 people passed through the Magic Café team in just over a decade. To help me get a sense of this flow I plotted their careers on a timeline: it's a river of talent, in some places calm and unbroken, a tranquil stream of steady commitment, but then there are periods when names turn over rapidly like rocks in the current, white-water rapids of chaotic turbulence. The first twelve months were a particular uneasy ride: only Jenny stayed the entire distance, doing her best to master the baking recipes before moving on at New Year. Some lasted just a shift or two, barely getting their feet wet;

others helped out for a few weeks, then stepped back onto dry land. Should you be curious, I include this timeline as an Appendix (*see pages 234-5*).

I'd got to know Cyd at the Dance Camp; the following year, the event moved to Sandy Lane Farm, and Farmer Charles had suggested I use an old milking station as a makeshift kitchen. I hadn't fancied this at all, busy as I was with other commitments, but Cyd had risen to the challenge, sufficient to contemplate setting up her own café. She welcomed the opportunity to learn from my fledgling operation. It was, she declares, *"inspirational"*. At the end of the year she too moved on to concentrate on creating what would eventually be Lily's Tea Room, a highly regarded establishment just up the road from Dorchester Abbey.

My *"small pool of expertise"* was scarcely more than a puddle. Perhaps I was simply too stretched to devote the necessary attention to training and tuition. Or maybe I was sending out the wrong message.

I'd had some experience over the previous few years in engaging temporary or occasional staff. It was generally a bit of a lark, something my friends were happy to share in. Running a full-time team, I came to realise, is quite different. I needed to respect people's other commitments – to their children, perhaps, or their incipient careers. How many hours in the week could they spare for the Café? There were some weeks when as many as a dozen names might appear on the shift plan. Not surprisingly, washing-up on a Friday night

A busy Friday evening, not long after the Café opened

was the least popular shift; frequently only a last-minute call-round managed to fill the slot. That was stressful!

Shortly before we'd opened up, with my sense of whimsy as yet unbowed by experience, I'd placed a card in the Inner Bookshop window, appealing for *"Apprentice Magicians"*. Maybe this is what attracted Matilda, keen to develop her circus skills; she stayed for a few weeks, but this wasn't the big career break she may have imagined. I needed to be more explicit in my invitation. This was not your bog standard café job, after all; this was "Something Else". Catering experience might be the last thing I was looking for. As I encountered each new hopeful candidate, I learned to look for that intangible quality: "having the right energy". Susie was definitely one such – a feisty "wee Scots lassie" with great sense of presence and fun; a proud mother of four, she always finished her shift with maximum speed and efficiency, signing off with a cheery "that's Me!" as she hurried out to greet her kids.

Stripey Joe the juggler

Towards the end of that first year I placed another ad next door, this time rather more specific: *"creative, enthusiastic and responsible person . . . must have flair for vegetarian cookery"*. Justin reckoned he fit the bill – or as good as: *"I'm creative, enthusiastic . . . and I wear flares"*. Justin was a born entertainer – how could I not be charmed? Since leaving college he'd been building a career as a professional juggler and jester, honing his skills in a variety of contexts, from medieval jousts to corporate conferences. By far the most demanding audience – and hence the most rewarding – would be a roomful of excited kids at a party. There was so much more to his art than simply launching balls into the air: he could whip his audience up into a frenzy of expectation, then perpetrate the most outrageous sleight of hand, all the while maintaining a cheeky, light touch banter, ever-ready to strike sparks off the unexpected.

Justin was a great companion in the kitchen, keeping me amused as we prepared lunch together. His was clearly a safe pair of hands – although not necessarily the fastest: each ball of bread dough needed to be carefully assessed, tossed from hand to hand to achieve a precisely even weight. His forte, inevitably, was showmanship, and the Solstice Celebration dinner, our first anniversary party, offered the ideal opportunity to appreciate his talents.

I had, rather apprehensively, agreed to be his fall guy, on the understanding that I wouldn't actually be sawn in half. But there would be no avoiding jeopardy. Ordered to lie prone, fresh eggs were juggled – successfully – across my body. Then knives were produced – how nervous I was of flying knives! – to be dextrously brandished and manipulated while I cowered anxiously, desperate for this to conclude without injury.

Justin wasn't done yet: brandishing a large scroll, this reckless jester proceeded to allege all manner of malpractice. What were these terrible crimes? There was certainly an accusation of dubious musical taste. So unfair – but I must pay the penalty!

> *That part of my show was reserved for the very rare occasions I would bring out my guillotine, which I'm always anxious about using as it happens so infrequently – I'm never quite sure I've recalled how to operate it safely. I remember the anxious look on your face as this rickety contraption was unveiled, much to the delight of your regulars . . .*

Justin on his narrow-boat in 2010

Such, after all, is the function of a court jester: to expose a despot to ridicule. To be thus publicly branded was immensely discomforting. For everyone else, of course, it was splendid entertainment: high hilarity prevailed, the ideal precursor for pudding.

Justin was still a kitchen regular by the time the winter solstice next rolled around. Friday evening supper was still a fixture, and I was still working much too much, but I had become more settled in the discipline of my routine, able to appreciate the company of such luminaries as Katie, Ceri, Quentin, Orange, Lilia and Sarada. Team spirit was developing, and fun was being had, projecting outwards from the kitchen, transmitted across the counter along with the food.

There was a suggestion that I ought to consider expanding the business, knocking through the wall into the adjoining workshop space. Mohammed's business fixing old TVs was falling victim to the changing times. Electronic gear was now flooding into the West from China, and prices were collapsing. Why bother fixing your old telly when, for more or less the same price, you could buy a brand-new model, with all the benefits of the latest digital technology? Mohammed's workshop, perpetually wreathed in a fug of tobacco smoke, was gradually filling up with obsolete and unwanted televisions, the enormous bulky widescreens of yesteryear. They might as well go straight to the dump.

I called in Rob to assess the state of this property, and started to fantasize about possible layouts. There was a fundamental problem in the disparity of floor levels, not only in the workshop itself, but also with the rest of the Café, which, as I'd learned, could only be solved by a combination of rubble and concrete. It was hard to imagine a transformation which didn't involve grave disruption to the existing business. My original plans had worked out so well, making the most of available space; what could really be gained, apart from providing a more commodious toilet area?

What settled my mind was the increased rent suggested by Mohammed. Icarus-like, my high-soaring dreams came tumbling down. Stick or bust? I was going to stick with what I had. Maybe it was already more than enough.

Justin wasn't available for the next Solstice party – I expect he had an alternative engagement. This would be on a Saturday evening; doubtless I had already stayed up late the evening before for the regular Friday supper. I'd devised a wonderful menu, and no doubt there was a full programme of entertainment to look forward to. But all I remember of that evening was mayhem: guests were starting to arrive, stepping through the door in all their festive finery, selecting their seats and anticipating a feast. I was confident that all was ready and in place, with just the Turkish-style carrot and apricot fritters to finish off in the deep-fryer – and then the fire-alarm sounded . . .

An incessant jangling, the distillation of panic and distress . . .

– which demands that everyone leaves the building, out into the December chill . . .

– and which can't be switched off. There is no access to the flat upstairs, because the regular student tenants have left for their Christmas break . . .

– and the emergency key I have insisted upon no longer fits the lock . . .

– and Mohammed can't be reached because it's Eid, and he's doubtless busy with Mosque festivities.

We call the fire brigade, which duly arrives with yet more jangling sirens. *"Where's the fire?"* There is no fire, just a disastrous landlord-related cockup. It doesn't occur to me until much later that my own ill-ventilated frying must have set off the alarm, so accustomed have I become to the alarm being set off by the students upstairs, toasting their late-morning breakfasts.

Camilla asserts herself, demanding that the firemen break into the upstairs flat. *"Can't do that, Madam, not without the landlord's permission."* Mohammed shows up, in his best shalwar kameez. Door is unlocked, the alarm disabled. And that's all I can recall . . .

This was the year that the calendar turned its crucial corner, amidst a frenzy of speculation about the possible collapse of civilisation triggered by a programming glitch, the so-called millennium bug. Surely now was the time to party! But I was far from being in a party mood. Instead, in that liminal zone between Christmas and New Year I embarked on a long-promised return to the magical land of my childhood, rereading Lord of the Rings for the first time in several decades. Shortly afterwards, I began to experience the symptoms of flu. I persevered against all odds, just like Frodo: I entered Mordor through the secret gate, marched across the blasted plateau disguised as an orc, stood on the very edge of the crack of doom – and then I could manage no more. In this ghastly interlude I wrestled with my evil twin, all the way through into the next millennium.

I was feeling distinctly wobbly when we reopened after the break. Full tilt was definitely beyond my capacity. A sign appeared on the door: *"We regret there will be no suppers served this Friday, due to a bad case of Millennium Bug. Back to normal next week"*. But I never did resume Friday evenings; and there were to be no more Winter Solstice Celebrations for many a year.

According to Chris Jardine's account quality and standards were diligently maintained, and spirits remained high. In my relationship with staff I was striving to balance friendship with being the boss; to be authoritative without being authoritarian. Sue Hughes, who helped out for several months round about that time, has fond memories:

You and I always got on well. I'd worked in catering before and I knew how stressful it was. You were calm compared to some of the chefs I'd worked with! You were also compassionate and caring. I always had my breaks and was able to chat to people and feel part of the team. I actually met some very nice people while I worked there.

Sue Hughes on the canal towpath, 2009

169

I remember coming in one afternoon and getting a phone call from [my son] David saying he'd been attacked by a friend (?) of his with what felt like a metal bar. It was only a hardwood stick but he must have hit my son very hard for him to say that. He was very upset, and even though he was being looked after by a friend you virtually pushed me out to go to him. I was so grateful . . .

Cait displaying her artwork at the 2000 Big Green Gathering

Stress found other ways to manifest. I am grateful to Cait Sweeney for the following well-remembered anecdotes:

Hafiz was at times under a lot of stress. Getting lunch out for 12 noon was the main gig; however, various breakfast options were also on the menu and each order would ratchet up Hafiz's stress level a notch as he would have to stop what he was making for lunch to prepare the breakfast.

On this particular morning there have already been numerous breakfast orders when a young man comes to the counter. Having perused the menu he says: "I'd like a toasted muffin with egg and mushrooms please and a cup of tea." "I'll just go and tell the chef" I reply, wondering how to deliver this request. There's no easy way so I just say: "That's another order for a toasted muffin with egg and mushrooms." At which point Hafiz steps away from whatever he was making, stares up at the ceiling and, taking a deep breath, emits a prolonged and none too quiet:
"Fuuuuuuuuuuuuuuuuuuuuuuuuuuuuuuuck!"

In the pause of silence that followed I imagine the hair of the young man at the counter being blown back by the force of it. I return and the chap says: "I don't have to have a breakfast, I don't have to have breakfast!" "Oh it's fine," I say, "take a seat and I'll bring it over when it's ready."

It's the end of the day, the café is closed and Hafiz and I are finishing the final chores when the phone rings. He answers it:

"Yes, it is a vegetarian café . . . Well, the salads are vegan and so is the soup . . . No, not organic . . . Yes, everything is made on the premises . . . Yes, we use fresh ingredients, some from a local farm shop and some from Tescos . . . I think the best thing is for you to come in and see what we do . . . No, I'm not going to run through the entire menu . . . Look, I've told you I'm not going through the entire menu with you, come in or don't, it's up to you!"

Hanging up the phone he says "I fucking hate vegans!"

Moments later the phone rings again "It'll be that woman, I'm not answering it" says Hafiz, "I will, I will!" I cry "Go ahead, be my guest" he says.

"Hello, Magic Café, can I help you?"

"I've just been spoken to very rudely by a member of your staff and I'd like to complain to the manager."

"Oh, that was the manager! Was there anything else?"

And finally, I'm not sure if this is actually my memory, I suspect I imagined it so vividly when Rom in fact recounted it that it's become mine too!

It's a busy lunch-time and there's been a possible over-sight on the staff rota time-tabling, in so much that two people, who won't be named, were on the same shift. Oh okay, it was X—— and Y——, both fine people I'm sure, but pretty useless in combination.

There's a rush on and the crockery is running low, X—— and Y—— are at the sink, one washing the other drying, talking nineteen to the dozen about some hippy shit and making very slow progress with the task in hand. Something snapped and Hafiz stepped out of the back-door, howling like a wolf at the sky. When he comes back in the kitchen Y—— remarks: "Relax man, take it easy!"

Yup, that's how it was. Easy it wasn't.

Sometimes you've got to let off some steam, level up the pressure. That's the point of catharsis. In turn, catharsis provides an opportunity for the restoration of harmony – a dynamic condition, the product of constant adjustment and negotiation.

To be sure, there were times when I grew fraught and frazzled; but, no, I didn't go nuts. The machine kept right on rolling.

Drinks		Lunch		Cakes & Desserts	
We use organic fairtrade Java coffee beans		*All food is freshly prepared on the premises, with daily changing menus; check the noticeboard for details.*		*(subject to availability)*	
Espresso:	£1.10				
Regular Coffee:	£1.10			Toasted Teacake, buttered:	£1.10
Latte:	£1.40			Cherry Coconut Flapjack:	£1.10
Cappucino:	£1.40	Special Hot Plateful:	£5.20	Paradise Slice:	£1.10
Double Espresso:	£1.60	Savoury pie:	£2.60	Lemon Sponge Cake:	£1.10
Iced Coffee Latte:	£1.50	Salads *(per portion)*:	£1.30	Apricot Coconut Delight:	£1.10
Hot Chocolate:	£1.40	Hearty Soup:	£2.60	Caramel Shortcake:	£1.10
Yannoh (Barleycup):	90p	Freshly baked bread roll:	90p	Date & Banana Slice:	£1.10
				Spiced Fruit Cake:	£1.10
Teas:	90p			Choc-Fudge Brownie:	£1.35
(Breakfast, Masala Chai, Darjeeling,		*Lunch is served from 12 noon*		Passion Cake:	£1.35
Darjeeling Green, Jasmine Green, Assam,					
Earl Grey, White Tea, Decaffeinated)		**Breakfast**		Cherry Vanilla Tart:	£1.60
Herb Teas:	90p			Chocolate Spiral Cake:	£1.60
(Peppermint, Rosehip, Sweet Berry Swirl,		*(Available before 12 noon)*		Lemon Cream Tart:	£1.60
Lemon Verbena, Blackcurrant, Echinacea,		Open Sesame ! Breakfast featuring		Blackcurrant Cheesecake:	£2.20
Yogi Tea Classic, Yogi Tea Jamaican, Fennel,		Toasted Sesame Seed Roll with:-			
Guarana & Blackcurrant, Lemon & Ginger,		--Mushrooms fried in butter: £2.90		Mango & Lime Sorbet:	£2.00
Camomile & Spearmint, Camomile, Rooibosch)		--Two fried eggs: £2.90		Ginger Icecream:	£2.20
Fruit Juice:	90p	--Fried egg & mushrooms: £3.20		Chocolate Icecream:	£2.20
(Orange, Apple, Grapefruit, Pineapple)		--Two fried eggs & mushrooms: £3.80		Strawberry Icecream:	£2.20
Organic Cordial Fizz:	90p	(All served with fried tomato & parsley)		Apricot & Amaretti Frozen Yogurt:£2.20	
(Cranberry, Elderflower, Ginger, Lemon,					
Lime, Blackcurrant)		Muesli Deluxe *or* Oat Crunchy		Fresh Fruit Smoothie	£1.80
Banana Milkshake:	£1.40	*with* **Banana & Milk** /Soyamilk: £2.30			
Mineral Water (fizzy or still):	45p				

Parade of Honour: Paradise Slice; Choc-Fudge Brownie; Cherry Coconut Flapjack; Lemon Sponge Cake; Passion Cake; Spiced Fruitcake; Caramel Shortcake; Apricot Coconut Delight; Date & Banana Slice.

The Tibetan Blessing

Where was it rooted, this resilience that brought the pendulum of my spirit to rest ever and again at a steady point?

I have, I hope, made it clear that my spiritual inclinations were not such as could find easy satisfaction in the embrace of a particular teaching, or a trusted master. The takeaway from my years in the Osho movement had, rather, been a wariness about becoming attached to one particular infallible method or path. But it occurs to me that I did, after all, have a guru, a special source of strength. Briefly, my Guru was the Magic Café itself.

Each morning, after I'd parked up my little red van and let myself in through the front door, there would be a moment of fresh dedication, as I acknowledged my creation, this wonderful space.

"Morning Haff!"

"Morning m'Caff!".

Thus the greeting, the magical relationship restated. Here was an emanation of myself, my fantasy made manifest, now forming its own relationships amongst the community in which it had embedded; which had its own particular needs, underwent sudden crises and existential dramas, and which demanded total ongoing commitment. I imagine parenthood can be something like this.

An early morning arrival. Note the stained glass triptych – magic cauldron; storm in a teacup; angel cake – by Richard Pantlin.

"This is how I choose to spend my life". Each morning, a fresh moment of submission to the task, a still point on which to pivot.

Doubtless I had brought in with me the menu I had printed out the previous evening, posting it up in the window. Already I was primed for the day's fierce schedule of activities that would restate one more time the essential purpose of this establishment – to Feed the Heart.

My own heart, dedicated to this very purpose, drew strength from the familiar fixtures and fittings, the joyous play of colours. I moved down the shop, toppling the chairs from their overnight perches, arranging them neatly around the tables, noticing which might need replacement, my fingers making fleeting contact with each piece.

This was fundamentally a very intimate relationship, between the Café and myself. One becomes very sensitive to the pulse of the beloved, instantly aware when something is awry.

Sometimes it's very clear that there is a problem. A board attached to the front window is an immediate signal that something terrible has happened in the night. A brick has been thrown; shards of glass lie scattered across the carpet and sofa. A note has been pushed through the door, from the local constabulary, alerting me to wee small hours thievery. A busy trail of ants leading all the way back to the kitchen from their home in the window parasol plant suggests that my ideal of Buddhist coexistence needs to be reassessed.

Or it can be more subtle; the absence of a hum, the first inkling that there might be a malfunction with the power supply. *"Stay calm"* is my first injunction: here is a problem needing to be analysed . . . I make it my business to understand the rudiments of electrical circuitry.

As I pass through into the back of the shop, maybe there is a splash against my cheek – one more contribution to a spreading dampness across the floor. The plumbing in the upstairs flat is once again in need of attention – raising the prospect of an awkward three-way negotiation between myself, the residents, and the landlord.

A flood downstairs might present a far more serious challenge. The basement walls are not entirely impervious to the fluctuating subterranean streams – or perhaps recent flooding has overloaded the drainage network, so that the basement floor is many inches deep in dubious fluid.

Whatever the presenting problem, one thing remains certain: lunch will be served at 12 noon. There is food to be unloaded from the back of the van and, with the arrival of the first staff members, the day's menu will be outlined, the necessary tasks divided up. Knives are sharpened, a keen eye is kept on the clock. As each stage is completed, I check in with my schedule: *"Right; what's next?"* And so the day progresses, a succession of tasks to be fulfilled.

One day, out on the street, I fall into a conversation with Lama Wangyal. It's not every street that has as presiding spirit a proper Tibetan lama, but there he is, sharing a namaste, smiling benignly. Shortly after the Café set up, Thrangu House moved onto the street from its temporary base on Bullingdon Road. Lama is, in effect, a missionary, here not only to shepherd the small community of diaspora Tibetans washed up on these shores, but to spread the blessings of the Buddha's teaching in the benighted West. It's a vision ardently propagated by His Holiness the Dalai Lama,

Thrangu House in 2021

striving to make the best of Communist China's heedless crushing of Tibetan culture. The flower might be battered and scorned, but its seeds have spread on the wind, settling and rooting wherever they fall. Last time I visited Freiburg, we stopped by just such a garden of delight, Kailash House. Its Oxford equivalent has built up a warm relationship with the Magic, visitors attending for yoga and meditation courses frequently popping over the road for lunch or tea. Lama himself has a particular fondness for our freshly baked bread rolls.

Lama's mission has evidently been quite a challenge. Its twin objectives are hard to reconcile: a popular religious tradition profoundly rooted in cultural folklore, with a rich iconography of boddhisattvas and demons, vibrant sound and colours, offers a bewildering buffet of sensation to westerners anxious for the balm of spiritual clarity. Lamaistic training specializes in the art of rhetoric: sadly, Lama's grasp of English has never managed to do this justice, so that a conversation struggles to enter into the depths of debate. Nonetheless, on this occasion he wishes to share his perception of my constant activity: it is, he recognizes, dharma work – in Buddhist terms, right practice, in conformity with Buddhist teaching.

I like to think that the Magic Café has been blessed accordingly.

My connection with Thrangu House went back some years. I'd catered for several of their courses and gatherings, most memorably on a boat cruise along the Thames, over which Thrangu Rinpoche himself had presided, serenely seated atop the cabin whilst the riverside scenery drifted past.

The very first meal served at the Magic, even before the fitting out was yet complete, had been in honour of another visiting Rinpoche, Ringu Tulku. A plastic sheet was hung across the back of the shop to screen the builders' work in progress. The builders themselves had been quite miffed at this premature outing, but I was delighted. The glorious colours seemed so appropriate for the visiting dignitary. Here too, I felt a blessing had been bestowed.

Several years on, and that blessing began to make itself apparent. One evening, my friend Raga appeared at the door with a young man of striking appearance, with graceful features and long dark hair. This was Bino, she explained, from Tibet. He needs a job.

Coming to the Magic Café was a big turning point in my life. I was living in Brixton, in a bad way. And then – an angel appeared at my door . . . just when I needed to leave, to start something new.

Raga had gone upstairs to investigate a plumbing problem! The young man who opened the door turned out to be much more fascinating than copper pipes. He was evidently in the wrong place . . .

My first memory of the Magic Café: it was my second day in Oxford, I was wandering around, was an hour late, Hafiz was freaked . . .

Bino had spaced out on the clock change. Soon, though, it became clear that he was far from unreliable. As we settled into a working rhythm, I began to learn about his remarkable background. He had spent his entire childhood, from the age of six, in a monastery, training to become a monk. It had been many, many years since he had last seen his family, who lived in the remotest part of India, a corner of Tibet that had somehow been scooped up into the British Raj. When he reached 18, he had decided not to confirm his vows: the wide world beckoned.

Oxford became a playground, a compensation for his lost childhood and adolescence. I was so impressed by his apparent steadiness and focus, it didn't occur to me that sometimes he hadn't slept, or was still hung over from his night-time revelries; some days at lunchtime he stopped by at Simon's Yard, the hippie hangout just down the road, to share a spliff. One morning he didn't show up at all; instead he called me to explain that he was barely able to move. Things had gotten out of hand the previous evening; he and a mate had tried to blag their way into a city centre night club, had

fallen foul of the bouncer; he'd woken up in a police cell, bruised all over, his glasses shattered. I went to his flat to check him out and make sure that he had what he needed. After an hour or two his ex-girlfriend showed up to look after him. It was, I suppose, a learning experience.

We were all learning: I was learning what a difference it could make, working with someone who knew how to be fully focussed on the job in hand.

Round about this time one more waif and stray appeared at the door: yet another young Tibetan, newly arrived from India. This was Tenzin; might there be a job for him? Tenzin had very little English, so I was a bit sceptical. But maybe Bino could help with this? My mind was settled by Tenzin's resolute assertion, perhaps the limit of his vocabulary: *"I do it."*

Over time, as he gained in confidence from the steadying environment, working with friends and expanding his English, details of Tenzin's story began to emerge. Here was a young man who had been subjected to desperate adversity, surviving through astonishing fortitude and resilience. He was now in his early twenties; a decade or so ago he had been obliged to leave his home in Lhasa in a hurry – I understood that his father had been implicated in an uprising against the Chinese authorities, and that this might have ended badly for Tenzin also. He was placed with a refugee caravan intent on escaping over the Himalayas – on foot – to India. There he completed his education at Dharamsala, in a school run by the Tibetan refugee community. When this was over, what should he do? His Indian-issue pass provided him with few options. There were some difficult times, not to be lingered over. Eventually, with the encouragement of his uncle, himself a refugee now living in Oxford, resolved to reunite his scattered family, Tenzin procured a travel pass.

It wasn't a genuine document, as Tenzin made clear as soon as he arrived

Tenzin in high spirits, 2007

in England. Immigration Control was immediately intensely interested; by their own slow-moving standards it wasn't long before his application for asylum was rejected. Again, this was a dismal time, of endless waiting and disempowerment. Officially, he wasn't supposed to be working, and it wasn't made clear that he could apply for a support allowance. This was my first acquaintance with the punitive, careless bureaucracy of the asylum process. I affected to misunderstand my commitments as an employer – it seemed so unjust. At least in the Café Tenzin could be assured of some nurture, some self-respect.

By good fortune, and with the support of the local charity Asylum Welcome, his appeal case was handled by a highly committed and meticulous lawyer, who was able to elucidate Tenzin's compromised family background. Asylum was granted, with indefinite leave to remain; after a set number of years, Tenzin was able to become a UK citizen. Recalling this long, tortuous, but ultimately successful process, I feel quite emotional.

A tide was turning at the Magic Café. I'd been seeing a chiropractor for help with my sore back; bones were manipulated, spine reset, money handed over. After repeating this several times over, I got the message: I was simply asking too much of my physical self. I needed to treat myself more kindly, and acknowledge my limitations. Following a series of massages from my friend Supi, I made my first encounters with acupuncture – adjusting my energies on a more systemic level. The result was unexpectedly profound.

Bino, not long after he settled in, had realised I was habitually overdoing it:

> One day, Hafiz ran out of the kitchen screaming *"I need a holiday!"* I'd never seen anyone in such a state, he was so stressed . . .

After a few months there came a point where he felt able to say: *"I could do that"*. Fresh from my acupuncture, instead of my customary response – *"it's all much too complex for anyone else"*, I simply replied, *"OK"*.

Bino took over for one day each week. I used this time to write down all my recipes, methodically working through my repertoire so that they might be easily followed by someone from a different background and culture. Gradually this amassed into a comprehensive resource. Up to this point, my recipes had been very largely held in my head, or written in quasi-hieroglyphs on compact file cards.

I would arrive in the morning with the groceries, unpack, and go through the menu and recipes with Bino, making sure he understood the method. Then I went home, confident that all would be well. This really was progress.

Jo showed up round about this time, asking after a job. I'm not saying he came from Tibet; in fact he hailed from the West Country, by way of Australia. Still, his story seems to belong in this chapter. I'm sure he won't mind.

During our introductory chat, sitting at the long table, he told me he'd arrived in Oxford to start a course at Brookes, to study comparative religion. I recognised him right away as a seeker – by his air of tormented earnestness, constantly in a struggle with a natural sweetness and generosity. It takes one to know one! The academic approach, I knew, was sure to be a dismal disappointment. What he was really looking for was to be found right here, even if, for the moment, he could only help out part-time while his college fantasy played out.

Jo makes it clear what he has for breakfast

My journey of healing and self-care began in Australia just before moving to Oxford. I met a therapist in Sydney called Karima (I think) who had been close to Osho. A beautiful older lady who advised me to surround myself with people who are good for me. I knew she was an Osho sannyasin and then without knowing I found my-self in your kitchen! From there my seeking took off!

I could write a book on how my time at the Magic Café greatly contributed to the shape and direction my life has taken. So many warm and fun memories. Too many brownies and the fun-niest thing in all of it was that in my years work-ing in the kitchen with you, little did I know that I was learning how to run a professional kitchen, and subsequently worked as a chef for the following 15 years . . .

I have reflected often on the great fortune to have shared time and space with the wonderful team in the Magic Café.

The next Tibetan to arrive was Kabita. She had grown up in Nepal, in a small village clinging to the mountainside in Manang, a province adjacent to Tibet. Much of her adolescence had been spent in a convent, absorbing the intensely religious Tibetan culture. Somehow she had arrived in England – I've learned not to pry too closely into the mystery of why anyone might wish to abandon their native homeland; perhaps she simply wanted a change. Thrangu House in Oxford was a sister institution to her own alma mater, so that's where she gravitated to. And from thence, she came to the Magic.

It was a good place to encounter a wider world, and to make friends:

Yes, I really enjoyed working in Magic Café. I have lovely memories of it. I met so many lovely people there. As I am from Nepal, I met lovely Tibetans, French, Brazilians, American. I remember a French lady Lydia, American girl Jasmine and Brazilian girl called Cath I think,

I got along with them really well. It was genuinely good friendship between us. Yes, I also remember a girl from Bosnia, she was really funny. It was good experience for me working there, lunch hours were mostly very busy especially on weekends. Camilla was always very kind to me, I will never forget that! And you gave us a job when our situation was complicated that time. So I sincerely thank you for those opportunities. Magic Café will always be my fun memory.

Kabita in 2021

A diasporic community, in exile from its homeland and dispersed through many lands, generates its own network of connections. I had experienced something similar as a member of the Osho movement: there is an easy welcome, as if for a long-lost friend, for anyone who can claim a similar background – or sense of loss. Information is passed from contact to contact – recommendations and warnings, like gypsy symbols at the gate: friendly welcome here; avoid this doorway; scary dogs. The internet, together with the proliferation of mobile phones, has globalised this process, immensely speeded the dispersal of news. The Magic Café, so Bino tells me, is spoken of in far-off Taiwan as a worthwhile destination for Tibetans. Face-to-face meetings, though, are far preferable. Bino and Tenzin become regulars at the annual Tibetan Community gatherings on the Sussex Downs, in the vicinity of the ancient Battle Abbey. From time to time their compatriots drop by the Café, sharing the latest gossip from absent friends.

One day Bino arrives fired up with excitement. He has made contact with his home village of Mechukha, in the remote province of Arunachal Pradesh, for the first time in nine years! An Indian official with that new-fangled thing, a modem, is there supervising the completion of the new highway: 25 years under construction, the first road ever to connect Mechukha with the outside world. Now Bino absolutely has to go there – his mother will be so glad to see him!

I will be losing Bino's help for some time, but I rejoice to be a part of this homecoming process. There is a marvellous evening at the Vaults, to help raise funds for the journey, and to celebrate our special friend. Justin performs his magic tricks. I meet many remarkable people, all here to wish Bino well.

Deki in 2007

Deki turns up. She is Tenzin's cousin, arriving from Lhasa with her mother and brother (also Tenzin). Her father has at last succeeded in bringing his family to safety – but the sustained effort has destroyed his health. Shortly afterwards, he passes away; I attend the wake at Thrangu House.

Deki has been studying at a Chinese university in Chongqing, Sichuan – part of the official process of sinification, by which Tibetan culture is being stifled and suffocated. Now she starts at Brookes, learning accountancy. Meanwhile, she helps out at the Magic – the start of a sustained connection, which will eventually see her as joint proprietor. She is well organised and diligent – and also lots of fun, with a knack of bestowing memorable nicknames on her colleagues and friends.

Shortly afterwards, Jiu Xien appears. This sounds like *"Jushy"* when I say it; Deki always calls him Jig-Jig. He comes from Amdo County, on the high plateau of Northern Tibet – cowboy country, even if nowadays the motorbike is taking over from the horse as preferred means of transport; broad-brimmed hats are popular. A handsome fellow, he has caught the eye of a visiting Italian anthropologist, Patrizia. They got married; now her research has brought her to Oxford University. It's an opportunity for Jushy to learn English – and, of course, to help out at the Magic Café.

Later that year – 2005 – Jamji joins the team. He comes from yet another corner of Tibet – Kham province. It's worth recalling how enormous Tibet is. Since the Chinese took over, borders have been redefined to China's advantage, but it is often compared in size to Western Europe. My Tibetan friends, in short, come from widely separate locations, and, although they share a common language and culture, their mother tongue is likely to be quite distinct. Standard Tibetan is their lingua franca: as they work together in the kitchen, I enjoy their incomprehensible chatter; now and again I catch a familiar word or phrase, like a fragment of modernity interpolated into ancient discourse.

Jamji had been one year in England before he arrived in Oxford, to visit the teacher with whom he commenced learning English in Tibet. As soon as he stepped off the bus on High Street, he was enraptured: by the beautiful old buildings, by the special atmosphere of the city. He has the sensibilities of a born artist: his recollections of that time are full of specific smells, sensations, sounds, colours – how could he not enjoy being in the Magic Café?

It was one of the best parts of my life when I was working at the Magic Café. I met such amazing interesting people. Also I was quite new in the UK so I learned lots of things about the UK. I was very lucky to work with Hafiz. We had so much fun. I used to work Monday and Saturday. Every morning when we prepare the lunch I used to make salads and I peel oranges. The orange smell made me so fresh in the early morning. And we listened to very beautiful classic music while we prepare the food. And early morning I remember the Sun coming through the window and the classic music and the smells of coriander and parsley. And Hafiz likes to tell stories – whatever we asked him he can tell us about the history and music. He likes talking and chatting, he is such an amazing man sometimes he forgets what he put on the stove and burned because he is so into our conversation. 😊

Jamji performing at the 10th Anniversary party

Can it be true, that I lost track of my cooking? I'm sure he is just pulling my leg! But I was certainly fascinated to hear his stories.

Jamji was indeed a born artist. His father was the valley's go-to man for temple art and restoration – a hereditary craft by which the iconographic traditions so essential to Tibetan Buddhist practice were passed on through the generations. He was in great demand following the systematic wrecking of monasteries during the Cultural Revolution. From him, Jamji learnt the secrets of tanka painting – the meticulous cosmographic mandalas conceptualising the order of creation – and the correct manner of sculpting and depicting the various arhats and boddhisattvas, the honoured temple guardians.

Music was also a fascination, sufficient for him to embark on a quest to find a master with whom he might study. He trekked through the mountains . . . across the border into India, all the way to Himalpradesh, near Ladakh, where he met his guru. Then he set off back home – a wandering vagabond. He was apprehended by Chinese police, who made sure he was put safely under lock and key: imprisoned without charge, for an indefinite stay. Only by desperate stratagem – convincing his jailors that he had a terrible contagious disease – did he manage to escape.

The Kalachakra seed syllable, or Tenfold Powerful One

All of this he has brought with him to the West. His artwork is a wonderful glimpse of an ancient tradition, still flowing through his fingers. Some of it was exhibited in the Café; I bought one picture, a stylised mantra, still adorning my study wall.

He played his flute for us one time, also, for our 10th birthday celebration. I think he is too shy with this – perhaps it is too imperfect a rendering of the music he hears in his soul. I heard something very special: haunting, delightful.

He was my favourite companion on a Saturday afternoon, as we wound down from the intensity of a busy morning and lunchtime. The café more or less emptied out, allowing us to tidy up in the kitchen, making sure everything was cleaned and in its proper place – and to share our stories.

And on Saturday evening when we close the café, sometimes there is lots of milk left in the jug. And I used to drink it all because I don't want to throw away. Sometimes we have to throw away some left food. And I used to say "SORRY GOD" when I throw leftover food in the bin. Because in Tibet we believe there is a food God, a fire God, water god and earth God . . . If you throw away lots of food and waste food or play with food, then we believe the food god will be disappointed in you. Then in the future you won't get good food. In Tibet, when children don't eat their food, we tell them "Se Lha Nyam". That means, God will be disappointed in you.

And I told that to Hafiz. After that whenever he threw some food in the bin he says "SORRY GOD" 😄 😄 😄 *That was so good.*

All this Tibetan-ness deserves to be celebrated: I help Tenzin prepare a meal for a special evening. Then, in the summer of 2005, it occurs to me to lend Bino the Café while Camilla and I take a holiday. It will be his own business, so he won't need to repay any VAT, hence make some good money. The café stays open, too, which keeps everybody happy.

THE RETURN OF
CAFÉ BINO

FOR TWO WEEKS ONLY !
FROM 7TH TO 19TH AUGUST

The Magic Café will be taking a break,
so that the boss can enjoy a summer holiday.
Do not panic ! Bino will be here instead,
offering a unique café experience.

OPENING MONDAY TO SATURDAY
10 AM - 6 PM
Featuring:
Eastern and Continental lunch menus
Exotic breakfasts
Coffee and cakes
Delightful atmosphere

COME AND LET YOURSELVES BE PAMPERED
BY BINO AND HIS GALLANT CREW

The Magic Café will return, fully rested,
on Monday 21st August

While I'm gone Bino invites all his Tibetan friends to help out; he gets to practise running a kitchen team. We repeat this experiment the next year – it's a big success. People are still talking about his watermelon curry!

I've discovered a journal from that time, and it is full of anxiety and self-recrimination; I worry about money, and that Bino appears to be earning more than me. The Old Nag is still hard at it! Nonetheless, even here there is a shift in emphasis. I'm feeling far less hemmed in, making space for personal development, and looking forward to fresh initiatives, stepping off the too-familiar treadmill. It has made a big difference, not being obliged to spend each and every day at work, with my hands constantly busy in the cake-mix.

And when I am in my Magic Space, I am sustained by the gift of friendship – from all of these wonderful people who have engaged so full-heartedly in this project. There has been a shift, too, in the quality of staff commitment – a greater willingness to absorb the discipline of the task, less of a hurry to move on to the next thing. Not only Bino, but Tenzin too is enthusiastically mastering my recipes, developing skills that will stand them both in good stead. When Bino moves to Brighton for a while, Tenzin takes over as Friday chef.

In China, possession of this marvellous image – the Tibetan national flag – would constitute a serious criminal offence.

"The Tibetans", so various in their character and backgrounds, share in the misfortune of having had their ancestral homeland ripped from their control. In the 1950s the Chinese Red Army had swept across the frontier to impose its authority, in the name of the imagined deity of historical materialism: feudalism must be swept away, liberating the downtrodden Tibetan peasantry to participate in a glorious new dawn. In the clear light of day, "Communism with Chinese Characteristics" is revealed as curiously similar to Western materialism. What emerged in England over the course of centuries, following the reordering of society at the Reformation – the destruction of the monasteries and the theocratic ordering of society; the repurposing of accumulated wealth towards worldly ends; the development of industrial technique; the ever-more aggressive thirst for new markets; and the enforced proletarianization of traditional cultures, both at home and in colonies abroad – has in China taken place at reckless, breakneck speed.

For Tibet and its unique culture this has been an immense catastrophe, a tsunami; I sense the waves still lapping up the Magdalen Road.

A photo of the Dalai Lama graces our kitchen shelf. Here is a man with true courage – vilified by the Chinese state as a "splitter". He is a sort of spiritual Tank Man, standing in the path of Irresistible Might; in his hand no more than a small bag of essentials, the ancient Buddhist teachings distilled into a single word – kindness.

In 2008 the Dalai Lama came to Oxford: a precious opportunity for all the local Tibetans to meet their hero and inspiration. For some this would not be possible: one academic I spoke with at a party – our conversation masked by party hubbub – told me of his worries for his family back in Beijing, should such transgressive behaviour reach official ears; he was obliged to keep his distance. Non-Tibetans would have no such worries – though they might have wondered at the array of saffron-clad protesters lining the street outside the Sheldonian Theatre, holding placards denouncing the Dalai Lama for inexplicable offences against their own dogma.

Could it be that these sectaries, devotees of the Shugden faith, appearing in force at each of HH's appearances in the UK, were being sponsored by the Chinese government?

The Dalai Lama kept his audience, his Western fanbase, waiting. First of all, he would meet his own dear people, in a private session at nearby Queens College. As they gather round him, he registers that one particular face is missing: *"Where is my friend from Lhasa?"* He is looking for Mr Dakar, Deki's father, Tenzin's uncle, the first Tibetan to settle in Oxford.

What is his special message for this select gathering? Simply that we are all human beings, rich or poor; just do your job well; everyone has the chance to be a good human. One day we will go home.

Present in this photo with HH the Dalai Lama: front row, second left, Deki's mother Neema; Deki, fourth from left; Tenzin, third from right, in grey robe; centre, Lama Wangyal, in red robe; Bino, back row, with wife Amelia and daughter Semkyi; in front of them, Patrizia and Jiu Xien (with golden scarf)

The World in my Kitchen

There's some stability now to the crew, with all this Tibetan bedrock. I can enjoy the sense of a wider horizon that my Tibetan friends bring to the kitchen. They have grown up under deep blue skies, ridden the wide prairies, imbibed the air gusting from the high Himalayas. The Magic Café becomes a meeting place for people from many lands.

East Oxford has always attracted people from far and wide. In the beginning, there had been Morris Motors, bringing Henry Ford-style mass production to Britain, drawing workers like a magnet from all corners of the kingdom. The fields from the Plain all the way up to Cowley filled out with streets and estates. Twice a day a stream of bicycles carried their riders to and from the factory. Old Mr Silvester, in the hardware store just across the road, remembered that time with nostalgia. Business had been brisk back in the day.

More recently, the population has diversified yet further, along with the economic base, and a rich cosmopolitan culture has grown up along the Cowley Road. Nonetheless, there's still a strong sense of "Town and Gown": a tension between the ancient sense of entitlement wielded by the University colleges, for the benefit of their transient student population, and the emerging multi-facetted communities, so vibrant and various.

I'd never envisaged the Magic Café as a student locale – there were more than enough of those already – but access to academia was by no means the only reason why young people might be drawn to Oxford. Chief amongst these would be: to have an adventure. Oxford – East Oxford, too – exerts a lure on curious spirits. And the Magic Café, once they had chanced upon it, would provide the quintessence of what they were looking for. Should they be tempted to stick around for a longer time in this marvellous city, a job here would provide the ideal mooring post.

Amongst the cascade of names on my staff timeline are many whose presence on the team was brief, fleeting, but perhaps those few weeks or months are remembered as one of the special experiences of youth, to be savoured long after their travelling days are done.

Deja, for example, spent several weeks with us back in the year 2000. She'd come to Oxford as part of her Big Adventure, reckoning that most likely the time would soon come when travelling would simply be too difficult. She'd picked out the Café from the Green Pages directory; gave me a call asking after a job, so I was waiting for her to show up.

Where was she? My eyes were looking in the wrong place! Deja, I discovered, was little taller than my serving counter. Scoliosis, a degenerative affliction of the spinal cord, caused her constant pain – but she was determined that it wouldn't crush her spirit. That was something inspiring for us!

Off she went – back to Vancouver, British Columbia. Whilst writing this chapter I got to wondering about her. Her unusual name – her parents were hippies who named her after their favourite LP! – made her surprisingly easy to track down. I was delighted to discover that she now has an 8 year old son – already taller than she is.

Deja with her son Hunter – plus ice cream!

Hello Hafiz! How lovely to hear from you. I often think of you when I have classical music on, especially whilst I am cooking!

And thats very cool that you are writing a book! I still lovingly use your 4 Seasons cookbooks! I had to convert the measurements to cups and teaspoons for my Canadian ways. But I love your salad with fennel! And my boy and I love the Million Dollar bars of course! You have such yummy recipes! Is your book going to be an Autobiography? Will it include more recipes? I am eager to see it when it is complete! You are one special man who has a lot of wisdom and I know you have encountered many amazing individuals and have had many wonderful adventures and hard trials in life too. I do feel blessed I was ones to have crossed paths with you for sure!

My memories are stronger from those final few years. My life had become less frantic, more measured, and the composition and dynamic of the Magic Café team shifted accordingly. Something remarkable emerged: a Brazilian-Polish-Tibetan-British nexus, that generated a trans-cultural conversation, an inspirational model of collaboration

I had learned to recognise what I was looking for, as I met a new prospect for the first time, sitting together at the long table. We would chat, and I would check in with my feelings. If we had already gotten so far, most likely I was already curious, intrigued. I'd encourage them to open up a little bit . . .

What strange chance has brought them to this particular door? What point have they reached on their journey, that makes this particular port of call feel so right? What stories might this person be willing to share?

With each fresh addition to the team, there is a corresponding shift in the group dynamic. New perspectives open up, and our shared fund of experience develops deeper resonance.

The ideal is to encourage a free flow of creative energy, a joyous inter-action. A happy kitchen will light up the whole café, infuse the food with a special sweetness, and send those good vibrations rippling out into the community.

How might that feel, for a young person just arrived from somewhere quite different? From Poland, say, still in a ferment of change following the recovery of national self-determination, opening up to new possibilities, asking questions that had long been off limits? Dominika, following in the footsteps of her good friend Dorota, arrived in Spring 2006, just a couple of years after Poland's accession to the European Union. She had grown up in the city of Wroclaw, where she had recently completed her studies in anthropology at the university.

Learning just this much about her background, I was already fascinated. Wroclaw, as Breslau, had been an integral part of Hitler's Reich, and before that, the second largest city in the Kingdom of Prussia, a major source of its wealth. In fact, it had changed hands many times during the course of history, and its population, along with its name, had shifted accordingly. Most recently there had been a comprehensive reset: at the end of the second world war it had been thoroughly smashed up and looted by the Soviet army; then it had been allotted to Poland, as some compensation for lands sliced away in the East. Entire communities were uprooted, trekking westwards to take up residence in battered homes just recently vacated by fleeing German families. Wroclaw University itself was, very largely, a reconstituted version of Lvov University, now lost to Ukraine. From this perspective, recent European history looks very different: fraught and tragic. Boundaries, loyalties, values – the sense of belonging, of identity – all is provisional, prone to disruption and betrayal. I need to remember that the name of Winston Churchill, who abandoned the Poles to this fate, plays entirely differently on Polish ears.

So much for my lecturing . . . let's hear from Dominika.

> *When I entered Magic Café for the first time, it was as if I had crossed the threshold into another world. The overwhelming smell of food, spices, perfect music and people who were there by chance. After talking to you Hafiz for the first time, I knew I had come to a place where I could slow down and learn, learn to live and be myself. I was just finishing my studies and I was afraid of the race for positions, for a job, I did not know who I was and what I wanted.*
>
> *Magic Café allowed me to see the world from a better side, work – yes, it is good, it is needed, but only if it brings happiness to you and others. That was the job at Magic Café. It gave me time to get to know myself and the world – a microcosm where Tibetan singing and good-naturedness mixed with Brazilian samba, Polish folk, Sufi wisdom and everything was completed by Victorian English, which I loved to listen to. Magic Café was a small world where I learned humility, peace and compassion straight from Tibet, where I learned the lightness of life and dance from Brazil, where I learned to search for the world and myself by listening to your Hafiz stories about Berlin, Pune and punk rock.*
>
> *I will never forget when Hafiz explained to Tenzin what punk rock is by dancing and singing Sex Pistols' Anarchy in England in the middle of the lunch time. And yet the music was not only the background of our work and talks, it set the pace, perfectly matched to the time of day, provoked discussions and events. Thanks to our talks about*

music, I found the best festival that I could dream of – Womad!

I remember that we were often occupied with discussions about the history of our world, you liked telling us about great English battles and conquests. Customers always looked into the kitchen with curiosity – what is also happening there when no one serves us?

I remember how the queue at the buffet was overwhelming us, it started to get nervous because it was Saturday's breakfast – everyone wanted their eggs, and then Rodrigo took me from his embrace and started dancing samba (Mama Africa song). All the tension was gone, everyone started laughing. I remember learning songs in English, Portuguese, Polish and Tibetan one by one. I remember a monk who used to come for the leftovers of dinner, always saying he didn't need anything, it was too much. I have always had a tendency to put too much on my plate, and you have calmly corrected me conscientiously, finally I understood that much was not better.

Dominika busy with the evening clean up

I remember how two old ladies came to the gossip and sat down at the buffet, for us it was the time after lunch, when the music was louder and we were cleaning, the ladies were very dissatisfied with the loud music, several times demanded that it be turned down, I lowered it bowing obeisances. In the end, you Hafiz got pissed off, turned the music to full blast and ran to the toilet. I realized that you don't always have to be service-minded and meet the expectations of others, and that sometimes it's worth saying no!

I remember a lot of our customers, Mister Soup and Roll, Miss Soya Decaf Latte – as we used to call them. I remember a very demanding lady who had complaints about something all the time, one day she gave us a fire, but the next day we found a letter of apology from her. Magic Café taught compassion.

I remember how there were phone calls with various offers and they always wanted to talk to the manager, and then you Hafiz made the decision – today Tenzin will be the manager. The feeling that we are equal, that we are a community and that it is possible to work in this way, in mutual respect and understanding the needs of the other, without hierarchy and artificial titles, accompanied me throughout a wonderful year at Magic Café. To this day, I believe that only in such an atmosphere of friendship and love can really good food be produced. And your love for Camilla, as you always said beautifully about her, is the one.

Thanks to you, Hafiz, I gave up eating meat and realized how rich and fantastic a vegetarian diet is. Of course, you taught me how to prepare meals, the importance of mindfulness, sequence and accuracy.

My studies of anthropology and culture removed me from spirituality, I looked at it as another theory to unravel. Thanks to my work at the Magic Café and my friendship with you and the guys, I started looking for spirituality again. I went to India for six months.

One day Dominika contributed a favourite CD to our playlist, which immediately became my favourite too. It's a recording of the Jamaican reggae band, the Twinkle Brothers, jamming with the Trebunia Family Band, musicians they'd met whilst passing through the Tatra mountains, on the border between Slovakia and Poland. This infectiously joyous collision of roots reggae with Central European folk dance is the very essence of cultural interplay, the soundtrack of our shared experience. Here, boundaries no longer shift – they have simply collapsed.

Then there is the Brazilian dimension. During my commune days I'd come to love the lilting Brazilian accent: swaying and playful, already halfway to becoming a song. I'd never met a graceless or grumpy Brazilian; however Jair Bolsonaro came to power remains an utter mystery. Surely this was the land of Pelé, of Antonio Carlos Jobim, of samba dance, capoeira and candomblé? As always, things are not so simple. There is a lot of darkness and tragedy in Brazilian history – slavery was abolished only in 1888, and its legacy remains profound. When I think about the Brazilians I have known, both in the Commune and working together in the Magic Café, what strikes me is their conscious choice to embody the best of their culture. There is a struggle to be endured, but no doubt where fun is to be found: in playfulness and in generosity of spirit.

Rodrigo at the Café farewell party

I had experienced this already with Michelli and with Catarina; with Rodrigo this energy was overflowing. If anything, Rodrigo was the conscious embodiment of good humour, his very presence in the room demanding an instinctive smile. I came to understand that he had imbibed this attitude with his mother's milk; propagating this was to become his life's mission. How fortunate we were to have him with us!

Strength, and resource, derives from the community. There is an obligation to contribute, with whatever one has. His gift was always the sense of delight in existence. Look! – it is snowing! – he has never seen such a thing before, and so, for us too, it is amazing, wonderful . . .

So many memories, so many stories – where to start?

One of the things that made Magic Café so magical was the sense of community. Not just connecting to the clients and knowing their names and stories, but the "internal community".

The people who worked there were more connected than many families. We knew each other's challenges, joys, birthdays and beyond. I remember when I was invited to make momos, the traditional Tibetan style pot sticker, with the Tibetan community. I think it was someone's birthday and they needed extra help. While we were making them, we were also chatting and laughing. A true sense of community.

Rafiz was also a community leader of sorts. Not just because he was the owner of the café, but he had (and I am sure still has) a beautiful way of sharing things, teaching us about the English culture or other things to us – the immigrants. We used to laugh trying to pronounce something in English when we were learning a new word or expression

194

from Rafiz. We learned how to cook many different dishes together, clean together, and serve together.

All of this gave me the sense of being part of an amazing community, where everybody did pretty much everything together.

And to this day, Magic Café is the best place I have ever worked – and Rafiz, the most magical boss of all!

I'm sure Rodrigo, cheeky fellow that he is, is deliberately mis-spelling my name. Perhaps this is connected to the Brazilian tendency to pronounce an R more like an H. Well, it's a theory. The next Brazilian to arrive, Renan, advised us to speak his name accordingly. Largely, though, we used the name Deki had bestowed – X-Man, on account of his many brightly coloured tattoos. Tall and gangly, with long, carefully plaited dreadlocks, he would make an immediate impression even with his shirt on. His smile alone would warm the room.

He was playing bass in a prog band. But really, what he liked was speed metal. And, of course, beautiful women. He was here in Oxford on a sort of coming-of-age adventure. I was happy to help out. His favourite schoolteacher had implanted the desire to attend the summer solstice celebrations at Stonehenge, so I gave him every encouragement. It was a glorious dawn – even without the wild hippie mayhem of yesteryear. Then he and Deki went to Glastonbury festival and had a lot of fun.

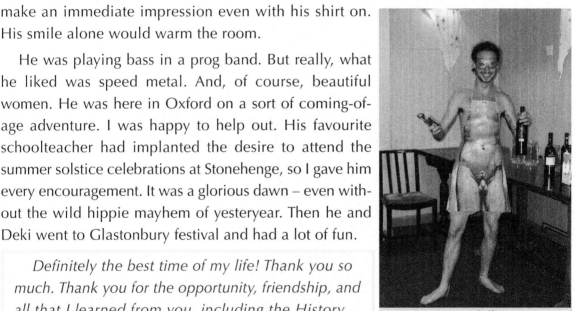

Renan modelling non-standard protective gear

Definitely the best time of my life! Thank you so much. Thank you for the opportunity, friendship, and all that I learned from you, including the History lessons, they were great.

By the time our period of working together was drawing to a close, he was harbouring a guilty secret: his work permit had expired. When he finally fessed up, I wasn't too surprised: I'd become familiar in commune times with the difficulties faced by Brazilians wishing to remain in Europe. Some had been able to claim Italian citizenship by virtue of having an Italian grandparent. Marriage of convenience was another strategy. Sometimes they had simply changed location from time to time to keep ahead of the game. Such is the tyranny of borders! It would be hard to consider my friends as desperate criminals. Evidently, neither did I consider myself as such.

I had benefitted so much from Britain's membership of the European Union. Hassle-free travel had allowed the European Rajneesh Commune to flourish, freely exchanging members between England, Holland, Germany, Italy . . . Certainly, eyebrows had been raised at the Dutch frontier, on my first trip to Freiburg, but that had been the extent of official concern. Work permits had been obtained with the minimum of fuss. What a triumph of visionary statesmanship it had been, to enable all of this!

We all rejoiced when the Berlin Wall was ripped asunder. Shortly afterwards, I was able to travel across into the Eastern Zone. There were still guards at the former frontier, but now beneath their peaked caps they were smiling broadly, waving us through. Some years later, once again visiting that city, I had been able to wander freely around a city once more united, free from roadblocks and impenetrable walls, all the insidious paraphernalia of oppression. It felt profoundly changed: reintegrated, no longer shy of embracing its shadow.

In the early years of this century, as the states of Central and Eastern Europe were welcomed into the European Union, all of us benefitted from an extended sense of identity. The Polish corner shops on the Cowley Road – Polski Sklep – that was us too. I remember the excitement of welcoming Romanians into the Café. And the joy of having Dorota and Dominika contributing their special essence to the kitchen team. But when Korana, from war-torn Bosnia, came asking for a job, what should I say? She is here on her own adventure, questing her own version of something else; could I really just slam the door shut?

Doubtless inspired by my daily communion with such creative spirits from around the world, I conceived a new project, to keep me busy through my unaccustomed downtime. I plotted out a second series of the Magic Cookbook: four more booklets, this time organised around the principle of geographical region. I would divide my recipes between North, South, East and West. And I thought of a wonderful means of navigation.

Selim drifted into my imagination, sitting cross-legged on a colourful kilim, purchased in the bazaar at Constantinople, beneath the towering minarets and soaring dome of the ancient Aya Sophia, temple of holy wisdom. It is a magic carpet, on which he journeys above many lands, dreaming of food; setting down from time to time for a splendid feast, before resuming his roving quest. The recipes in each booklet amount to a sort of "captain's log", all carefully quantified and elucidated, along with a light garnish of quasi-mystical musing.

It would be easy to see Selim as a signifier for myself; I have no problems with this interpretation. I thoroughly enjoyed our travels together, as depicted so delightfully by Camilla. Each illustrative challenge was triumphantly surmounted: jolly festival wellies; a green man peering through tangled foliage; a Bayeux Tapestry tree; a dancing Krishna; a Chinese dragon; a swooping crane . . .

The booklets appeared annually, with the final instalment ready at the end of 2008. They sold from the counter in a steady trickle, just like the previous Four Seasons booklets. I'd confidently had printed a substantial number of each, at Green Print just down the road; down in the basement the stack of boxes was accumulating. For Selim's final adventure, I saw fit to reduce my order – just 500 copies. Something was telling me to step on the brakes.

There's a distinct valedictory quality to this last booklet – South. Of course, I realised that the series was coming to a close, and that my beloved Selim deserved a fitting finale. On this final adventure, the element of quest is heightened: he is driven by a promise of "the treasure that lies waiting for you at the end of the world", and he is given an enchanted key with which he might unlock this secret. While he flies above the desert sands, the oases and caravanserais, he dreams of his favourite dishes: dolmades, spanakopitas, tabouleh, falafels, tzatziki, basboosa, date and ginger fool . . .

As we turn the final page, the end of the world makes itself apparent:

On the Beach

Finally, the last sand-dune has been traversed, and ahead lies only the ocean, sparkling in the fiery sunshine. Half-buried in sand, lapped around by waves, Selim notices a carved wooden chest, and instinctively clutches at the silver key hanging at his breast. The treasure at the end of the world!

He can wait no longer, the key is turned, up springs the lid. A rush of released pressure knocks him clean over, and when he staggers back to his feet, there is Suleiman the Djinn, grinning mischievously from earring to earring.

"It's all yours", says the Djinn, pointing at the gleaming contents of the treasure chest. "Here are your precious memories, each shining like a gold piece, each a joy to handle, engraved with symbols only you can decypher. Nice of you to drop by."

"Wait a minute," reflects Selim. "This treasure I have already, but still I have my unanswered question . . . what I really want to know is . . . what's for afters?

"Ho Ho Ho . . ." Suleiman laughs a deep rolling laugh, radiating outwards like ripples upon the ocean, sparkling like flashing jewels, reverberating and booming with the surf, becoming a golden haze fragrant with musk and spices . . . and then they are gone, and there is only the sun, sinking steadily down into the eternal ocean.

Party Time!

All through this enchanted decade, Jon, whom we met earlier organising the Magic Arts programme at the Asian Cultural Centre, had been attracting people to regular events at his home in the village of Elsfield, just outside Oxford. By a combination of persistence and good fortune he had managed to secure possession – for an extended moment, at least – of a substantial thatched cottage, complete with attached ten acre nature reserve. It was the ideal location for a small artists' community, an idyllic environment to raise his children, and a fabulous venue for community gatherings and parties.

Jon and I had recognised one another as magic brothers. Just as I envisaged the true purpose of communal eating to be inherently sacramental, so was he inspired by the potential for transcendence in a group of people gathered together in focussed activity. Parties at Garden Cottage would always feature some sort of ritual, generally reflecting the progression of the seasons and informed by mythological tradition. It was all quite light-hearted: there would be an opportunity for dressing up, with perhaps a fairy-lit procession through the woodlands, followed by a cosmic drama of sorts in which all, should they so wish, might participate. In the aftermath, a circle would gather around the sacred bonfire, well stoked in bonhomie and camaraderie.

Pete Galpin was a regular performer at the Magic Café. Here he's playing at the Elsfield Bonfire, shortly after personifying Orpheus.

Food would be a bring-and-share banquet, an opportunity for me to experiment with some new dish – always well-received! These were for me happy occasions, on which I could check in with my friends on a more personal basis than in the midst of the café hustle and bustle. There was indeed considerable crossover

199

between Elsfield regulars and Magic Café customers. Here too was a con-sciously orchestrated exercise in community building.

What, after all, is the point of a party? Whether it be a wild rumpus or a more structured coming-together, somebody will have spent time and energy organising it; perhaps, like Jon, creating elaborate artworks to support the intended theme. Most likely they will find it difficult to abandon themselves to the intensity of the moment that they have so artfully engineered, drawing their satisfaction instead from witnessing the success of their enterprise – a brightly coloured stone skilfully flung, casting ripples out across the com-munal pool.

Thus is the world reshaped and renewed: there is an invitation to enter into an inchoate zone, where boundaries might be dissolved, hidden depths fathomed, new connections drawn. You might make a new friend, or simply let go your cares in a life-enhancing bop.

Parties can be quite demanding, even for the guest: I do regret frequently being much too tired to appreciate Jon's achievement to the full. In commit-ting myself to the Magic Café, I needed to reserve the major part of my creative energies for my chosen project. These were years in which my danc-ing feet remained still, my guitar gathered dust, and the energetic meditation techniques I'd once championed became no more than a curious memory, recalled for the amusement of my staff.

To be honest, I did feel some nostalgia for the carefree times of yesteryear, as I observed the human drama unfolding from my vantage point looking through the kitchen hatchway.

For many people, the Café was the kicking off point for a wild party, every Friday night. But the party wasn't at the Café – it was at Don's House, just around the corner.

I'd got to know Don as a colleague of Craig and Elise; he was the brains behind the Oxford Green Party's electoral success. He was certainly a clever guy, who had earned a lot of money configuring Java programming – but he was also a maverick genius, for whom rationality was just a bit too dull.

At our Friday night suppers, he acted the life and soul of the party, offer-ing a template for good-humoured indulgence. When I stopped offering the suppers, the party moved over to Don's – morphing into a sustained bacchanale, stretching long into the night. Don was done with the long march of ecological campaigning; now he championed cultural transformation as the revolutionary road. Hedonism, he announced with missionary zeal, was the true way forward. I don't recall him ever quoting William Blake, but his approach was essentially thus:

The road of excess leads to the palace of wisdom; for we never know what is enough until we know what is more than enough.

I liked Don, and enjoyed his company when he dropped by the Café. I was amused by his deliberately outrageous claims – it was from him that I first heard that the Apollo moon landings never actually happened. It was a challenge, a come on – but I wasn't going to get drawn in. I'd already done all that crazy stuff! I went one time to the party, but by midnight I was heading home . . . it was pumpkin time, and I needed to get myself rested and ready for a busy Saturday. As I left, a troupe of drummers came marching down the street, beating out an energetic tattoo. Poor neighbours!

For all those good people who became habitués of the Friday night revels, I understand that this libertine environment could be life-changing, disclosing unsuspected avenues of experience. The house itself had been transformed into a trompe l'oeil playground. One door opened onto a woodland glade straight out of fairyland; another into an enveloping, well-cushioned crimson womb; the downstairs loo was a dayglo grotto, with gnomes and kobolds peering out from a

Don Smith astride his subterranean throne
Photo by kind permission Oxford Mail

tangle of tree roots. It was a good place to get out of your head.

I see Don as a "Giver of Permission", and a Trickster. Both of these roles are valuable and transformative – and also perilous. Powerful forces are unleashed. For me, Veeresh and Frank Natale – Osho too – had performed these functions: I will be forever grateful. They had each striven to create a Magic Theatre in which (so to speak) the Emergency Exit was well enough sign-posted. Could it be that Don was incautious of the risks he subjected himself

201

to? His unexpected early death – mourned by so many, including myself – casts his story in a more sombre light. RIP.

It was interesting to mull this over with Bernadette, now back in her native upstate New York. She had been helping out at the Magic – on and off – for many years. In that time when life hadn't yet cohered into a steady narrative, the Magic Café had provided a place of refuge.

> *For me, The Magic Café is a big, big piece of the pie that is my heart! Every second was so deeply profound to me in every way . . . I haven't ever tried to understand why, I just know it is, and will always love and cherish my time there! It was like home to me. It was a safe space, a familiar place and a place I truly loved.*

Bernadette enjoying a wild time at Don's

She was a regular at Don's parties – and also, curiously, had attended workshops at the Humaniversity. Both had left her feeling wary, cautious of the unbounded licence. Compared to which, participating in the Café as a team member suited her far better:

> *Thank you for teaching me so much, not just about cooking and serving and just being, but for . . . well, actually, yes, just being! That has been my biggest education to date, not to say, I haven't had other experiences that have educated and formed me, I have, but not like that. Not with grace, you have extreme grace in your being and presence that permeates and that's why everyone loved you and wanted to be around you. I've never experienced it since, but I still search for such souls!*

For Bernadette, the Café was her Magic Theatre. Okay – sometimes it felt like running a circus, too: me the ringmaster, with so many star performers, each with their own idiosyncrasies and special skills. How strange, that these amazing people were content to be busy in my kitchen washing dishes and chopping vegetables.

Kathy was another who contributed to the team spirit, on and off over many years. Lucy (we'll come back to her later) recalls:

> the laughter that would bubble up whenever Kathy was there with us – and the way that she would tell a story – just anything that had happened to her – in a way that was irresistibly, delightfully, and sometimes shockingly funny.

Whoever thought a job could be this much fun?

> **Kathy:** My favourite job ever! I LOVED working with the lovely Magic Café team. It never felt like I was going to work, only like I was passing a happy day with friends, chatting and listening to music while being happily engaged in veg chopping. You created an amazing place to work and be, Hafiz. Thanks for inviting me to be part of it.

Also an intermittent regular was Sharron Kraus, a woman of rare talent. She had originally come to Oxford to pursue her enquiries into difficult philosophy, but it had become clear that her true calling was to music – specifically that edgy genre, "dark folk". Here was a far more effective means of exploring the secret recesses of the soul. Her compositions spin a web of enchantment, drawing us deep into the forest shadows, esoteric dramas of destiny and fate. I was astonished when I first heard her perform, one Saturday lunchtime: her voice at once tentative and deliberate, vulnerable, reaching towards the edge of mystery – just her and her plangent finger-picking banjo.

Sharron performing at Andy and Naomi's wedding, 2010

Part-time employment suited her well, with a boss who regarded her presence in the kitchen as a privilege, and took a relaxed view of her occasional absences, while she went on tour in various parts of the world.

> I have lots of happy memories of working in the café – mostly of making good friendships and having interesting conversations whilst chopping veg!

I remain disappointed that Dolly Parton still hasn't recorded Sharron's song "Twins", a dark tale of incestuous amour in the deepest part of the wood. Had Sharron's Café experience contributed to her oeuvre? Her second CD

203

features the track "Angelica Caraway", a romantic ballad of unrequited love inspired by the jars on my spice shelf. It's an honour!

Photo: Kate Raworth

I was always happy to see Edward Pope coming through the door. Here was someone who takes great delight in whatever life has to offer; who does his best to share that delight with whomever might be willing. Passion Cake was his regular indulgence.

I used to enjoy the Saturday lunchtime music in the Magic, specially when it was Sharron Kraus. Not sure if I ever did one of those slots myself . . . The Magic Café seems to figure in my memory as a place where dates often met. I had one there I chickened out of by hiding in the toilet and another that started well but ended disastrously (for both of us). I'm not sure if your memoir wants these sort of stories though!

Andy Letcher must hold the record for most inappropriately qualified washer-upper – two PhDs, for goodness' sake – but once again here was someone with an ambivalent relationship with the intellect. He would much rather be a bard – or at least a Scholar Gypsy. Wisdom was, he recognised, to be found not so much within the pages of a book but in lived experience. He would speak of his studies at the University of the Hedge – even whilst part-timing as a lecturer in Comparative Religion at Brookes University. His most esteemed teachers, so he claimed, were his Welsh Friends – by which he meant, the magic mushroom *psilocybe semilanceata*, also known as the liberty cap. This was no idle boast: he had been commissioned by Faber & Faber to write an authoritative overview of the subject, to be published as "Shroom".

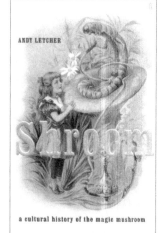

a cultural history of the magic mushroom

Needless to say, working with Andy provided much opportunity for fascinating conversation. Perhaps some of this fed into his book – I'm glad to be included in his list of acknowledgements. Some of our debates still continue in my mind, forever unresolved. He is tangling with the mystery of consciousness, as illuminated by the psychedelic experience. In his book, so it seems to me, he is torn between the scientific method and the implosion of rationality which is the mushroom's gift. I imagine he too is still trying to work this one out . . .

Andy is also a brilliant musician and song-writer, yet another star in the dark constellation of esoteric folk. His chosen instruments – self-taught – are the Northumbrian pipes and the mandolin. Early on Mayday morning he could be seen in full bardic regalia in front of the Clarendon Building, leading the joyous "alternative" celebration of incoming summer, away from the jammed-together crowds beneath Magdalen Tower. Not that I was able to witness this myself – I had a café to run! As some compensation, he might show up at the kitchen door round about mid-morning, still displaying his extravagantly Mayed-up face and costume.

The Hurly Burly Whirly Very Early Band, 2010

He kept me up to date with something else I was missing, too: the weekly parade of talent at the Catweazle Club, now relocated to Princes St, just off the Cowley Road. Andy was a regular performer, either solo, or with his wonderful band, Telling The Bees. "Cracking Weazle last night", he might say, as we cleared the dishes on a Friday afternoon. Evidently, for him this was an essential source of creative nourishment. I could do with some of that!

As I felt able to let go some of my cooking duties to Bino and Tenzin, so did it seem more possible to attend Catweazle myself. Here was indeed a magical zone, a shared experience of individual creativity. The key ingredient, rigorously imposed by moral force, was an absolute stillness during performance. In this intense attentiveness, nothing lies between artist and audience: there is direct communication. I had witnessed this in Buddha Hall, in the Pune Ashram; otherwise, outside an intimate relationship, we have lost touch with this possibility. How generous and special that Matt Sage has enabled this ritual of artistic communion over so many years!

Sitting in such an atmosphere, imbibing its spirit, it is impossible not to feel a yearning to contribute, to make one's own statement of being and belonging. And along with this, there is the spectre of possible failure, of ridicule. Many of these performances verged on perfection, doubtless the product of a lifetime of sustained practice. Rapturous applause would have been well deserved. Others fell more into the category of "plucky but flawed". These too were kindly, warmly received. It occurred to me that I could at least aspire to the latter category.

I treated myself to a lovely new guitar. I checked in with a vocal coach, who helped ease me through an utter crisis of confidence, and who made me aware of what I was choosing to sing about: a bunch of songs about peril on the ocean waves, sudden shipwreck, and the yearning to be back on dry land. One afternoon in the Café I was sitting across from a most genial long-haired fellow: "Hello, mate . . .", he says. This turned out to be Eddie, a brilliantly gifted guitar player, who consented to give me lessons on his boat moored up on Port Meadow. It did me good, leaving the Café for the after-noon, heading down to the river to take some well-informed tuition. There were times when I had to remove my shoes and socks to wade through the flooded towpath . . .

Bringing my guitar and my shaky skills along with me to the 'Weazle, I discovered that it was actually okay to be plucky but flawed. Halfway into a song, and the next chord is suddenly a total mystery . . .

The Magic Café invites you to

A taste of Catweazle

A special evening of food and entertainment
Featuring a sumptuous three-course vegetarian feast, with performances from a galaxy of Catweazle stars

Inspired by Kate Raworth's photographs of Catweazle performers, on exhibition throughout April at the Magic Café

Matt Sage
Alan Buckley
Colin and Jane
Sophia Blackwell
Telling the Bees
Edward Pope
Jean Bramley

Saturday 14th April

at the Magic Café   Tel 01865 794604
7.30 pm prompt.   Tickets £15
Available from the Magic Café and at Catweazle Club
Please bring your own drinks.

Kate Raworth – subsequently to be acclaimed for her vision of "Doughnut Economics" – has built up an impressive portfolio of performance portraits, which she asks Camilla to display at the Café. Not only this, but she suggests a special evening to launch the exhibition. It is a marvellous opportunity to connect Club and Café.

"A Taste of Catweazle" will offer not only a marvellous feast – an intricate combination of my favourite Middle Eastern cuisine – but also a lavish programme of entertainment. We have been able to choose our favourite performers, seven acts in total, all of whom are sure-fire stars. For this special evening, Groovy Sue will transform the Café space with her artfully draped fabrics, and Camilla is to take on Matt's role as impresario. Tickets sell out fast.

If I had to pick one standout moment in the history of the Magic Café, this might well be it. It was a coming together, a celebration, and all went according to plan.

Ed Pope pulled out his battered balalaika from a plastic bag, to delight us with a couple of his idiosyncratic ditties, Jean accompanied her inimitable singing with improvised percussion, courtesy of bubble wrap, Colin and Jane transfixed us with the intensity of their duetting, Alan

Camilla (far left) talking to Kate before the feast

and Sophia each recited from their well-honed oeuvre, and Matt himself treated us to some of his finest compositions. Following Catweazle tradition, the cabaret was divided into two halves; unconventionally, delicious desserts were served in the interval. As grand finale, Andy appeared with Telling The Bees – featuring Colin and Jane on bass and fiddle, and Josie on Cello.

Fabulous!

Photo: Kate Raworth

A significant date was approaching: our ten year anniversary. It had been on my mind for quite some time, not least because it marked the termination of my lease agreement, and I was uncomfortably aware that my landlord, Mohammed, was keen to set a significantly higher rent. Despite the pleasure to be had working with my colleagues in the Café, it was impossible to escape an undertone of anxiety about money. In my day-to-day engagement with other businesses in the street, it seemed to me at that time – 2007 – that I wasn't the only one with such a feeling. A discomforting haze of uncertainty obscured the horizon: did I really want to commit to another decade of business, with all its vicissitudes and bureaucratic hassle? I resented Mohammed's claim on my hard-earned treasure, just as I wearied from the constant demands of the government agencies. Scariest of all, the spectre of professionalism, in all its joyless stolidity, loomed out of the fog.

But a ten year birthday party was hard to resist. The Catweazle evening had been such a success, and the final instalment of my Magic Cookbook at last complete. There was after all plenty to celebrate. I swallowed my misgivings and agreed, at least on a temporary basis, to Mohammed's terms; we could settle on the details later.

Once again, it was time to pull out all the stops, to create one more evening to remember. Here's how I described it to my brother, writing just a couple of weeks into the New Year:

> I wanted it to be sort of like going to heaven and checking out with all your old mates, remembering all the good times, giving thanks for what we have achieved over the years. Well, a good time was certainly had, and it did feel like a significant milestone had been passed. I had proved that I had achieved what I set out to achieve, and experienced the satisfaction of knowing my efforts have been appreciated.

In truth, what I actually recall from that evening is rather more down to earth – and more difficult to acknowledge.

Amongst the dazzling array of talent I had succeeded in corralling for the promised entertainment – which included Jamji playing his mystical flute – I had asked my good friend Jon to provide some interesting diversion. Not wishing to cramp his style, I gave him no specific instructions. He had done us proud at our opening party, with his inspired "Full Café" game; I was confident of some more splendid fireworks.

The Cabaret was to put us in a good space for the promised dessert; Jon would surely lead us there in fine style. I have the puddings ready to roll, as Jon begins to speak.

I recently spoke with Jon about this performance, which he professed to have entirely forgotten. But he took my recollections, hitherto withheld, in good spirit:

> *The thing about being an artist is that there's always the possibility of total failure. I mean, that time at Ian and Lynn's wedding, when I performed Carmina Burana, what was I thinking? I can't sing in tune, I didn't know the words . . .*

I assured him that I remembered that occasion with the greatest joy, that it was indeed one of the wildest things I have ever witnessed, recalled frequently with a happy nostalgic smile. I was sitting next to Jon as he launched into Carl Orff's O Fortuna – also known as the Old Spice theme – and found myself pressed back into my seat in shock and awe. Imagine a boatload of Vikings at the end of a rambunctious evening, high on plundered mead, stomping their bearskin boots, roaring out the choruses. THAT was fun!

Now he is telling us about the putative winter solstice celebrations at Stonehenge, which might be inferred from the positioning of the various stones, and what this might mean in cosmological terms. There is rather more information here than can easily be digested, at least on a full stomach, and I wonder when he might be coming to some outrageous denouement. His disquisition ranges wider across the misty reaches of the Bronze Age, and I begin to lose my sense of time and place. Looking around the room, I can see I'm not the only one. The collective spirit has frayed, attention is wandering. Jon reaches the end of another page. There's evidently a long way yet to go. I check the clock: it's been thirty minutes already . . . forty minutes . . . I share panicky, despairing glances with Deki, who is doubtless wondering when she will ever get home . . .

My heart, opened wide in the spirit of generosity for this special evening, crumples together, dismayed at this disaster. One wish alone remains:

"Just make it stop . . . please make it stop!"

The Magic Spatula

All through this decade I'd been checking in with my journal at New Year, noting down some reflections on the past twelve months, and maybe looking forward to new possibilities ahead. There had been some years which seemed mired in gloom and weariness: a relentless treadmill, on which the only change had been the comings and goings on the staff roster. Personal life had been more or less subsumed by the demands of the Café, holidays barely sufficient to recharge my exhausted batteries. Poor Camilla!

The transition from '07 to '08, as recorded in my journal, has a very different quality. I look back with satisfaction at the conclusion of my Magic Cookbook project and the "completion ritual" of the 10th anniversary party, and I am feeling well rested. There is a sense of excitement at the prospect of changing fortunes – an ancestral legacy looks set to transform our family finances. Plus, my sense of self appears to be floating free from its identification with the Café. I had taken up meditating again, and was noticing how this shifted my internal narrative.

I had become accustomed, as I opened up the front door on my first day back at work, to find a seasonal message from a business sales agency: "Thinking of Selling Your Business?" This had always been filed straight away into the bin – but not this year. Somewhat guiltily, I folded it into my pocket.

I could sense there was a process underway, a weather change, which just needed some time to clarify. By the end of January I felt able to write:

I did wonder how I'd managed to completely ignore the Café in my resolutions for the new year.

This has been the week when the penny dropped – not only do I desperately want to give it up, but I feel absolutely fine about it, it is not a shameful or a sad thing, or stemming from failure; rather, as I wrote to [my brother] John, I could be content that I have achieved what I set out to achieve. I have given it my best shot, my whole heart, and now my heart seems to have moved on.

This week I am swept by my emotional storms – it's hard to keep a grip on running the café, I can't seem to swallow back my anxieties and resistance like I normally do.

By the evening it is all clear, clear enough to announce to Camilla – I'm gonna sell up, as soon as possible.

She needs a bit of persuading . . . But my mind – and my heart – is clear, all sorts of possibilities suppressed for so long start to suggest themselves – but chiefly, the sense of release from a no-longer tolerable strait-jacket.

A tarot reading helps too. I draw 6 of Disks, Success, crossed with Ace of Disks (big money); for conscious, the Death card; for unconscious, 8 of Cups – Indolence. The past is the Tower, the future 3 of Cups – Abundance.

So clearly, a time for necessary change, and transformation, and reclamation of neglected possibilities, facilitated by auspicious circumstances. That's what I'm hoping anyway.

My emotions are all over the place – need some Chi treatment – everything in the Café is suffused with poignancy, and I'm not allowed to speak my mind! I'm hearing how much people love the place, but I can take this as an acknowledgement rather than as a burden. I really am ready to quit – though quitting is a process that needs seeing through – carefully – to the end –

The last person out of the café yesterday asked me, was I a sannyasin? I said, yes, but it's not like a church . . . it's about following your heart, that's why the Café is as it is – what I couldn't say is, now my heart is saying something else – the question is, what?

I called up the Selling Agent, and we made a date. Did I really have something to sell? – I didn't even have a lease agreement, but at least I hadn't gone to war with the landlord. The man in the suit assured me that I did indeed have an attractive business. It could even be worth a substantial amount: half the annual turnover, I learned, was the standard selling price. Arrangements were made for some discreet photography, and shortly afterwards an attractive prospectus was made available on the market. My beloved Magic Café, the child of my imagination, the focus of my creative energies for the past ten years and more, was now a product on the shelf, for whomsoever might fancy their chances in running an idiosyncratic hippy business, someone else's manifested dream.

I had signed a document allotting sole selling rights for the next six months to this company, who stood to gain a substantial portion of the eventual price in return for their marketing expertise. Was this one of those fabled "deals with the devil"? Was not the Magic Café, if not my very soul, at least its progeny? It was a hard call, but I had made my choice.

I'm fed up with a lot of things, now I can admit it. Every day shopping at Tesco, the same faces in the carpark, running through the same recipes, the pressures of keeping my staff on the move – I'll be happy to let it all go.

What sustained me through this time – apart from Camilla's unstinting support – was an awareness that this could be a meditation all of its own: the experience of letting go of something very precious, but – perhaps – peripheral to one's essential nature. There was something of George Gurdjieff about this: the renowned mystic and teacher would tease his disciples by insisting on complete commitment to a project – say, digging an all-important hole – then, of a sudden, calling out *"Stop!"* Osho had a similar method; perhaps the Ranch experiment is best understood in this way. Like he said: *"I am cooking something else."*

It was all a big secret. Why this felt so imperative, I find it difficult now to explain. Was I concerned that news of imminent sale might taint the Café's reputation amongst its customers, or was there some sense of shameful reckoning which I was hoping to postpone? Maybe I just wanted to avoid the inevitable constant explaining which publicity might attract. Wasn't publicity the business of the sales agency?

I certainly wasn't helping them along, consciously or no – and they weren't doing so well on their own account either. This was after all 2008, the year in which capitalism came within a whisker of collapse. It wasn't a good year to be selling a hippy business, however tempting the prospects for improved turnover – boosting the prices of everything! – might appear. To my knowledge, there was only one interested purchaser: I think they were quite bewildered at how much trouble it might be for so little gain. Wouldn't a sandwich bar make more sense?

I began to regret my commitment to the commercial agents. Perhaps there were other possibilities – even if these would have to wait until my contract expired. I was already busy with plans for a life beyond the Café. I fancied treating my enquiring mind to a blast of academia, registering for an MA course at Brookes University. Mind was evidently champing at the bit, endlessly rehearsing the causes of the First World War, or the role of the humble bicycle in the collapse of the British Empire, for the benefit of my curious staff, while attempting at the same time to keep track of the Saturday morning breakfast orders. Wouldn't it be great to have nothing else to do but read and think, for one entire year? My prospective course would begin at the beginning of September – time was running out.

One effective means of venting my turbulent emotions proved to be performing at the Catweazle Club. Even if I wasn't allowing myself to properly explain my choice of song, I could at least give expression to my process. I had the privilege of marking my 50th birthday with a (plucky but flawed) rendition of Richard Thompson's song "Time to Ring Some Changes". Matt had even done me the honour of asking me to kick off the show. *"Don't change too much, will you Hafiz?"*, he remarked quite sweetly after I was done. But all was still a secret . . .

Secrets being what they are, word inevitably seeped out. *"I hear you're selling up"*, Sharron confronted me one day. *"The Magic Café will live forever"*, was my quick, dissembling response. Who was I fooling?

I'd thought I had a purchaser . . . and then that fell through. Was there still a Plan B? What about Team Tibet, the core of dedicated staff which had accrued over the past few years? Bino, it was true, had relocated to Brighton, but perhaps he could be tempted back. But none of them, surely, had access to financial resource – so essential to sustaining a business, let alone providing me with some recompense that might cushion my impending loss of income.

I lost patience with the Sales Agency and their Loadsamoney dream. How much did I really need? Enough to tide me over for a couple of years, I reckoned. So now I was ready with an offer: my beautiful Magic Café, one loving owner, now available at a bargain half price, for someone willing to give it special care. Perhaps some sort of cooperative might be organised?

I had a sense of gears turning, possibilities being explored. What were the prospects of an effective team emerging, complete with that all-important "whatever it takes" mentality without which no enterprise can succeed? I had noticed Jiu Xien, newly back on the team, paying particular attention to my suggestions. He got on the phone to his wife, and came back in a state of high excitement: they would buy the business – if I was really serious! This was something I hadn't foreseen – a way forward, like a logjam breaking, pent-up energy rolling freely down the river . . .

Events speeded up. I worked with Jiu Xien as much as possible, showing him everything, explaining the particular reason for each of my actions and choices – that nothing was random, it had all been carefully thought through. He was paying close attention, treating me as an esteemed teacher, all the while evolving a new perception of self. He was going to be Boss! For Jiu Xien, this was a big, unexpected adventure suddenly underway.

I made sure he understood his obligations to health and safety, booking him a place on the Environmental Health training course.

With my summer holiday approaching, I suggested that Jiu Xien and Tenzin try running the Tibetan Café together, to see how that might go . . .

And when I return, I can barely contain my excitement:

Two more weeks to go . . . I'm enjoying the sense of imminent liberation. I can own up to the world, confident that it is indeed going to come to pass.

People ask me, "is it true?" and "are you upset?" – to which I say, truthfully, not at all, just hugely relieved, and glad that the story is in for a happy ending, a fitting close for an undertaking conducted with all my heart.

Then they say – are you having a party? And I invite them all over for our farewell 'do'.

Last weekend I closed off my holidays and re-entered the race to the finish line with a special night of wonder at the Burgess Field (i.e. 'the wilderness') in honour of Andy's 'forty-fication', abjuring an evening up at Elsfield in favour of the promise of 'shaman-juice'.

– which was duly forthcoming – a delightful experience, sitting around the campfire, in the drizzle, lovely music constantly swirling, merry company, and all completely smashed and silly. I'd forgotten about all this . . .

As I took my gracious leave (prior to stumbling back across the blasted heath) I announced my plans to my good companions – brought myself into present time – which I take to be the special gift, the boon, brought back from the wilds of adventure (my journey to the sea of possibility).

Lovely lovely.

Something important is about to happen, and I need to make this register on the deepest level. I am feeling like Shakespeare's Prospero, at the end of The Tempest. I have become accustomed to wielding power in my little kingdom, transforming the elements, shaping events according to my will. All has transpired more or less according to my wishes. And now it is time to let it all go. I am resolved to make an absolute break, so that there is no temptation to slip back into catering. All my equipment will be included in the sale; even the CD collection, the carefully considered soundtrack of my days, belongs more with the Café than myself.

Many years before, when I was still searching through junkshops and bric-a-brac for items that might be useful in my fledgling catering career, I had come across a small tool: a kitchen spatula, an oblong piece of flexible plastic attached to a shaft bent in such a manner that the hand might float above the item being smoothed, or caressed. In technical terms, this was a crank-handled spatula. Such a marvellous tool, the perfect extension to a hand held steady: Brownies, Passion Cake, Caramel Shortcake, all otherwise hard to manifest – and in combination with that wickedly-named turntable, the Lazy Susan, the means by which the signature spiral might be imposed on our rich Chocolate Torte. Jenny, my first baking assistant, had christened it the Magic Spatch, the enabler of so many things. As it began to show signs of wear and tear, I searched everywhere for a replacement, but in vain.

Here, I realised, was my equivalent to Prospero's mighty rod of power. I wasn't proposing to snap it in pieces, but I would make a little ceremony by which its creative virtue would be transferred to Jiu Xien. And what he in turn made of it would be none of my concern.

Renan and Tenzin look on as Camilla applies the final magic touches to our cake.

The last Saturday of August arrives. There is one final feast to prepare, and a special cake to decorate. This is ritual food – a passion cake embodying all these years of effort and imagination – to be shared with the community one more time.

It's time to let go of my Mister Magic Café persona. One legacy of my commune days had been an understanding that energetic work is supported best by red clothing. Bright red T-shirt and maroon apron have been my constant working uniform; now I retreat into the basement for a transformative gear-shift. Pulling on a sky-blue shirt, already I feel different.

Many friends are here, staff past and present, regular customers, well-wishers . . . It's not a packed house; whoever feels the need to be here is here. There's a goodly number of musicians. Paul Duggan, who has tended the piano over the years, tuning it with a patient ear, cajoles it once again into a roistering boogie-woogie workout. Maeve steps up with her ballads and blues, and one last chorus of Feed Your Heart. Frei Zinger unpacks his flute, adds some tootling descants. Andy straps on his pipes for a song celebrating the pleasures of being jobless and carefree . . .

And then it is time for our little ceremony. There is the Magic Spatula, nestled in the raffia breadbasket, atop a scarlet napkin. I take it in my hands, hand it to the new man . . .

Sweet release!

Job done.

1 Sept 08

Monday morning, at liberty to do whatever I want. I'm sitting by the pond in University Parks, letting this wonderful new reality sink in – I have cut myself free from the café, and all is well.

Last photocall for the Magic Veterans: Renan, Rodrigo, Hafiz, Tenzin, Deki, Jiu Xien, Shahin, Elaine, Libby

After an evening bathed in love – farewell to the Magic (cf Prospero) – how special was that? – an experience to feature in Lifetime's Greatest Hits – worth the effort of Ten Years and More's hard work and dedication.

Wow

So many special moments, meeting each of my special guests, all bestow me with love (and a scarf from Lama).

I feel so fortunate – good old Jiu Xien – stepping up so boldly, so sincere in his ambition – I bestow upon him the Magic Spatch – and so it is all passed on.

Cares and worries float away from off of my shoulders – no more tedious bureaucracy, mad demands from environmental health, shepherding staff . . . just a few days before I had to talk Jiu Xien and Tenzin down from sacking each other – just remember – you're mates. And so they are.

And then I sang for them all – a bit dodgily, I know, 'cos Rodrigo re-corded some snips – though it felt sweet at the time – a final serenade for the good ship Magic Café, and all who sailed in her . . .

2 weeks later

Now I have seen the newly-renovated Magic Café in its new colours – and I can be assured that it is a different place – the old Magic Café has relocated into the realm of once-upon-a-time.

So I can move on, confident that, after all, the magic is still in my pocket.

Oxford - was it a dream?

This magical landscape, with its ever-pertinent question, was a fixture in the Magic Café loo ever since Al Cane exhibited his photo-shopped fantasies, shortly after the the Café opened.

218

At Some Distance from the Pivot

We have been scoping down the long years by means of that marvellous device, the act of memory. This is a curious instrument: all is refracted through a lens, a shape-shifting engine, which we may justly term the emotional attachment. Properly twiddled and tweaked, all springs into life and shape; remove it, and meaning falls away. Historians should take notice.

There he sits, the historian, adjusting the barrel of his signifier, training his attention on the events of long ago. It ought to be a science, like the experiments conducted by those splendid fellows Hooke and Boyle, but it just ain't so. Today he's feeling grumpy – no need to pry too closely into the why. All he sees on the other side of the lens looks similarly tainted by grouch and grumble. Come back another day, well-rested and benevolent, and this sense of well-being is projected back into another age as if freshly minted, the original source.

Thus the hazard of proposing one's own recollections as true history.

I have made much, in this story, of the various names I have borne in the course of my life, and the manner in which these have shaped my identity. So here's another, which I acquired the moment I walked away from my creation: *"The Man Who Used To Run The Magic Café"*. It's an awkward handle, which resists being squeezed into an easy acronym. Being addressed as such, I am instantly called upon to take a position. Is there regret? Pain? Hurt?

To be sure, the immediate, overwhelming, reaction, was relief. That tremendous burden, the ball and chain of my commitment, was gone, melted into thin air. And if anyone might be so bold as to praise my achievement, the manifestation of my dream, I might even declare that my dream had gotten twisted into nightmare.

Perhaps I was simply indulging in cheap rhetoric. What was certainly true, was that I was exhausted, drained, a flat battery. Far from the confident expectation that my magic pocket would soon enough be host to freshly bubbling creativity, there was for a long time nothing at the end of my dabbling fingers but pocket fluff.

I would find myself continually drawn to kitchenware shops, still driven by residual desire for a crank-handled spatula. I swear I saw one once, on display in some old-fashioned shop in Woodstock; time was pressing, so I promised myself I'd return some other day. Setting out at last on this expedition, I felt a twinge of bad faith; then, on the way, my car was involved in a minor collision. When I eventually arrived at Woodstock, the shop was nowhere to be found . . .

I grew accustomed to regulating my recipes to fit the domestic arena, just enough for me and Camilla. Only once each year would something resembling old times occur: I undertook to help out with the Green Café at the Oxford Town Hall, the annual pre-Christmas fundraiser for the Green Party. After a couple of years I learned to relax into this: this café was a collective effort in which my contribution would be most welcome – but it wasn't my overall responsibility. I marvelled at how I could slip into this role of easy cooperation, and at how much fun that could be. And at the end of this one day, I was sure to feel extremely tired.

The Magic Café wasn't far from our new house, so I would see it regularly as I went about my life. How did that feel? It was a double pleasure, I might reply: firstly, that it was still there, resilient, when all could so easily have ended up in the skip; secondly, that it was no longer my business. If I did enter, my visit would be fleeting; here was somewhere almost too familiar, from which I had banished myself.

Then I had been diagnosed as coeliac, so it simply wasn't safe to eat anything I hadn't personally prepared. Cafés in general were off my menu.

Cycling back home one evening, after my day's work at Asylum Welcome, my attention was drawn by a glimmering flashlight in the otherwise dark Café interior. Curious, and sensing that I might be of some use, I ventured inwards, to discover Tenzin peering into the electricity junction box. From the recesses of memory I summoned up my emergency procedure: what to do when the electricity suddenly fails. After a couple of exploratory thrown switches, illumination was duly restored. And that made me glad. You could justly say it was a lightbulb moment.

Historical memory is of course a collective construct, into which I blundered from time to time, since it wasn't quite where I expected it be. I became aware that, in certain quarters, the Magic Café had acquired a sort of legendary status – with the implication that I too might have accrued some heroic virtue. At the end of last year I was minded to post a photo – one of those from our opening night, featured at the beginning of this book – on the local community Facebook page, and was greatly heartened by the response.

There was a gurgling and rushing in my river of dreams, and a sleek, hefty shape split the surface, splashing back down in an explosion of crystal droplets, and leaving in its wake a sparkling new idea. I would write a book, and it would be called "I Am Cooking Something Else", to tell the story of how the Magic Café came to be. And so here we are . . .

Just as the Café represents a coming together, a well-held public space in which the spirit of community can manifest and proliferate, so should this account be much more than one man's self-serving boast. I have done my best to present as many voices as possible – and if they all tend to tell a similar tale, who am I to argue?

Here's one more, provided by Lucy, whose attunement to the energy of the heart chakra fitted so well to the pre-vailing Magic Café ethos. I was always happy to welcome her back to the team!

What can I say about the Magic Café?

I think it may be the only café in the whole of Oxford that I didn't get fired from!

That says a lot already.

I loved being in the back – in the kitchen – chopping vegetables into VERY specific shapes . . . and the feeling of community that would arise between us as we worked . . . the conversations that were wide-ranging, from stories of your time in the Osho community all the way up to the crazy end of that era that you were a part of . . . and the way your knowledge of history could infuse and enrich a whole range of topics and all the moments in which you were just happy to be with us, cooking delicious food for the masses in your own kitchen.

Tenzin, Jamji and Deki – the gentle and mysterious Tibetan spirit that persists in all of them and that I found soulful and beautiful to be around . . .

And as familiar faces started to arrive for mid-morning coffee and cake the community would diversify and extend beyond the kitchen.

I remember the delight of being able to slip into The Inner Bookshop next door and to have Thrangu House just up the road and the Lama coming in for lunch.

The way that nobody batted an eyelid when children were rubbing carrot cake with cream cheese frosting into the carpet

And women could relax and breastfeed little ones.

Locals of all different ages dropping in alone and with friends for a warming and nourishing bite to eat in a place that had soul with zero pretensions . . .

Thank you Hafiz for offering up your dream to the community and for sharing the ride with us!

It's been lovely for me, hearing from so many old colleagues and friends. But what is still missing, of course, is the wider experience, the daily coming and going of the café clientele. While there are many willing to testify to a broad, diffused, glow of satisfaction, it is rare for this to crystallize in a single, memorable moment. Who notices a delightful tapestry, if it is simply part of the backdrop of existence?

Children have grown up here, confident that their play will be unmolested, that there will be friendship and fun, and that, if mum and dad behave themselves as they ought, there will be cake – or ice cream! It will be a place of remembered happiness to keep them company through life.

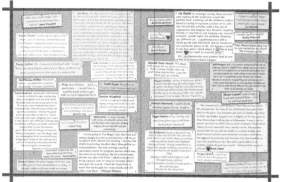

I hope that it has done something similar for grownups, too.

Based on comments made on Facebook and elsewhere, I've made a collage of some of those happy memories, which you can see just over the page. Thanks to everyone who contributed!

So, a lovely café with memorable brownies, or something more besides? Why, of all things possible, was this my chosen arena of action?

Should you have been paying attention to my wide-ranging, if occasionally digressive discourse, you may have noticed that I am fascinated by the process of change – which sometimes goes by the more dignified rubric of history. Change may be gradual, almost imperceptible, or it may be sudden and catastrophic. In my lifetime, it has mostly been the former – at least in that part of the world I call home. There are places I have lived which still bore witness – in the damaged or shattered cityscapes, and in the memories of older generations – to warfare and civil breakdown. Neighbours set against neighbours, and everybody loses. Now, turmoil and upheaval have engulfed so much of our world, and it seems to me that we should not be complacent that we are immune to such disasters.

In the centre of Oxford are two monuments to the same event: the ceremonial burning to death, by royal command, of the Archbishop of Canterbury, Thomas Cranmer, in 1556. A simple cross embedded in the Broad Street roadway marks the location of this dreadful bonfire; around the corner, erected nearly three centuries later, the far more imposing Martyrs' Memorial enjoins us to be wary of the perfidious Church of Rome. A fracture in our society, a relic

X marks the spot

of doctrinal disagreement, has persisted, been nurtured even, down to our own time. It was still common currency in the town of my childhood; even more so in Ireland just across the water. What happens when a community ceases to meet together as friends, or targets one part of society as the scapegoat for all ills?

We currently have a government recklessly stoking hatred, deliberately manufacturing a "hostile climate" for those perceived as undeserving incomers. It fills me with dismay.

In the face of this ever-present danger, the Magic Café has been my response.

ahhh, your lovely Magic Café – cornerstone of alternative East Oxford – **Janet Stansfeld**

Sue Shaw: The Magic Café was always more than a café for me. From its start at the Asian cultural centre, it was a place of nurture and sanctuary: a point to meet and make friends, or just hang out and listen to music with coffee and cake. Over the years it grew and changed (as we all did) – expanded into an ex-junk shop, got a bigger menu – but its essential character remained. At its heart, was you, Hafiz, always cheerful though sometimes harassed, orchestrating with meticulous detail the many helpers, food production and ambience, to make sure everything was perfect for the rest of us. I spent hours there enjoying ginger ice cream and spiced soup: took my new partner and elderly parents, went into labour, breastfed my baby, let my toddlers play – and once astonishingly found 'little pig' among the heap of toys, after he had 'run away' months before. I lunched there with friends on a regular basis, and while the Magic Café existed, there was always someone to talk to and somewhere to go. I miss it now.

Sophia Trinder: I loved hearing Topaz at the Magic, and Jon Fletcher, Jane Griffiths and Colin Fletcher. I loved being able to turn up at the Magic and know I would meet a loving community of friends there, all gathered to hear each other's music. Such wonderful times!

Tracey Collins: Oh, it was such a brilliant café. I loved it there. So many happy memories of 'Music to Munch to' ... great contribution to the heart of a community.

Katy Jennison: It was a wonderful place for meeting friends, both by design and by accident, and for me it had a symbiotic relationship with the Inner Bookshop next door. I loved the magic food, and I miss your magical chocolate brownies!

Paul Thomas Phillips: Wonderful place – so talented in creating a wonderfully welcome community

Philip Torr: Brilliant ... Such a great place ... I would love to read the book of the magic café; so much happened there!

Nadia Saadi: Best place in Cowley. Can't wait to read this!!

Sarah Lionheart: I practically LIVED there! I moved to Oxford in 1991, and by May 1992 was pregnant with our first, Katie. The Asian Cultural Centre was next to my GP practice and I attended alternative antenatal talks there plus found Hafiz selling Very Good food. I needed the good food, so I was there on the two ? lunchtimes you were open, begging you to start a café of your own which you resisted and baulked at, until you eventually realised it was possible as your food was so good. That centre holds good memories. When you moved to start the Magic Café me and daughter Katie moved with you, dropping by whenever we could as every time we would find some of our friends there eating the yummy food.
Heaven!

A place that touched so many of us. Grateful to have been part of the Magic Café family – **Michelli Jelly**

Dominic Woodfield: Used to love having a working breakfast with laptop sitting next to the live role-players with their armour, cloaks and foam swords!

Elaine Nicol: I so loved Saturday with music, any day for community and the best notice board for finding lodgers, like-minded folk and fab networking!

Such a wonderful place – Karen Kay

I loved going to The Magic Café, the food was always deeply nourishing and delicious and the atmosphere both vibrant and relaxing. I met my first child's Godmother, Heather Abel, through the noticeboard there. She was running a spiritual awareness course for pregnant women which was the start of our friendship. My third child's baby-shower was also held there. I asked everyone to bring a prayer, wish or song for my baby which I later put into a book. I liked the food there so much that we bought the recipe books and still often cook them. – *Philippa Williams*

Loved their cookbooks, the bean salad was one of my staples for years! – **Laura Davies**

Simon Collery: So many happy memories, one of the places I love about Oxford, so many people, coffee and home-made ice cream.

Liz Goold: *So nostalgic seeing these pictures and reading all the memories! Loved the yummy food, checking out the infamous notice board or trying to squeeze a notice on it, sinking into the big armchair with a big cup of cappuccino and magical choc brownie, meeting friends or new folk or just hanging out, musical sessions, candle-light, the windows steaming up, different art - a gathering place with a lovely quirky vibe that holds special memories of a particular phase in life. still brings a smile to my face when I think about it. ☺ Thank you Hafiz. ♥ Can't wait to read the book!*

- PS also remember your yummy food at one of the first Oxford Dance Camps!

It was a great place – **Rahima Kenner**

Loved it there – **Kat Allsworth** ♥

Still miss it – **Maeve Bayton**

Happy memories. Magic Café was part of the reason I ended up in East Oxford – **Jon Fletcher**

I loved it here as a child! – **Ruby Driscoll**

Paul Mackilligin: Why has no one mentioned the food? The food was great!

Hannah Rose Ireson: *The Magic Café saved me on many occasions from sinking further into my post-natal depression. Love the food and ice creams.*

Will Pouget: *Haf I remember doing my first pop up with you, back in 2000 it was really successful and it give me real confidence to move forward from just serving sandwiches and salads at Alphabar which led to me to establishing the Vaults and Garden . . . thanks so much for supporting me and my career . . . I also remember going to wild parties with Bino at Don's house and seeing Bino in the café the next day both of us having not slept!*

Maggie Crosbie: *me too. A real haven. When I had the odd afternoon off without baby, it was straight to the Magic Café for a friendly welcome, immediate and delicious food, that amazing cake with the cherry on top, great coffee, and read the newspaper cover to cover. Heaven. Thank you.*

Miriam Levene: Lots of happy times with grandchildren – and my well-behaved dog.

Damian Haywood: *I used to be an absolute regular for me. Loved it*

Payam Nabarz: It was a lovely café, one of few places you could taste the barakat in the food.

Liz Hodgson: *it was a haven for me when I was very ill in the late 90s and went there to eat rather than try cooking with my aching hands and depleted energy at home. Always somewhere to bump into people and keep connected, as well as arrange to see people on purpose – Vital.*
Always a relief not having to wade through meaty options!
And I remember Camilla's lovely quilt on the wall one year.
Thanks for the memories!

You created such a special place. Nice that you have done this retrospective. So many of our community have great affections for the place. Last breakfast out with my brother was there in 2003. My brother stopped over in Blighty on his way back to New Mexico from a hiking trip on Kilimanjaro. It was a rare in-person visit since we didn't live on same continent. I lived off of Sidney St so of course MC was a nearby venue. Anyway two months later he was with his family on a winter holiday near Banff Canada and did a solo snowshoe excursion while there. He triggered an avalanche and that was that. Our breakfast at your café would be our last. But what a great place to remember. Thanks for getting in touch— feels good to convey it. All best. ♥ **Scott Urban**

Bridget Walker: *I used to go when the Inner Bookshop was there. Always loved the food.*

Marinaes La Salva: Thank you for the magic! For everyone and anyone as we all felt included in that gorgeous den

We are actors in a global drama, and the Magic Café has been a meeting place for people from many lands. Much has been shared – information, friendship, experience, music, even chocolate brownies – and much has been taken away. In particular, I would like to point out some of those wonderful people who have drawn on their time in the Magic Café team to develop their own vision of righteous response to the demands of our age.

Rodrigo has been based in Portland, Oregon, for some years now, doing his best to spread good cheer. Why weren't people as joyous as they ought to be? After tackling this head on, promoting himself as "Brazilian Happiness Coach", he has at last opened his own venue – Brazilian Favela Café – where he can diffuse his energy more broadly. Now where did he get that idea?

The café is called FAVELA Brazilian Café, as I wanted people to feel they are part of a bigger community, just like in favelas, where people truly have to rely on each other and help one another.

Thank you so much Hafiz for creating the community business that I'm now sharing in the USA. My café is just a humble attempt to be as magical as yours. Hugs!

Bino has settled in Boulder, Colorado, with his wife and daughter. As "Chef Lama", he's been running the R&D department of the local Google catering operation – a tribute to his creativity and skill. When not busy with that, or exploring Native American heritage sites, he's been teaching meditation at Naropa University, a Buddhist-based foundation. I asked him what he tells his students:

One morning, chopping to Chopin (I think it was) in Magic Café I had a sudden realization. To do a meditation you don't need to be sitting in a lonely cave in the Himalaya.

I realized that you can meditate while chopping vegetables: as you know, how much I love chopping vegetables, and everything that I chop has to be precise, and kind of, the training of my being in the monastery and in the cave, all this kind of came together, and from then on . . . don't talk, classical music, focus on what you are doing, the knife in your hand, each piece of vegetable, the way you are in your body . . . that was my first realization, and ever since then I've been cooking now for over 20 years, never thought that one day I would be a chef.

To the students usually what I tell them, when I teach meditation here at the Naropa University, is that meditation is a great way to learn or familiarize oneself with whatever one is doing, could be writing or making something, that we can adapt those mindfulness aspects on to our daily lives . . . Main thing is, just leave behind all this expectation about doing right or wrong . . .

The example that I give them is, when I had the revelation of how you can meditate while chopping the vegetable is that I never had expectation of becoming a chef or anything it's just carried on, just gradually build up and improve and improve and final goal is that, you know, I think I am kind of accomplished chef at the moment, I can say that proudly and I think this is all because of working in the culinary world and building up my own tastebud and my own style and that is the fruitation of doing something without expecting result right away.

The Little Lama Café, Naropa University

It looks like Bino has taken his own advice to heart: just recently he has opened his own establishment on the Naropa campus – the Little Lama Café. I'm sure this will be a big success: he has something very special to share.

Renan is back in Brazil, running a pub called Rock the Casbah in the city of Curitiba: offering a fun collision of English rock music and Arabic-style food. It keeps him busy, but does it keep him out of mischief?

The last time I connected with Jo, he was in Goa – but he has been moving around quite a lot:

I'm living in Goa where I run a start-up kombucha brand. I am very fortunate to have been here through the recent global situation. Most of my close friends are here also and we're all settling into the 'suse-gad' lifestyle.

I don't spend much time cooking these days as I'm too busy perfecting my ferments. I source my teas directly from the wonderful gardens of India and have brought my passion for fine food and drink wholeheartedly into my work. The kombucha market is ready to boom here and I have a phenomenal product. Watch this space!

I did a good stint running my own (mostly vegetarian) catering company in Europe. With all my work getting cancelled last summer I have decided to call it a day and focus 100% on my project here. The time we spent together in the Magic Café set me up to be a chef. Little did I know at the time that I was gonna take the reins and feed the people. I worked mostly in community settings, including regular gigs at Osho centres around Europe.

I took sannyas in 2006 in Pune. I never really found my place in Osho's teachings and with hindsight I see that this is because I was looking for a living master. I have however received great benefits from all that Osho brought to the world.

I was in touch with Bino recently. What a precious man. It was sweet to speak after many years. I have reflected often on the great fortune to have shared time and space with the wonderful team in the Magic Café.

I am a long-time student of Dorje Ziji Tsal Rinpoche (Candice Rinpoche). My dear Guru is the magic thread that weaves through my life and enables me to face the challenges and celebrate the joys.

A little closer to home, Andy is now settled with his family near Totnes, close to Schumacher College where he is senior lecturer in ecological studies. He has created the MA course in Engaged Ecology. This is so clearly the right place for him to be!

He found a spare few minutes to record me a voicemail, from which I have extracted some nuggets . . .

Back in the day, The Magic Café was the right place too:

> *I remember our interview, you just took one look at me, said, "yeah!, you've got the right thing . . ."*

Something similar must have happened at Schumacher:

> *I'd sent my CV on a whim – thought nothing would come of it . . . invited to lunch, I only realised halfway through it was actually an interview, but what for?*
>
> *As soon as I arrived for lunch, I felt a deep sense of familiarity: the community vibe, tables brimming with the most wonderful organic vegetarian food . . . just like the Magic Café fostered a deep sense of community, brought people of like minds together – so I wasn't fazed by anything at the interview, I felt immediately at home . . . it opened up the path to the job I'm in now, so "Thanks!"*
>
> *I also miss our conversations. Some of the best conversations I've had at the college have been while cooking or washing up!*

Some of my old friends are still in Oxford. There are days when you can find Jamji at Gloucester Green market, offering delicious momos and "Shiwah's Magic Chai" from his own pop-up catering stand, Tibet Stove. At other times he keeps busy with his art, practising his music, or exploring the wilder parts of the British Isles – the bits that remind him of the open vistas of his homeland.

I bump into Tenzin from time to time, which is always a pleasure – generally he's on a bicycle coming to or from his place of work. The Magic Café has provided the foundation for an enduring career as a chef, especially

Tenzin busy making momos
in the Magic Café kitchen

prized for his skills with cake-making and vegetarian dishes. "He so fast", says his cousin Deki, admiringly. Sometimes he helps out with a shift or two at the Magic Café.

Ah . . . the Magic Café – how goes it with that dear old institution?

Enforced closure during the pandemic has been an immense challenge for all hospitality businesses; how could a small business make it through? As I shopped at Wild Honey for my wholefood supplies, I felt sad to see the Café next door closed up, dark and moribund. Then, in late summer of last year, there were some signs of life, of things being shifted around inside. Soon there was a small team of workmen busy laying down a new patio at the front, stripping out the interior fittings and embarking on a comprehensive redecoration.

With the refit complete, it was a joy to behold. The Café, to my eyes at least, had for many years appeared uncertain of its identity, a provisional approximation of something it used to be. No wonder I felt uneasy being there – it was as if it were calling out for attention, and I was resolute in my turning away. Now all was freshly imagined. The colourful walls – which successive paint jobs had long since stripped of harmony – were gone; instead, an overall fresh white creates a light and airy atmosphere. Colourful artworks march happily down the shop, and the lighting is organised rather more effectively than I had ever achieved. The noticeboard is back in the centre of the space – though would it ever, in this era of IT networking, fulfil such a role as it had formerly? The serving counter has been entirely rebuilt, to suit the needs of a more hygiene conscious age. It is quite different – but also, in important respects, very much the same.

I'd brought along my old photos of the original refit to show the building crew; it was good to spend some time with my memories of this special place. I started to recall all those good times – and some of the difficult ones too. I made a date with Deki to show her my pictures and tell her about the history of her Magic Café; she was fascinated, taking the album home to

Pride of Magdalen Road – the Magic Café has aquired new neighbours: on the left, Jess & Matt have created an attractive healthfood store; on the right, Yeshe & Julie have just opened their new restaurant, Taste Tibet.

study with her mother and young son.

Not long afterwards came shocking news: Covid had hit the whole family, and Deki's mother was gone. This disaster cut through to me too.

Deki is resilient, and with lockdown gradually easing up, she has been able to immerse herself in café business. She is also excited about my project. I asked her to contribute something for this book:

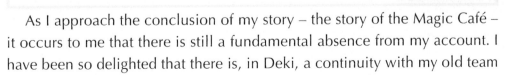

The Café always has been in my life, I am in touch with it almost everyday, it is part of my life and I can't imagine living without it – during the times I have meet so many lovely people and learnt so much more. Now I am so lucky that this Magic Café runs by me and my friend Jahan. We have made this café even more beautiful and special for our local community and people around. I am very excited that Hafiz is writing a book of the history of The Magic Café and sharing our stories.

As I approach the conclusion of my story – the story of the Magic Café – it occurs to me that there is still a fundamental absence from my account. I have been so delighted that there is, in Deki, a continuity with my old team that I have failed to acknowledge what her partner Jahan has brought to the Café. I need to check in with her, but I'm a little bit nervous, because I sense some awkwardness between us . . .

Jahan: "Magic Café Lady"

I turn up at the end of lunchtime, reckoning that this will be a propitious time to chat. We sit together, and it is suddenly clear what a wonderful, special person this is – so open-hearted, bright and dynamic – truly a creative spirit.

She admits to having been a bit wary of me, on the various occasions when we have briefly crossed paths. Now, all that seems to have dropped away, and she is eager to share her story of the Magic Café. For her too, it seems the refit has at last allowed her to take full possession – even though, as I learned to some surprise, she had been busy pouring her passion into the Magic Café since shortly after I departed.

Jiu Xien had recruited her, and she was immediately smitten with the idea of a friendly neighbourhood café – something which Jiu Xien, for all his boldness and enterprise, never really understood. She wanted to take it on as her own, to invest it with the love and attention she knew it called out for; but events didn't run quite so smoothly as she'd hoped. Jiu Xien sold it on to another; still she hung on, held her nerve. In my fanciful way, I imagine that the Café itself was whispering to her: *"one day we shall be together . . ."*

She and Deki were at last able to take on the business as partners. They are, as Jahan relates, an effective, complementary team, quite different in character, but never in serious disagreement. Fortunate Magic Café!

As we sit there, at the table purchased by me so many years ago in some long-gone junkshop, I notice various familiar faces stepping up to the counter. Jahan greets them each by name, acknowledging their regular orders. As she remarks to me, there is nowhere else like the Magic Café: it's so much a part of the community. It's still here because the people keep coming. Children have grown up here. And she is widely known as "Magic Café Lady".

You can imagine my heart swelling when I hear this.

Perhaps yours is too . . .

I can feel a song coming on, as the credits start to roll:

Come on in –

Feed your Heart – at the Magic Café . . .

Feed your Heart – at the Magic Café . . .

Feed your Heart – at the Magic Café . . .

This Magic Café was made for You

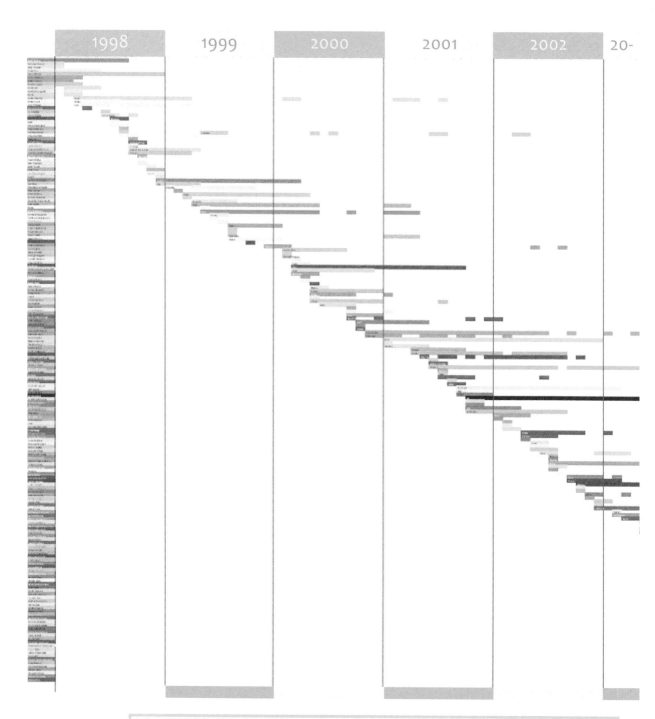

The Magic Café staff timeline: There are 182 names compressed into the left hand bar, all those who served on the Magic Café staff. Each coloured line represents an individual Café career.

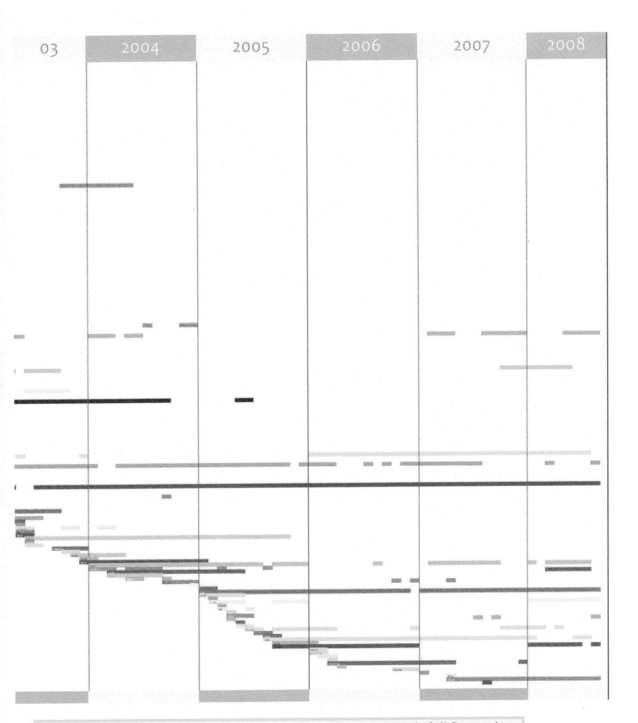

The longest line, chestnut brown, corresponds to Tenzin's full five and a half years. Next up is Bino's blue line, measuring about one year less. My heartfelt thanks to everyone who contributed to this amazing team.

Index

Index entries in bold signify Magic Café team members.
Page numbers in bold denote photos or illustrations.

The Magic Cookbook

My two collections of the Magic Cookbook – Four Seasons and Four Directions – as featured on pages 120-2 and 196-8 – are still available in their original booklet format. If you would like to order copies, you could either ask me in person, should you bump into me round and about Oxford, or send me a message via the Magic Pocket website (*www.magicpocket.org*).

Had I not been spending the past year immersed in bringing this present book to fruition, I would have been busy furthering my other website – *www.magiccookbook.online*. So that's my next project, which will include recipes from those existing booklets as well as more recently concocted dishes. These new recipes will all, necessarily, be Gluten Free.

It is also my intention to make all of these recipes more widely available in book format. That's plenty to keep me occupied!

An invitation

I hope you've enjoyed reading "I Am Cooking Something Else". It's been a lot of fun putting this together, and a big effort too, so I'm really hoping it gets spread around. It would be great if you could pass on your experience to others.

If you purchased the book on Amazon, please leave a review on that site. Otherwise, goodreads.com offers the opportunity to give voice to your opinion. Spread the word!

Should you wish to contact me, you can post a message on the Magic Pocket website *(www.magicpocket.org)*.

Printed in Great Britain
by Amazon